THE BUSINESS OF SHOW BUSINESS

THE BUSINESS
OF SHOW
BUSINESS

A Guide to Career Opportunities
Behind the Scenes in Theatre and Film

JUDITH A. KATZ

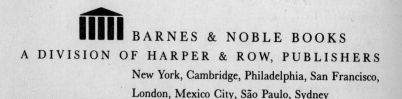

BARNES & NOBLE BOOKS
A DIVISION OF HARPER & ROW, PUBLISHERS
New York, Cambridge, Philadelphia, San Francisco,
London, Mexico City, São Paulo, Sydney

PN1580
K3
1981

FIRST EDITION

Designer: Sidney Feinberg

Library of Congress Cataloging in Publication Data

Katz, Judith A.
  The business of show business.
  Includes index.
  1. Performing arts—Vocational guidance—United
States. I. Title.
PN1580.K3   790.2′023′73   80-8689   AACR2
ISBN 0-06-014847-0   81 82 83 84 85 10 9 8 7 6 5 4 3 2 1
ISBN 0-06-463534-1 (pbk.)   81 82 83 84 85 10 9 8 7 6 5 4 3 2 1

For Jamie

If a man has a talent and cannot use it, he has failed. If he has a talent and uses only half of it, he has partly failed. If he has a talent and learns somehow to use the whole of it, he has gloriously succeeded and won a satisfaction and a triumph few men ever know.

—THOMAS WOLFE
The Web and the Rock

In an effort not to genderize the job descriptions, the author uses the universal *he* throughout.

Contents

Acknowledgments *ix*

Introduction *xi*

**Part I: A Quick Overview of the Business
of Show Business**

 1. How and Where Films and Plays Are Put Together 3

 2. How Unions Affect Theatre and Film Jobs 9

 3. Types of Theatre and Film 11

Part II: Administration

 4. Administrative Job Descriptions 25

 5. Administrative Profiles: 35

  Maxine Fox, Producer of the Play *Grease* on Broadway 35

  Sidney Kiwitt, Warner Brothers Business
   Affairs Expert 45

  Bob Moss, Producing Director of Playwrights Horizons 51

  Peter Saphier, Universal Pictures Production
   Executive 57

Part III: Production

 6. Production Job Descriptions 65

 7. Production Profiles: 72

  Vinnette Carroll, Artistic Director of the Urban Arts Corps
   Theatre and Creator of *Don't Bother
   Me, I Can't Cope* 72

  Paul Monette, Hollywood Screenwriter 77

  Richard Fischoff, Associate Producer of *Kramer vs. Kramer* 82

  Robert (Bob) Allan Ackerman, Director of
   the Broadway Production of *Bent* 89

  Lewis Jackson, a New York Independent Filmmaker 97

Part **IV**: **Production Crafts**

8. Production Crafts Job Descriptions   109
9. Production Artisan Profiles: 131
    Susan (Sandy) E. Morse, Editor of *Manhattan*   131
    Mel Bourne, Production Designer of *Annie Hall*   137
    Zoya Wyeth, Equity Stage Manager   142
    Fred Schuler, Camera Operator of *The Deer Hunter* and
       Director of Photography of *Gloria*   147
    A. Christina (Stia) Giannini, Costume Designer to
       Agnes de Mille and Alvin Ailey   153

Part **V**: **Supporting Services**

10. Supporting Services Job Descriptions   161
11. Supporting Services Profiles: 173
    Geoffrey Sanford, Hollywood Literary Agent   173
    David Denby, Film Critic on *New York* Magazine   177

Part **VI**: **Finding a Job**

12. The First Step   187
    Epilogue   195

    Appendix A: *Jobs in Show Business*   197
    Appendix B: *Resources*   213

        Internships and Training Programs   213
        Employment Clearinghouses and
          Placement Services   220
        Grants and Festivals   222
        Schools   224
        Colleges and Universities   225
        Unions, Guilds, and Professional Associations   228
        Theatre- and Film-Related Publications   236
        Bookstores   242
        Libraries and Study Centers   242

    Index   245

Acknowledgments

This book could not have been possible without the help of the sixteen people featured in the career profiles. I thank them all for their openness and willingness to share. I also thank my friends and agents Katinka Matson and John Brockman for their confidence and inspiration; my editor, Jeanne Flagg, for her help; my parents and good friends, especially Adele Marano, for their support.

And I thank the following friends, associates, and strangers who took time out from their incredibly busy lives to tell me about their work and otherwise help me write *The Business of Show Business:* Nancy Littlefield, Director of the Mayor's Office for Motion Pictures and Television; Tom Tulley of NABET; producer Patti Grubman; Vice President of Warner Communications Norman Samnick; Ira Eaker of *Back Stage;* composer Jimmy Hasskel; merchandising expert Les Borden of Columbia Pictures; industrial filmmaker David Tapper; cinematographer Ed Lachman; story editor Terri Lee of David Susskind Productions; President of the Los Angeles musicians' local Max Herman; Joe Farrell of the National Research Group; box office treasurer Scott Fuchs; Barbara Robinson of the I.A.; graphic/optical designers R. Greenberg Associates; Earl Karpin of the L.A. Crafts Service Union; the *Santa* crew and office staff; Ellen Rudolph, former president of OOBA; Denise Hamilton of the New York Foundation for the Arts; Audrey Nass of the Pittsburgh Public Theatre; Harriet Slaughter of the League of New York Theatres and Producers; Albert Dureyea of Precision Film Lab; Kristin Beck of Radio City Music Hall; Harold Blumberg of Eaves-Brooks Costume Co.; Richard Kaplan of the Astoria Motion Picture and Television Center Foundation; Donna Lerner of the Walter Reade Organization; Suzanne Stevens of Lincoln Center for the Performing Arts; Gail Bell of the League of Off Broadway Theatres and Producers; Barbara Keleman of the National Survey Research Group;

Elaine Cohen, director of East Coast Television Warner Communications; Martin Guest; Barbara and Irv Captan; Amos Kollek; the show biz dentist Dr. Ben Koplik; Jody Caravaglia, Madeline Porter, and Merri Anne Milwee, photographers; Nancy Johnson, costume supervisor; Josh Weiner, still photographer; Raphael Etkes; Herb Gardner, author of *A Thousand Clowns;* and other generous, knowledgeable friends and associates too numerous to mention.

Introduction

In the beginning of a career in show business, the hardest view to come by is an overview. You are too busy climbing up to look around. It is the purpose of this book to provide you with an overview, and in doing so, help you become a working member of the professional theatre and film community. If you are just starting out, it will enable you to see things in a broad context, like looking at a map before embarking on a journey. If you are already on the way, it will provide you with a new vantage point and perhaps help you understand where you fit into the picture.

This book was sparked off by a question put to me when I was director of education at the Roundabout Theatre Company in New York. It was my job to channel prospective interns into assignments that would further their career goals. When I asked what those goals were, the replies I invariably got, even from sophisticated graduate students, were vague and undirected. They wanted to "get into" theatre or "get into" film or "eventually" to produce and direct. One day I was startled by an honest response to my question: "I don't know. What've you got?"

Hearing that straightforward response gave me new insight into my job. If I was to help these people filter into the "business," I would have to tell them what their options were, present them with choices. Just as a person seeking employment in a corporation must have a more specific goal than "I want to run the company or be president," a person seeking employment in theatre or film must be realistic and have a specific job in mind when he or she goes out looking for work.

I recalled my own dilemma in looking for a behind-the-scenes job some ten years earlier. When I did as my friends did—look in the *New York Sunday Times* employment section—I found "Repairman" listed under TV careers and nothing, week after week, under film or theatre. Having graduated from the High School of Performing Arts and Adelphi University's theatre department, I was supposed to have "show biz" savvy, yet I had no idea of what jobs existed behind the scenes or where to look for them.

The problem with the entertainment industry is that you have to get in before you can learn what's available, the first of many "Catch 22" situations. I dealt with this at the Roundabout by organizing a series of seminars, each conducted by a working professional who told about his job and how he built a successful career. It worked. The interns began to get a handle on the situation.

Even after I left the Roundabout, I continued to ask people about their jobs in theatre and film. Their responses form a major section of this book.

There are six parts in all. The first gives a brief account of how films and plays are put together and describes the various kinds of theatre and film that exist today. This should give you a sense of the flow and scheme of things in these two facets of the entertainment world. Television, although very much a part of show business, has not been included for a number of reasons, mainly because the subject is too vast; there are so many television job titles it would require a separate book to do them justice.

The next four parts identify and describe the jobs, then take an intimate look at what some of the key jobs are like in practice. The descriptions should give you a good idea of the kinds of work and what they entail. Naturally, each working situation is somewhat different; just as no two secretaries do the exact same things, no two gaffers do. The jobs were researched at unions, theatres, and film companies across the country. They are titled as accurately as possible in the jargon of the industry, yet it should be kept in mind that they are theoretical. If you find contradictions between the job descriptions and any of the careers in practice, it only means that a variable in the particular situation influenced the job that way.

All the jobs in this book are grouped according to theatrical tradition: administrative, production, production crafts, and supporting service jobs. This is done to simplify organization and to call attention to the similarities that exist between some theatre and film jobs. In the field you'll find film jobs categorized somewhat differently, the main difference being that any job involved in the creation of a particular film—be it that of agent, writer, studio executive, or cameraman—is considered a production job.

The career profiles are given in sufficient detail so that you can see the step-by-step progress involved in building a successful career; you see that those who eventually make it once held menial jobs, had doubts, and got depressed. You cannot repeat their experiences, but you can learn from them. They all have certain things in common. Each of their careers began with a dream, and, as simple as it sounds, were built on hard work, tenaciousness, and good timing. Although it may seem that you have no control over the last, in a way you do. Disraeli said it best: "The secret of success in life is for a man to be ready for his opportunity when it comes."

The section on finding a job sifts out tips from the professionals and provides you with some direction as to where and how to go about looking for work. The two appendixes contain invaluable information you will want to hold onto for future reference.

Just as in any business, contacts are essential to getting ahead. Contacts are cultivated, not inherited. Only two of the people profiled here knew anyone when they started out. In fact, one of them (a top cinematographer) came to this country knowing no one, in or out of the business. Keep that in mind as you read the book. Keep in mind also that competition is tough, but don't dwell on it or you won't get beyond it. Too often, clearly talented and intelligent people are tyrannized by discouraging words and negativism. Yes, some fail, but mainly because they are not realistic and not willing to start at the beginning. More important, some succeed. It is my hope that with this book to turn to, you will be one of them.

PART I

A QUICK OVERVIEW
OF THE BUSINESS
OF SHOW BUSINESS

It is a business like any other. But, in order to be successful at it, you have to love it.

—PATTI GRUBMAN
Producer

1 How and Where Films and Plays Are Put Together

> You've got to be flexible in this business. If you're the rigid type who likes everything to fit in the right hole—stay away. There's no two situations that match. A tolerance for chaos is important.
>
> —JOE FARRELL, Entertainment researcher

Films and plays are put together and presented to the public in a variety of ways, most of them complicated and expensive. A great number of people holding assorted jobs and working for various organizations are involved. This wasn't always so. In the early years of the film industry, everything that had anything to do with making motion pictures was accomplished by the "studio." That included financing, producing, and exhibiting. Everyone who worked in the "industry," as it liked to be called, worked on-staff for a film studio and answered to a powerful studio boss. Films were made with studio actors, directors, producers, musicians, and crews, and were shipped off and shown in studio-owned theatres across the country. The pace was fast and the supply was short; the demand for movies was built in because the studios were supplying their own cinemas. All this changed in 1948 when an anti-trust suit forced the studios to divest themselves of their theatres and concentrate on producing. That meant distributing to independent exhibitors. The demand for new films slackened and was further reduced by the onset of television. Fewer films were made, on-staff personnel were "canned" and replaced with free lancers, and a "new" Hollywood began to take shape. The "new" Hollywood that evolved in the 1950s and 1960s continues to function today.

Hollywood now uses studio money, studio executives, studio facilities, and studio distribution networks, but for the most part leaves the actual production work (i.e., the making of the film) to independent producers and their production companies. Almost everyone works free lance in the "new" Hollywood. That includes producers, screenwriters, directors, actors, crews, editors, and publicists. Very few films are made "in-house" (by the studio without the services of a production company), and when they are, a studio executive hires

3

a producer, screenwriter, and director to make the film for the studio. The main difference between films made in-house and those made by independent production companies is that in the first case the studio owns the property (screenplay, novel, or story) and in the second, the production company does. Most films are instigated (property bought, screenplay developed, financing sought) outside the studio by independent producers who put films together in a variety of ways.

One way is to make a long-term deal with a studio whereby the studio agrees to finance and distribute all the producer's projects for a predetermined period. During this time (generally a minimum of three years) the producer maintains an office somewhere on the studio lot and his films are shot in the studio facility. A studio executive is assigned to each of his films to "oversee" expenditures and nurse the project along. The producer and his staff remain autonomous, determining which films they will and will not make. At the end of the time period the producer may decide to stay on (if the studio agrees) or take himself and his company elsewhere.

An example of how this arrangement works is the relationship that existed between Columbia Pictures and Stanley Jaffe Productions in the making of *Kramer vs. Kramer*. Stanley Jaffe had a three-year contract with Columbia Pictures to finance and distribute his films. His production company office was housed on Columbia's lot and his films were made on their facility. During this time, Jaffe found the property and decided to produce *Kramer vs. Kramer* (for specific details, see Part III). He hired writer/director Robert Benton to adapt the novel and direct the film, and he cast Dustin Hoffman, Meryl Streep, and Jane Alexander in the leads. Columbia Pictures assigned production executive Sherry Lansing (now president of Twentieth Century-Fox) to watch over it. The film was made by Stanley Jaffe Productions and distributed by Columbia Pictures. Both companies (along with any profit participants, i.e., creative people with "points" in their deal) shared in the film's profits. At the completion of the three-year contract with Columbia, Jaffe entered into another long-term deal, this one with Twentieth Century-Fox.

Most independent producers do not have such deals. They must arrange for financing and distribution networks each time they find a property they want to develop and produce. They have projects in various stages of production with many of the studios. Only when in production do they keep an office on the studio lot. Although run on a picture-to-picture basis, this type of studio deal generally includes financing and distribution, and here too the studio and the production company share in the film's profits.

Another way producers (we can drop the independent because no producer works full time for a studio) put together films is through untraditional means (tax shelter money, private investors, corporations selling stock in the film, theatre companies, or any other money that does not come from the studio). These films get made without studio interference or input. Once produced, they are shown to independent distributors and studios with distribution networks. Occasionally, a major studio acquires and distributes such a film, but only one it believes to be potentially very commercial. Failing that, the producers try to attract the independent distribution companies. Among other things they will send the film to festivals around the world (Cannes is the most popular) to show it to foreign and domestic distributors. This approach is financially risky and lends itself only to low budget films. The ideal situation is to have a good (that is, financially advantageous to the producer) distribution deal set up prior to the film's completion.

Because so much of successful producing depends on the property, the studio and independents compete for and woo talented writers. Their story department executives vie with each other for the first look at "hot" manuscripts from the book publishing companies. Writers who've sold a screenplay to one company are deluged with lunch invitations from the others. Millions of dollars are spent optioning properties. Deals are made on books and screenplays not yet written on the basis of an idea or an outline. Big-name actors and directors too are wooed by studio production executives and independent producers. Everything is done to keep them happy and "put" (including giving them mega-buck contracts). Competition for talent is keen in Hollywood, and the ability to attract it is an important element in successful producing.

There is no one way that feature films get made and released in "new" Hollywood; most of the people involved are independent spirits and the wheeler-dealer possibilities are endless. Nor is there one place where features are made. The "new" Hollywood borders go beyond Los Angeles. New York, Texas, Canada, Georgia, Detroit, and Indianapolis (the home of the productive Mel Simon Productions, financed by Mel Simon, real estate tycoon turned film producer) have been luring filmmakers with the promise of easy financing, tax shelter money, nonrestrictive unions, talent, good location sites, and government help in cutting red tape. In addition, almost all the major studios and production companies maintain "think tank" offices in New York (where the publishing world is) or other major cities. A number of states have created film commissions to attract filmmakers and thus provide gainful employment for their citizens in behind-the-scenes roles. For people looking for work in the industry, this newly expanded Hollywood means greater opportunities to find it—not necessarily outside their own home town.

In old Hollywood a film got made when a studio mogul decided to make it and told his producers to do so; in new Hollywood a film gets made when a producer chooses to do it and can attract sufficient financing. In the Hollywood of the 1980s and 1990s films are likely to be made in a completely different manner. Already, Francis Ford Coppola is looking toward the future with innovative ideas in movie producing. He has converted his production company, American Zoetrope, into Zoetrope *Studios*, a facility complete with soundstages, editing rooms, special effects shops and on-staff actors, writers, directors, and producers reminiscent of the "golden days." It will be a financial struggle to keep it going, but if he does, he will in effect combine old Hollywood's on-staff system with new Hollywood's flexible ways and electronic technology. His "think tank" office is in San Francisco, his studio in the heart of Hollywood. Another interesting development is that the federal court gave permission to Loews Corporation, a major film exhibitor, to produce and distribute films. This decision modified the anti-trust orders that had inadvertently brought about "new" Hollywood. What effect the decision will have on "new new" Hollywood remains to be seen.

If there is one prediction everyone in Hollywood agrees with, it is that the pay-television revolution will greatly influence the Hollywood of the eighties and nineties. Already, owners of electronic networks (i.e., Home Box Office, Showtime, Warner-Amex) are changing the way film entertainment is being delivered to the public, and are developing films and other programs especially for pay-television, video disks, and cassette machines. There is a power struggle going on between the television networks and major movie studios and the new electronic networks—who now offer production companies an alternative source of financing and distribution—that once resolved will restructure the entertainment industry and provide new opportunities for behind-the-scenes people.

The business of making films, like most everything else, is in a constant state of change and is affected by many things, including the economy, legislation, tax laws, politics, and technology. It is important for anyone interested in the industry to keep up with the internal stirrings and external forces that cause these changes and to always have an eye toward the future.

Theatre production too has undergone major changes in the past two decades. The reason is twofold: the high costs of commercial production and support of the arts by government and private foundations.

Until the 1930s, American theatre was commercial theatre, with no room for experimentation or vanguard themes. Plays were financed almost entirely by mercenary "angels" with little interest in the performing arts. They invested with producers who could make them rich and in plays that would make a profit. A play was written, and the playwright would look for a producer with investors; the success or failure of the production was measured by the amount of money it brought in, period. In 1931, Cheryl Crawford, Lee Strasberg, and Harold Clurman, in an attempt to break away from this commercialism, formed The Group Theatre. The Group's aim was to broaden the art and content of the American theatre. Lee J. Cobb, John Garfield, Stella Adler, and others got their start in The Group Theatre. Although The Group lasted only ten years, it was the precursor of the noncommercial theatre movement in this country. It's fortunate for commercial theatre that the movement came into its own when it did (late 1950s), for at about the same time costs began to skyrocket. These two events, occurring simultaneously, greatly affected the future of theatre production.

Although it was far from their intention, the flourishing noncommercial theatres provided the commercial world with material and a testing ground for new plays. Theatre in the 1980s will continue to be greatly affected by the symbiotic relationship between the two.

Today, commercial play production works like this: A producer finds a property in the form of a manuscript, at a not-for-profit, or regional, theatre company, in this country or in a theatre abroad, especially in London. He options it, employs a general manager, forms a limited partnership, and raises the money from private investors ("angels"), other producers, theatre owners, movie companies (*The Best Little Whorehouse in Texas* was partially financed by Universal Pictures), and anywhere else he can. Most commercial producers maintain a theatrical office on a year-round basis but keep the staff down to a minimum. Many of those involved in putting a theatrical production together (e.g., ad agency, general manager, press agent, theatrical attorney) maintain their own offices, where they service a number of clients simultaneously. They therefore can afford to be kept "on hold" by a producer until their services are needed. Producers actually hire these independents only when they're ready to produce something. Once the producer has decided to go ahead with a project, he hires the director (unless the writer insists on choosing the director), a press agent, and an ad agency; the director casts and selects the designers and stage manager; the general manager hires the company manager. The producer finds a suitable house (one that is atmospherically right) and the crew is hired. Some commercial productions are taken on a try-out run before coming to New York, others go directly from rehearsal to Broadway. Often, if a play is a success on Broadway, "bus and truck" and "sit-down" national touring companies are sent out to perform the play across the country and even the world. The producers (general partners) and the investors (limited partners) share in the play's profits, as do the profit participants—playwright, director, choreographer, composer, or general manager.

Noncommercial theatre is produced by companies financed through grants from government agencies (e.g., the National Endowment for the Arts), state agencies (e.g., the New York State Council for the Arts), private foundations and corporations, individual donations, and earned income. Many noncommercial theatre companies are resident companies, in that they maintain a permanent structure and staff of administrators, production, and technical people. Plays are chosen by an artistic director and productions are mounted with on-staff (as well as guest) directors, designers, and actors. Any profits the theatre earns go back into its coffers for future endeavors.

A great number of the noncommercial theatre companies are dedicated to finding and developing new American plays and playwrights. In one way or another the companies support new playwrights and provide them with a workshop atmosphere in which to function. Often, these workshop productions are developed and ultimately produced commercially. In the past few seasons over half of the plays produced on Broadway came from the not-for-profit arena; the remaining half were revivals, classics, and new untried plays.

Theatre, too, has expanded its borders. Whereas once New York was considered to be the only place serious professional theatre took place, today regional theatre is flourishing. New and more sophisticated theatres are cropping up across the country all the time. Years ago, a play that didn't make it on Broadway was considered a flop; today, some of our best contemporary playwrights survive very nicely without ever having their plays produced on Broadway.

There is much "producing-in-law" going on in theatre today. Noncommercial producers are teaming up with commercial producers; commercial producers are joining forces, and noncommercial theatre companies are working side by side to produce theatre. All this activity has led to a thriving American theatre, both commercial and noncommercial, with more opportunities than ever for behind-the-scenes fledglings. As with film, theatre production is in a constant state of change, affected by government policy, the economy, and technology. Those sensitive to the direction in which theatre is moving will be one step ahead of those who are not.

2 How Unions Affect Theatre and Film Jobs

Unions are a strong force in the entertainment industry. Their demands affect the structure, employment opportunities, job responsibilities, and salaries in both theatre and film.

In the theatre, producers must enter into contracts with the various unions (of actors and stage managers, technicians, managers, musicians, etc.) each time they go into production. The unions designate each production as a particular type (e.g., Broadway, Off Off Broadway) and prescribe the rules and regulations that apply. Designation is based on the number of seats in the house, the location of the theatre, the budget, and such variables as whether the show was written for children or dinner will be served during a performance. Also, theatres are identified as union houses and nonunion houses. Producers and union members must adhere to the dictates of the particular union contract. The bringing in of these contracts, in a way, gave officialdom to unofficial activity and in so doing influenced the structure of the theatre. In other words, while economics or a philosophical attitude may have given rise to a particular theatre activity such as Off Off Broadway, the union's sanctity forced it into becoming an authorized movement with rules and regulations.

In film, too, producers enter into contracts with the various unions and the film then becomes a "union film." Only union members are allowed to work on union films and only nonunion people on nonunion films—independent films where the producer somehow got out of entering into a contract with the union(s). Union crafts people determined to work on nonunion films lie and say they are not union members, often using an alias as protection, although this is not necessary in some states where union locals are more flexible.

The unions influence who will work in the industry in other ways. Entrance to some of the crafts locals (unofficially) requires that you be related to a member. There are ways to get around this, but it takes fierce determination. In other cases all you need for entrance is the offer of a job on a union project, but of course no one will offer you such a job unless you are a member of a union!

Unions have a lot to say on the subject of job responsibilities, or who does what for whom. The union contracts spell out exactly which of its members are allowed to do what and in what capacity they are to be employed. In the job description sections of this book, the union descriptions are used wherever possible, but these are theoretical and not nearly as neat in practice, even on union projects. On nonunion projects, job responsibilities overlap much more, owing to smaller crews and a less restrictive atmosphere. One reason union films and plays cost so much more to produce is because the unions dictate how many behind-the-scenes personnel must be employed (often many more than are needed) and how much they must be paid. On the positive side, union salaries, even on menial jobs, are much higher than nonunion salaries and the benefits are extensive.

A frequent complaint against some of the unions is that they require members to spend an exorbitant amount of time in entry-level jobs, even if they are capable of doing more advanced work. Another complaint is that in some cases, members of a New York local are not allowed to work in Los Angeles or join the Los Angeles local because they are residents of New York.

There are many "Catch 22" situations involved in dealing with the unions, especially at the beginning of a career. Some people cope with this by delaying joining a union and working on independent films and in noncommercial theatre. Others join up as soon as they can and deal with each situation as it arises. The entrance requirements of each union and local are different. In some cases a long and complicated exam must be passed; in others a job offer on a union project is enough, and in still others again, especially those where nepotism prevails, constant (pleasant) nagging and questioning might get you somewhere. Once you are admitted you have no more assurance of obtaining work than you did previously, but generally speaking, your status is upgraded. A list of related unions and guilds is included in Appendix B.

3   Types of Theatre and Film

> Everyone always talks about features, features, features. There is much more to this business than features.
> — NANCY LITTLEFIELD, Director of the Mayor's Office for Motion Pictures and Television, New York City

There is more to show business than Hollywood films and Broadway plays. A variety of show business activity takes place all across this country. Much of that activity is open to beginners, certainly more so than Hollywood and Broadway. Many behind-the-scenes people start out in one kind of theatre or film and move on as they gain experience. Below you will find descriptions of various kinds of theatre and film activities. You will better understand your career alternatives if you are aware of them from the very beginning. These descriptions will also help you to see how the jobs mentioned in this book take on different responsibilities from one area of theatre and film to the next.

Theatre

Commercial Theatre.   Commercial theatre means theatre for a profit; by definition it is a moneymaking entity. Because it supports itself through ticket sales, commercial theatre generally concentrates on plays with wide popular appeal. It aims to make a profit for producers and investors by entertaining the public. The best known and most highly regarded commercial theatre district in America is Broadway, but there are other theatres around the country and Off Broadway theatres in New York that house commercial theatre productions. A number of these survive by showing "packaged-in" touring companies of successful Broadway plays.

Commercial theatre is only performed in commercial theatres (houses with union status) and only employs union personnel, whether they be actors, designers, crafts people, stage managers, company managers, press agents, or house staff. Anyone who can raise the money to do so can produce in the commercial marketplace but, generally speaking, it's not open to beginners in any capacity.

Broadway.   The term "Broadway" has come to mean excellence in theatre. It has become synonymous with the whole of commercial theatre activity but, in actuality, is the forty-two "legitimate" houses between 41st and 53rd Streets in New York City and the plays that are presented on those stages. Broadway theatres are owned and operated by theatre organizations such as the Shubert Organization and the Nederlander Organization (who together control 70% of all Broadway houses) and by independent theatre owners. Only union personnel are allowed to work on Broadway, making it difficult for the nonunion beginner. There are theatrical impresarios (Alexander Cohen, David Merrick, and Hal Prince are among the best known) who specialize in bringing shows to Broadway, but nothing except lack of experience is to stop a noncommercial producer or complete novice from trying. Broadway productions are quite expensive to mount; it is not unusual for a musical to have a $2 million budget. Broadway audiences are said to be among the most sophisticated and affluent in the country.

Off Broadway.   Of all the theatrical activities in the country, Off Broadway is the most difficult to pigeonhole, because its identity keeps changing. The "movement" was begun originally so that plays could be produced at a lower cost than on Broadway. Actor and technician unions allowed for a low pay scale and less stringent operating conditions. The theatres, many in low rent districts in and around Greenwich Village, were smaller and thus easier and cheaper to keep up, making it financially less risky to produce Off Broadway than on. Off Broadway was the place to take the avant-garde, experimental, or adventurous play with artistic merit but little or no commercial appeal. As the unions demanded higher rates and costs soared, this changed. Off Broadway came to mean New York City commercial theatre outside of Broadway. It became a "Baby Broadway," the place to take commercial productions that couldn't survive on Broadway, where the houses have at least seven hundred seats. Today, there are two types of Off Broadway activity, commercial and noncommercial. For the one-shot commercial producer, Off Broadway still functions as an adjunct to Broadway, with a slightly different audience makeup, supposedly attracting a more serious theatre patron. There are also a number of seasonal not-for-profit companies functioning Off Broadway. Most of these began as Off Off Broadway theatre companies; when they were able to raise their funding to the point where they could pay standard minimum salaries for Off Broadway, they were designated "Off Broadway" by the unions. Just as Off Broadway theatre activities are a mixed bag, so are Off Broadway job opportunities; union, nonunion, on-staff and free-lance jobs are all available.

Noncommercial Theatre (a.k.a. Not-for-Profit Theatre). Noncommercial theatre began to take shape in the 1950s with a tax reform act of the federal government. By this act an individual was allowed to donate money to a cultural not-for-profit institution and get a tax writeoff. In 1965 the federal government created the National Endowment for the Arts, and publicly supported theatre became a reality. Soon after that state councils on the arts, foundations, and business came through with financial support for noncommercial theatre. With this new source of income, the avant-garde and experimental theatres flourished and expanded, first to Off Broadway, next to Off Off Broadway, and then to regional theatres across the country. What had once been unorganized activities became serious and productive theatre movements. "Noncommercial theatre" is an umbrella term that refers to all theatre activity that does not aim to make a profit—Off Off Broadway, regional, grass roots, cultural institutions, and university theatre. Profits earned from noncommercial endeavors go toward paying employees and expanding and improving the theatre company. Depending on the sophistication and work of the theatres, support comes from donations, government, private foundations, volunteerism, ticket and subscription sales, and a combination of the above. There are both seasonal and one-shot producers working in the noncommercial arena, and goings on range from little community groups working out of a church basement to resident companies housed in multi-million-dollar institutional theatre complexes. Since so many not-for-profit theatres depend on contributions for their survival, arts managers with fundraising savvy are in demand here. Generally speaking, the unions do not have a stronghold in noncommercial theatres, making it accessible to the behind-the-scenes neophyte. It is the place newcomers find internships, volunteer stints, and entry-level jobs, and the place the experienced find year-round on-staff positions.

Off Off Broadway. Off Off Broadway is one of those "children of the sixties" activities that managed to survive and flourish into the seventies and eighties. Before it evolved into what it is today— New York's well-organized, thriving noncommercial theatre movement—it was theatre at play. It started in the early 1960s at Joe

Papp's Shakespeare Theatre, Ellen Stewart's La Mama Etc., Joe Cino's Caffe, and in lofts, basements, dingy rooms, and theatres around town where people wanted to do theatre without worrying about paying rent and salaries. It was a sixties activity without a name; the newspapers referred to it as *off* Off Broadway.

A number of things happened to turn this rambling activity into the Off Off Broadway movement. First of all, Off Broadway went "commercial"; second, commercial theatre costs soared so high producers were afraid to bring a new show to the commercial marketplace; and third, perhaps the most influential factor, money, in the form of tax-exempt contributions, became available to cultural institutions with not-for-profit status. Those companies that got their acts together with regard to fundraising and grant writing flourished; those that didn't fell by the wayside. Today, there are over two hundred Off Off Broadway Theatre companies that stretch from 120th Street down to SoHo, many with full resident staffs and unique artistic identities. Since Off Off Broadway is a place for testing potential talent, ideas, projects, plays, and ways of working, it is the ideal place for hopeful beginners; it is to today's behind-the-scenes fledglings what vaudeville was to the young of its day. Off Off Broadway is the place to go to look for internships, volunteer programs, experience, contacts, and work. The Off Off Broadway Theatre Alliance (see Appendix B for details) is a clearinghouse of information for all Off Off Broadway theatres. Until recently, unions were nonexistent in the Off Off Broadway arena.

Regional Theatre (Resident Theatre). Regional theatre refers to the flourishing noncommercial theatre activities outside New York City, and specifically to the resident theatre companies both inside and outside New York that are members of LORT—the League of Resident Theatres. Some of the better known resident theatres are the Mark Taper Forum in Los Angeles and the Arena Stage in Washington, D.C. Regional theatre began as community theatre. It grew and developed into the professional activity it is today when government and private foundations started injecting monies (in 1966 the Ford Foundation donated some $60 million to regional theatres and symphonies). Today, regional theatres are enjoying enormous popularity, so much so that new ones are cropping up all the time. Many concentrate on presenting new plays, others do revivals and classics. A great number of Broadway productions were first mounted in regional theatres.

Regional theatre companies are run by either an artistic director or a producing director and employ permanent staffs of production, technical, promotion, box-office, and administrative people. Some have permanent acting companies and resident playwrights. Regional theatre is supported by contributions, subscription sales, and single ticket sales. The varied and competitive ways in which they raise money create a need for a work force with expertise in fundraising, grantsmanship, long-range planning, and marketing techniques. A number of regional theatre companies offer internships (with and without stipends) and entry-level positions. Both union and non-union people are employed.

Cultural Institutions (Arts Centers). Cultural institutions are noncommercial theatre complexes such as Lincoln Center and the Kennedy Center where all kinds of performing arts activities—theatre, film, dance, opera, symphony orchestras, and educational theatre—take place. These vast institutions (most have three stages as well as concert halls) house resident companies and book guest companies and performers. Some institutions maintain schools, libraries, film and music societies, and other special programs. Constituents of the institution share expenses, corporate services, and monies from corporate fund drives. Each maintains its own staff. A corporate staff administers the work of the institution (overall programming, booking, corporate fundraising, public relations, general administration, public service, etc.). A personnel director is generally responsible for hiring the institution's administrative staff, while each company hires its own. A number of cultural institutions maintain costume and scenic shops, which also makes them a source of employment for crafts people. Because of their large size and varied activities, cultural institutions are a good place to seek work, particularly for those interested in all the arts. They employ union and nonunion personnel.

Grass Roots Theatre (Community Theatre). Grass roots theatre is theatre for and by the people. Grass roots companies spring up in every town and hamlet of the country; some are funded by government and private foundations, others subsist solely on volunteerism. A number of grass roots theatre companies are involved in social purpose (Theatre for the Forgotten brings theatre into the prisons; New York Street Caravan brings it into the ghettos) and some are involved in theatre for theatre's sake. Whichever kind it is, grass roots theatre is an ideal place for the behind-the-scenes begin-

ner to soak up experience. Such theatres are always looking for volunteers to stage-manage, design sets and costumes, paint sets, and do
all other behind-the-scenes jobs.

*Showcase Theatre ("Equity Waiver Theatre" in Los Ange-
les).*   Showcase theatre is theatre for the sake of showing off talent.
In New York and L.A., a showcase is put together by acting schools,
grass roots companies, groups of friends, playwrights, actors—anybody wishing to present something to someone. If the "company"
has no available space, it will rent a "showcase" theatre, one that is
sanctioned by Actors' Equity as such, and invite agents, producers,
directors, friends, and relatives to watch. Some Off Off Broadway
productions are considered showcase because they don't pay their
actors a salary, but generally showcases are one-shot productions to
introduce an actor or a play to agents, producers, and directors.
Showcase is a good place for novices to get their feet wet. Showcase
producers are generally eager to accept volunteers (no one gets paid)
to do behind-the-scenes jobs. Because people at different levels of
their careers do showcases, this is a good place to make valuable
contacts. Such productions are often announced in the trade papers.
Union and nonunion personnel work showcases.

Summer Stock Theatre.   Stock theatre consists of hundreds of
theatres that are in operation throughout the country during the
summer months. There are four types of summer theatre operations:
Council of Stock Theatres (COST) or "star" houses, tent and musical
theatres, Equity regional playhouses, and nonunion resident theatres. Behind-the-scenes staffs range from a few amateurs (Mickey
and Judy putting on theatre in the garage) to a full staff of resident
professionals. A variety of material is presented on the "straw cir-
cuit," depending on the type of operation. Commercial pre-packed
shows, classics, new plays, and Broadway-bound plays appear in
summer stock. Cast and crew include show biz "up and comers" as
well as veterans (often attracted for such fringe benefits as free ten-
nis or a pretty coastal town).

Stock offers many things to behind-the-scenes newcomers: a
chance to meet and work with theatre professionals, a productive
work schedule, challenging problems (such as mounting ten plays in
ten weeks), an opportunity to build a favorable reputation among
theatre colleagues, and in some cases a weekly salary. Summer stock
is traditionally the place the show biz novice pays his dues and gains
some "street sense" about theatre. Volunteers and interns sweep
stages, vacuum lobbies, paint sets, "gofer" coffee, and do everything

else that no one else will do, and they do it all for the roar of the crowd and smell of the greasepaint and a dingy little room, for they rarely get paid. Untold numbers of theatre professionals earned their first show biz stripes working behind the scenes in summer stock. Depending on the type of operation, both union and nonunion personnel are employed.

Dinner Theatre.   Dinner theatres are located all over the country, generally in the suburbs or in rural communities where no other theatre exists. There are dinner theatre chains (e.g., Coachlight Dinner Theatres) and those that are independently owned (e.g., Burt Reynolds' Dinner Theatre). Dinner theatre tends to be light theatre; comedies and musicals are favorites (as Walter Kerr said, "Nobody wants to see Oedipus gouge his eyes out over dessert"). For the most part, dinner theatre tends to be "packaged-in" theatre—theatre produced elsewhere and moved intact. Resident staffs (bookers, box-office personnel, stage managers, and crafts people) run the shows. Staff members, particularly stage managers, are expected to do more to compensate for the small administrative staff. Working in dinner theatre is often an opportunity to work with "star" actors and get some well-rounded experience. Union and nonunion personnel are employed.

Dance and Opera Companies.   The growth of seasonal dance and opera companies in the country has increased the need for administrative, production and technical personnel with a love and understanding of dance and music. Many of these companies maintain full resident staffs, while others employ people on a free-lance basis. Most are not-for-profit companies, making the arts manager with fundraising know-how much sought after. Union and nonunion personnel are employed.

Children's and Educational Theatre.   Several theatre companies in the country specialize in producing plays that have special appeal and relevance to the young. Some are commercial, others are funded; some maintain resident staffs, others hire on a project-to-project basis. There are children's theatre companies that function independently (e.g., New York's Paper Bag Players) and those that are associated with a resident theatre company. All hire administrative production and crafts people and most accept volunteers to do behind-the-scenes work.

In addition, there are "arts-in-education" organizations that perform varying services to young audiences, such as enrichment programs, teaching the performing arts, film education programs, and curriculum study through the arts. Arts organizations hire resident and free-lance people; those with an arts-in-education background are especially favored. A number of universities (e.g., Emerson College in Boston, New York University) offer studies in children's and educational theatre.

University Theatre.   Theatrical activity within a university embraces anything from the training of actors, playwrights, directors, producers, arts managers, and critics to a professional repertory theatre such as the one at Yale. Directors and choreographers are generally invited to work on university productions because of some past theatrical achievement. Volunteer directors and designers are often sought after to work on student-run productions, making university theatre another good place for production people to get their feet wet. A number of universities offer paid fellowships in theatre and directing to graduate students in good standing.

*Industrial Shows.**   Large corporations such as Milliken and Avon often produce live multimedia theatre to introduce their new product line to salespeople and customers. The shows generally last a couple of days to a week and offer behind-the-scenes crafts people good salaries, an opportunity to work with stars, and exposure to multimedia techniques. There are production companies (e.g., New York's Jack Morton Productions) that specialize in producing this type of show.

Film

Theatrical Film.   Theatrical films are what most people mean when they talk of a movie or film or motion picture or picture. As a category, these are films of at least ninety minutes in length made for theatrical release, that is, to be shown in movie theatres for entertainment purposes. Theatrical films are animated or live action, and are based on original screenplays, books, and magazine articles (e.g., *Saturday Night Fever* was based on a *New York* magazine article). They are made both independently and with studio money; newcomers have a better chance of getting to work on the independently made nonunion films.

Feature Film.   Although this term is often used interchangeably with "theatrical film," a feature is by definition any film of feature

---

*Industrial, educational, and TV commercial projects are not, strictly speaking, a part of show business. They are mentioned here only because of the opportunities they offer the behind-the-scenes novice.

length that entertains, regardless of whether it has been made to be shown in a movie theatre or elsewhere (television, cable, home video cassette, etc.).

Hollywood Film. A Hollywood film is a big budget feature made with money from one of the "majors" (such entertainment conglomerates as Columbia Pictures Industries, Gulf & Western Industries, MCA Inc., Twentieth Century-Fox Film Corporation, United Artists, Warner Communications Inc.). Hollywood films are distributed on a grand scale with the anticipation of huge profits. Good or bad, they are always commercial. They aren't necessarily shot in Hollywood but almost always feature a Hollywood star in the cast. Crews on Hollywood films are fully unionized and the jobs are strictly categorized. It is rare but not impossible that a behind-the-scenes person gets his or her start on a Hollywood film; almost all the staff from producer to gaffer have had previous experience.

Independent Film (a.k.a. "Indie"). An independent film is a feature that has been financed through untraditional means (i.e., money from any place other than a studio). Independent films are made in New York, Hollywood, and regionally, and may or may not be commercial in nature (those that are eventually get distributed by one of the major studios or distribution companies). "Indies" are generally budgeted much lower than traditionally financed films and are produced by anyone from veteran producers to ex-shopping center developers; anyone who can raise the money or who has the means. It is not uncommon for a screenwriter, determined to get his script made into a movie, to turn himself into an independent film-maker for the occasion. "Indies" are often staffed by fledgling writers, directors, and crews that are predominantly nonunion and generally fall into two categories, noncommercial personal films and commercial "copies" of the popular genre of the day.

Made-for-TV Film. Made-for-TV films are just that—feature films or films of mini-series length made especially for television release. They are made by many of the same production companies that produce theatrical films and by a few that specialize in television film (e.g., David Wolper Productions, Titus Productions), and are sold to the networks. Crews are union and the personnel breakdown is the same as on Hollywood films, making the made-for-TV field a difficult place for nonunion people to find work.

Made-for-Pay-Television and Home Video Films. As the pay-television revolution takes hold, more and more films and other programs are being developed and produced especially for the electronic networks. This new product of the entertainment industry is produced by the independent production companies and by the pay-television networks themselves (e.g., Home Box Office, Showtime, Warner-Amex). Free-lance crafts job opportunities are the same as they are on Hollywood and made-for-TV films, with the addition of video technician jobs. On-staff development, programming, and acquisition jobs with the electronic networks offer an exciting opportunity to get in on the ground floor of an industry and for this very reason attract much competition.

Documentary Film (Non-Fiction Film). Documentary films are made for theatrical release (*The Sorrow and the Pity* and *Best Boy*), and for television release (Frederick Wiseman's *Hospital*, *Welfare*, and *Meat*), and for educational purposes. The documentary film employs smaller crews and less equipment than does the feature film and uses no actors. It is a good place for craft and production people to gain early experience. There are a number of successful documentary filmmakers in the country, and some (e.g., the Maysles Brothers) do hire enthusiastic beginners. It is also possible for beginners to experiment on their own documentary films with a crew of one or two, a decent portable camera and equipment, a good location, and a provocative theme. Some documentary films are eligible for grants and others for not-for-profit funding.

Industrial Film (Business Film). Industrial films are financed by and made for the business community by filmmakers who specialize in this kind of work. Industrial films serve a wide variety of purposes from public service to selling tools to special training (e.g., a film on the dangers of smoking sponsored by the American Cancer Society or a film training salespeople in the techniques of selling "extras" sponsored by a car manufacturer). Industrial films are shown to groups, businesspeople, employees, and other nontheatrical audiences. Generally, a professional distributor is hired to make certain the best target groups are reached. Industrials range in length from ten to ninety minutes. Innovative film techniques are applauded and are financially in the realm of possibility. (More than one technique originally developed by industrial filmmakers is being used by feature makers.) The industrial filmmaker is generally the proposal writer, scriptwriter, producer, and director all in one, but depending on company size, free-lance and on-staff people are employed. New York is the center for industrial filmmaking; still, industrial film companies can be found in most of the major cities. Crews are often nonunion.

TV Commercials. Television commercials are produced by commercial production companies for advertising agencies that act in behalf of their business clients. Most "spots" are written by an ad agency copywriter and bid out to a number of production companies that specialize in producing commercials. Once a production company has been chosen, the spot is handed over to the production company producer and director. TV commercial production companies usually maintain on-staff personnel (producers, directors, casting directors, etc.) and hire free-lance crews. The crews are smaller (TV commercials are thirty or sixty seconds long), but are composed of basically the same jobs as other crews. New York is the center for this type of activity, though production companies can be found in Los Angeles, Miami, Atlanta, and a number of other cities. This is an excellent place for would-be's to test out their abilities and get experience (often without moving from home). Both union and nonunion personnel are employed.

Educational Film. Educational films and filmstrips are made by educational filmmakers for corporations, educational publishing companies, schools, universities, libraries, foundations, and for educational television stations for the purpose of passing on knowledge. Topics range from the basic (teaching the alphabet) to the sophisticated (TV's *Nova* series). Educational films are used as tools on all levels of education. There are film companies that specialize in writing and producing the educational film. Generally, these companies are skeleton staffed and hire a number of free lancers (writers, directors, crews) to make the films. Union and nonunion people are employed. Grants and not-for-profit funding are sometimes available.

PART II

ADMINISTRATION

The Administrators

Administrators manage, supervise, oversee, and make decisions. Some administrative jobs are highly creative and require talent and imagination as well as a strong business sense.

The administrators are the catalysts behind the scenes of theatre and film.

4   Administrative Job Descriptions

Arts Manager.   A term rather than a specific job title, it refers to the people who manage not-for-profit theatres and have expertise in management areas, including fundraising, grantsmanship, trusteemanship, long-range planning, and corporate accountability. For additional information, see the profile of Bob Moss on page 51.

Booking Director.   See Program Director.

Box-Office Personnel.   Selling theatre tickets is a more complicated task than one might think. It involves the collection of all revenues from ticket sales, including box-office, mail, and phone orders. Most theatre owners employ a *head treasurer, treasurer,* one or more *assistant* or *apprentice treasurers,* and a *mailroom "girl"* or *"boy."* The head treasurer is responsible for hiring and for doing or assigning the following: He responds to ticket requests over the phone and at the window, pulls tickets for individuals, theatre parties, and complimentary tickets, and works the box-office computer for that purpose. He prepares the box-office statement at the end of each performance (including revenues taken in, attendance, and discounts), makes up bank deposits, keeps track of tickets as they are "racked," and generally supervises all box-office business. This is a union position in most commercial houses and nonunion in many not-for-profit theatres.

Company Manager.   In theatre, the company manager is the producer's and general manager's on-the-spot representative. It is his job to remain with the company (cast, crew, stage managers of a particular production) at the theatre at all performance times. He works with only one company at a time and answers to the general manager. Together with the production stage manager, he handles company business. Some of his tasks are to check each night's take, oversee production expenses, disburse payroll to cast and crew, negotiate contracts, arrange for actors' housing when necessary, and make sure actors file tax withholding and social security forms. He should be familiar with union regulations in case of a dispute with the company. A company manager always accompanies a "bus and truck" company on the road and acts as liaison between the company and the producer's home office. This is the perfect job for aspiring general managers. It is a union job in commercial theatre and an apprenticeship program is available through ATPAM and the League of New York Theatres.

Comptroller (a.k.a. Bookkeeper). Resident theatre companies and some film companies employ a comptroller to account for all monies received and spent. Most times, however, this job is handled by an outside accounting firm. When it is handled in-house, the comptroller analyzes each department's budget and reports to the general manager, company manager, or outside accountant on disbursements and expenditures. He maintains financial records, posts all financial activity to the general ledger, prepares a monthly financial statement and quarterly and year-end payroll tax reports, and for not-for-profit theatres gathers information on grant proposals. For related jobs, see *Production Auditor* and *Studio Executive— Administration*.

Director of Audience Development. This noncommercial resident theatre job is to increase the size of a theatre's paying audience. The director of audience development identifies potential markets (schools, organizations, religious groups, etc.) for each play in his company's repertoire. He develops marketing strategies and campaigns (direct mail, brochures, phone solicitations, flyers) and coordinates all activities with the advertising and public relations department. The director and his staff are interested in increasing a theatre company's subscription audience as well as its single sales. An *assistant* is sometimes employed to make phone calls to potential markets, prepare flyers, and code brochures for demographic studies. For related jobs, see *Subscription Director*.

Director of Funding and Development. This noncommercial resident theatre job is to research, develop, coordinate, and implement all fundraising activities. It's this director's job to develop unearned income—income not earned from ticket sales—from local and national corporations, foundations, government agencies, and the general public. Some responsibilities are to research, write, and review grant proposals, identify and develop new funding sources, review funding publications, prepare progress reports to contributing organizations, acknowledge and keep records of gifts, and coordinate special events such as fundraising luncheons and special theatre parties. The director acts as liaison between the theatre's board of directors and the various funding committees. An *assistant* is sometimes employed to do research at funding libraries, prepare invitations to fundraisers, call patrons for funding purposes, and generally assist.

Distributor.   There are two types of film distribution operations, studio owned and independently owned. The people who work for those operations "lease" films to exhibitors. The studio distribution people lease only those films produced or acquired by their studio. The independent distributors see all available films (i.e., independently produced, foreign, made-for-TV), attend film festivals, and purchase films to distribute. Both operations distribute to various markets (a.k.a. "windows"), such as foreign and domestic theatres, cable TV, network and syndicated TV, overseas TV, electronic systems, and in-flight entertainment. Distribution *print people* are responsible for having prints of films made for the various markets, preparing them for foreign markets (with subtitles or dubbing), and seeing that they get to where they are supposed to be. Distribution *salespeople* explore markets and book the films into the best theatres for the best possible terms. Independent distributors hire local ad agencies and oversee marketing and ad campaigns. In New York, distributors are responsible for placing all media; outside New York, they share this responsibility and expense with the theatre owner. For additional information, see *Studio Executive—Distribution*.

General Manager.   This theatre job is found in both commercial and noncommercial theatre. It is a nonunion position. The general manager is responsible for the business affairs of all companies of a play. In commercial theatre, that might include a Broadway company and several national touring companies. In noncommercial resident theatre, where the job is on-staff, it includes all the companies in the year's ensemble. He keeps track of each company's activities through the respective company managers. His responsibilities include: supervising company managers, production stage managers, comptrollers, attorneys, theatre managers, and press people, and acting as the producer's right hand. He prepares and monitors budgets, oversees staff efforts, determines vendors to undertake jobs (e.g., costume and carpentry shops), and approves purchases. He negotiates contracts. He is responsible for the allocation and disbursement of funds, financial recordkeeping, cash receipts, and general office management. In the past, general managers worked out of producers' offices; of late, they maintain their own where they service a number of clients. They generally work on a fee basis, charging a producer an initial fee to set up a show and a weekly operating fee thereafter. Some general managers demand and get a percentage of a play's profits.

House Manager.   This theatre job is found in commercial and noncommercial theatres. The house manager is responsible for physically maintaining the "house." He supervises the house staff engaged to clean the lobby, lavatories, dressing rooms, and house area. He handles any audience problems or complaints, runs the Actor's Fund Drive and other charity drives, disburses salaries to the house staff and collar money to the ushers ($1 a week to clean and maintain the usher's collar), pays all house bills (e.g., light bulbs), retains ticket stubs for box-office cash reports, and maintains lobby displays and review blow-ups. He maintains communications backstage through the stage manager and gives the "all clear" to start the show. In noncommercial theatre he recruits volunteer ushers.

Literary Manager.　See *Story Editor.*

Packager.　Theatre packagers put together productions of previously produced plays and book them into summer theatres, dinner theatres, and other regional commercial houses. The packager (sometimes an agent) secures the rights of the show from the original producer, assembles a cast, arranges for duplicate costumes and sets to be built, and approaches theatre owners regarding bookings. Self-employed packagers are also referred to as COST (Council of Stock Theatres) producers.

Producer.　Both film and theatre producers are responsible for putting together a project, financing it, developing it, and functioning as a buffer between the parties involved. Producers initiate projects (i.e., by hiring writers to work on original ideas), seek out properties to be adapted, package projects (by finding and attracting directors and stars); they promote projects, seek funding for projects, move projects (e.g., from the noncommercial arena to Broadway), and they remain involved with a project from concept through production and exhibition. There are many kinds of producers—often they will team up to get a project off the ground; one might have a property while another arranges the financing, and so on.

　　Theatre producer.　In theatre, there are *Commercial* and *Noncommercial producers.* Noncommercial producers (*a.k.a. Arts managers* and *Seasonal producers*) work in theatres with not-for-profit status (often ones that they began), and are given titles related to their function in the organization. Generally, they are responsible for keeping their theatres afloat, choosing the plays to be presented each season, overseeing all creative work, hiring key personnel, making public appearances in behalf of the theatre, attending fundraisers, representing their theatre at arts service organization meetings, and governing all activities. For additional information, see the profile of Bob Moss on page 51.

The commercial theatre producer's first task is to find a play he believes will succeed financially. In order to do this he reads new plays, goes to readings, showcases, and other non-commercial productions of plays, and initiates ideas (e.g., to do a revival). Once a producer options the rights from the play-wright to produce his play, he raises the money from individ-uals (angels), other producers (who then become *co-producers*), theatre owners (such as the Shuberts), film companies, and occasionally uses his own. He hires a general manager (who hires the crew) and a director (who hires the cast and designers), a press agent, an ad agency, negotiates for a house, and together with his staff makes decisions on bud-gets, deadlines, creative matters, and marketing strategy. He appears periodically at rehearsals and accompanies the com-pany on its out-of-town run. He makes himself available to his press agent for interviews with the media and is involved with marketing and advertising his play to the public. He maintains control over and sells the rights to touring companies, and maintains contact with and disburses profits to his investors. For additional information, see the profile of Maxine Fox on page 35.

Film producer. Producers are considered to be the catalysts of "new" Hollywood in that they make films happen; the stu-dio chieftains were the catalysts of old Hollywood. All film producers are considered *independent producers* since none work for the studios on a full-time basis (although some have long-term deals with a particular studio). As with theatre pro-ducers, a film producer's first responsibility is to find a "mar-ketable" property, which he does in conjunction with his staff of "creative filters." He then develops the property into a screenplay and arranges for financing and distribution either through traditional means (the studios) or anywhere else. "Creative-type" producers seek out and initiate projects, se-cure properties, package and develop screenplays, and main-tain a strong involvement through the release of a film. "Financier-type" producers (sometimes referred to as execu-tive producers) are more concerned with finding commercially sound properties to invest in. Often, the two types will team up to produce a film, hence the reason for the many screen credits (Executive Producer, Producer, A So-and-So Produc-tion, Associate Producer, Co-Producer). Generally, one pro-ducer is ultimately responsible to the investors, be it a studio or individuals, and for bringing together the major elements of the film and acting as arbitrator when problems arise. There is also the job of *line producer*—a free lancer hired by a producer or studio to handle production problems and follow through on details. He or she stays on top of a project for the producer(s) and/or studio, keeps track of the budget, represents the company in dealings with the union and labs, and supervises the production managers—an excellent position for someone interested in ultimately producing on his own. For additional information on film producers, see the profile of Richard Fischoff in Part III.

Production Auditor. This film job entails handling the daily bookkeeping on a film while it's in production. The auditor enters all expenditures, maintains contact with the film's production accountant, production manager, and production office coordinator, and provides the producer(s) with weekly accounts based on their original budget and actual expenditures. It is a good production entry-level job for anyone with accounting skills.

Production Estimator. This film job involves breaking down a script with regard to cost and submitting the findings to a production executive. It is done in the development stage prior to any commitment by the studio.

Production Manager. In film the production manager is the producer's representative, responsible for managing the entire production on a daily basis. He is among the first of the staff to be hired. On films with one or more units shooting concurrently, each unit has a unit production manager and often an assistant unit production manager. These jobs are described below.

A production manager arranges and schedules all production elements and allocates company funds. He budgets productions (based on departmental estimates and a duration of shooting estimate) and prepares a shooting schedule, arranging for sequences to be shot in the most economical and practical order. He determines the need for and then hires the appropriate number of union personnel. He selects and organizes permits for location areas and studio facilities. He sees that all contracts and clearances are signed. He notifies the cast and crew of work calls, scenes to be shot, sets to be used, equipment and personnel required. He arranges for transportation for staff, cast, crew, and equipment, and for living quarters for personnel required on location. He authorizes all orders and expenditures, and disburses company funds. He expedites and coordinates the work of all departments.

Unit production manager. Acts as the production manager's representative, responsible for managing the unit he is assigned to. His duties are the same as those of the production manager but his entrustment is a particular unit of the production. At certain times, if the production manager is on location or absent for other reasons, the unit manager will take charge of the production.

Assistant unit production manager. Employed when additional production management is required. The assistant will "gofer" and act as expeditor for the production manager and the unit manager(s). He will sometimes serve as liaison between the various managers and the production office. This is an excellent entry-level position.

Production Office Coordinator. The production office coordinator runs a film's production office during the pre-, post-, and production time. All films in production maintain some space (be it at the studio, the production company, or temporary rented space) where administrative matters are handled; the office coordinator heads up this office. He supervises all other office workers (secretaries, clerks, production auditor, production assistants), takes important calls in the absence of the producers or production managers, acts as liaison between the set and the production office, keeps up with the daily bookkeeping if no auditor is employed, and generally assists the producers and production managers in any way possible. This is an excellent above-entry-level position.

Program Director. This theatre job is found in arts centers with several resident companies and theatres. It is the program director's job to seek out and arrange for guest companies to fill in for out-of-season resident companies. For example, if a resident opera company performs for only six months, the program director is responsible for filling the house for the remaining six months. He identifies eligible companies, presents them to a board of directors, and negotiates contracts with the companies chosen. There is also the job of *booking director* in arts centers. He or she arranges for outside bookings with companies and individuals wishing to rent space within the complex for a concert or other one-night stand. He does not seek out talent.

Reader. See *Story Analyst.*

Receptionist. Theatrical and film production offices employ a receptionist to answer the phones, meet and greet visitors, type letters the secretary is too busy to type, order lunch and generally run the front of the office. This is an excellent entry-level position.

Secretary/Assistant. Film and theatre producers, studio and film company executives, general managers, stars, entertainment lawyers, agents and others all hire secretaries to answer and screen phone calls, write and type correspondence, and in general help with the workload. *Production secretaries* are so called because they are hired to work specifically on such production-related tasks as typing a casting list, production notes, script revisions, "sides," and contracts. But they find that everything from opening-night party invitations to the director's grocery list passes their desk. Aware secretaries take advantage of the pivotal position they are in to learn administrative and production procedures inside and out. This is an excellent entry-level position.

Story Analyst (Reader). This theatre and film job can be either free lance or on-staff. In L.A. the job is unionized. Readers read and review properties (hard-cover novels, scripts, plays, unpublished manuscripts) and prepare written reports on them for a story editor or literary manager. Their reports consist of a synopsis of the plot, an evaluation of the kind of work it is (star vehicle, ensemble, big budget, etc.), and recommendations with regard to its commercial and aesthetic potential. An excellent entry-level job, particularly for those with related work experience.

Story Editor. Story editors work for film studios and production companies, and are responsible for getting a first look at new properties in behalf of their company. For this purpose they meet and try to attract agents, writers, and publishers. They are responsible for developing original story ideas as well as finding suitable properties. Once material is submitted to them, they arrange to have it read and evaluated by readers, and pass on favorable findings to their superiors. In theatre, the job is known as that of *Literary Manager* and differs in that the person is concerned only with new plays and playwrights. The job is found with theatre companies that specialize in mounting new plays; otherwise the task of finding new material is left to the producer.

Studio Executive. Most of the major studios are affiliates of large conglomerates and as such are organized like any corporate structure, with a chief executive officer (CEO), division head(s), executives, and executive assistants.

The head of the studio is responsible for all film divisions, studio operations, ultimate revenues, and all executive decisions (they're the ones who can say yes). The division heads are responsible for maintaining productive and financially sound operations, for approving or disapproving actions related to their division, for managing division affairs, generating projects, and assigning executives to specific assignments.

The further up the corporate echelon the executive is, the greater his financial responsibility; those at the very top answer only to the CEO and stockholders. Division heads with real clout are officers of the parent company as well as executives of the studio. Each film studio awards different job titles and responsibilities to its executives, based on what the individual brings to the position and the existing hierarchy. Rather than provide job titles, the most common divisions are described below; again, each studio has its own structure. Generally speaking, for each division described there is a head and a staff of executives and assistants. (See the profile of Sidney Kiwitt on page 45 and that of Peter Saphier on page 57.)

Acquisitions. Acquisitions people are responsible for finding and attracting outside properties (projects not initiated and/or produced by the studio) and for supervising their progress and eventual release. They are also responsible for making profitable acquisitions deals for the studio. Acquisition deals can mean anything from acquiring a finished film to an independent producer's idea or the long-term services of a production company.

Administration (general). Studio administration personnel consist of lawyers, accountants, and others who are responsible for the smooth running of the company. *Lawyers* draft contracts based on memos and conversations with business affairs executives, production executives, and lawyers representing the other party (agent, actor, production company, etc.). *General accountants* are concerned with general expenditures, *production accountants* with monies and financial records of particular films. Many studios employ a *labor relations expert* to represent them in negotiations with the union.

Advertising, publicity, and exploitation. In-house advertising and promotion people develop approaches to market movies. Once the strengths and weaknesses of a project have been identified by the marketing department, the advertising and promotion people set out to present these points to the public. They oversee preparations of ad campaigns, press releases, stories, interviews, trailers, and all other work created to attract their market to the theatre. They hire and direct the work of ad agencies, public relations firms, free-lance illustrators, and publicists. When an independent has produced the film, they work closely with them on all aspects of advertising and promotion. For related jobs, see Part V, Supporting Services—*Advertising, Publicity.*

Business affairs.   Business affairs people (most are lawyers) review negotiations and contracts with anyone the studio does business with: agents, writers, producers, directors, unions and guilds, distribution companies, theatre owners, video and disk producers. Once a studio executive makes a verbal commitment to do something, a business affairs person is brought in and consulted. He is responsible for assuring the best possible financial and legal deal given the circumstances the executive presents. He explains the deal to the legal department, which in turn draws up a contract and returns it to the business affairs person for review and approval.

Distribution.   Studio distribution departments "lease" pictures—those produced by the studio and those acquired by the studio specifically for distribution—to theatre owners. *Distribution executives* are responsible for assuring maximum exposure and revenues for each studio release and for booking films into the best theatres at the best terms. *Salespeople* are responsible for leasing films (selling the rights to show) to worldwide, domestic, TV network, TV syndication, cable TV, and other markets. *Print people* arrange for quality film duplication (for each market, as each has specific requirements) and for the trafficking and tracking of prints in circulation.

Marketing.   Marketing people are concerned with developing approaches to marketing specific movies and mapping out (along with the advertising department) strategies. Marketing teams identify a film's strength, determine how and when the film should be released (TV season, Christmas, summer), who its audience is (age group and gender), which media would be the most appropriate for reaching its proposed audience, and so on. They assess the movie's box-office potential and determine an advertising budget for it. Marketing executives rely heavily on the work of *market researchers*, both in-house and independent.

Production.   Production department personnel are responsible for making films. Some production departments are subdivided into literary affairs (story department), development, creative production, and physical production, each with its own set of executives and assistants answering to the production head. Other production departments allow their executives to float from one area to the next, depending on their interests and talents. Regardless of the company structure, the production team is responsible for choosing, developing, packaging, fostering, and making successful movies for the studio to release; and for wooing to and supporting talent (producers, directors, writers, and actors) at their studio for that purpose. Once a *production head* approves a project, he assigns it to a *production executive,* who acts as liaison between the producer and the studio. The production executive represents the studio and its money, and in its behalf nurtures the film along, makes creative suggestions, approves hiring and firing decisions, watches over monetary flow, keeps track of editing progress, and generally oversees the film's progression.

Subscription Director. This noncommercial theatre job is to develop a theatre's subscription audience—patrons who subscribe to a theatre for a season rather than purchasing tickets for individual plays. The subscription director and his staff design and implement renewal campaigns, correspond with subscribers, fill subscription orders, assign seasonal seats, and work with the advertising staff in designing subscription brochures and flyers. In smaller theatre companies, this job is handled by the head treasurer or director of audience development.

5 Administrative Profiles

Maxine Fox, Producer of the Play *Grease* on Broadway

It's a theatrical producer's job to make theatrical events happen. They find a property, raise funds, choose a staff, act as a creative buffer, and supervise the marketing of the play. They are responsible for the artistic and financial success of the production. Although there is much "producing-in-law" going on in the theatre (and in film) today, traditionally the responsibility falls on one person, the producer.

"I provide entertainment that people pay for. It's my job to sell tickets and to choose projects I can sell tickets to. The way I like to produce, the producer is involved in every aspect [of producing]. He is the only person who sees the whole pie; everybody else sees only their slice."

Maxine Fox, a woman in her late thirties, is a producer in the old-fashioned sense of the word, in that she takes responsibility from beginning to end. Together with her former partner/husband, Ken Waissman, she ran the New York theatrical office of Waissman & Fox and has produced, among other things, the longest running Broadway show, *Grease*. For her, the producer's job is a craft, a series of skills to learn and perfect.

"Once you together with your [theatrical] lawyer option a play, the next step is to organize. You give yourself an ideal opening date and work back from there. You set a rehearsal date and give yourself a goal for raising money and hiring the director and finding a theatre. You do many things simultaneously. If you don't have a general manager, you talk to different general managing offices until you find the right one. Once you do, you negotiate their fee: an initial fee for setting up a show and a weekly fee from the show once it's running. The general manager suggests a company manager. At the beginning, you work with your general manager to set up your budgets, a production budget and an operating budget. These give you an idea of how much money you must raise, how much it will cost you to operate the production, what the potential gross should be, what the potential profit is, how long it will take to get the investment back at three quarters capacity, half capacity and a full house.

"The lawyer draws up a prospectus and offering circular and a limited partnership agreement (which sets up the terms and conditions under which you take someone's money). You 'offer' the play to anybody you know who could invest in it and afford to lose the money. A theatrical investment should be for intelligent fun. It's more fun than the stock market. Investors could lose their money in one night or could make a killing. Fortunately, *Grease* turned out to be an example of a killing. You sell in units; each unit has a dollar figure attached to it. In some cases you don't take anything less than one unit, in other cases you'll take a fraction. While you raise the money you finalize dates and nail down personnel, hire an ad agency and press agent.

"As a producer you have thousands of choices to make, several of which will determine the fate of the show. One is the direction the publicity and advertising is going to take. You learn who your audience is and direct a very specific campaign at them. You have to be objective and listen to what's being said about the show, not what you want to hear. If you think there's life in your box office, you

Kenn Duncan, Ltd.

MAXINE FOX

can beat bad reviews with an intelligent and well-managed ad and PR campaign early in the show's run. Also you must determine where a show will try out, whether it should try out at all, what theatre it goes into (out of town as well as in). You choose a theatre that's atmospherically right for your show and hope you can get it. All these choices are important. Once the show opens, your job changes. You not only have to maintain the quality of the production and make sure the ads and publicity are continuing to sell the show, you also have to make money for your investors. There are many ways to generate income apart from the Broadway production: with road companies, a movie sale, a record sale, TV, merchandising. Sometimes we produce these ourselves; other times it's a matter of leasing the rights. With the exception of road companies, these rights are known as subsidiary rights. Subsidiary rights income is shared by the author and the company [i.e., the producer and his investors] 10 percent to 40 percent, with the author receiving the greater share. Investors are paid back before any profits are taken. Until that time, producers earn money by drawing a weekly producer's fee from the operating budget.

"When I'm not in production, I'm involved in finding a new property. I attend little showcases and readings. People audition musicals for me. Authors send scripts, agents send scripts. I listen to authors' ideas; I generate ideas myself and hire someone to write the book, music and lyrics to see if it all becomes what I want it to become. If it doesn't, I have to be objective enough to drop it right then and there."

Maxine Fox has known she wanted a career in show business since she was six. She caught the "show biz disease" in her first dancing class in her native Baltimore and went on to the lead in the high school play. Her drama teacher had only one complaint about Maxine's acting—she was always looking around at what everybody else was doing. She studied drama at Boston University, one of the few schools at the time (early sixties) where one could major in theatre from the freshman year. The summer following her first year, Maxine took a stock job in a Baltimore tent theatre with the Music Fair Organization, New York theatrical producers who specialized in producing "star packages" for summer stock theatres. She headed the prop department and assisted the house manager. The producers came around and saw Maxine at work. They liked her spirit, eagerness and commitment, and offered her a job in their New York office.

"I place a high value on a college education; you learn conceptual thinking that you really need later on. But when I had to make a decision to do theatre or study it, I came to New York and finished my schooling in the offices of Broadway. I was hired as a receptionist. What I did was assist; I could anticipate someone else's needs and fulfill them. I was not as good in the secretarial department. I answered phones and made calls for the producers and (slowly) typed their letters. They were producing a bus and truck production of *Carnival* at the time and I was asked to be the production secretary, at no additional salary. I worked with the director and choreographer and it was a fantastic experience. The director and choreographer were the production stage manager and dance captain of the Broadway show, so I could go over there and watch them work. No one told me to do that but my instincts told me it was a fantastic opportunity. That's how I managed to get backstage on Broadway for the first time. It was a good entry-level job. I learned the names of countless agents, producers, lawyers, people involved in the business. The sooner you become familiar with who does what and the names of the theatres and producing organizations, the more valuable you are. I didn't know that then, I just did it because I wanted to know."

After a year and a half Maxine left the Music Fair Organization and for the first time actually looked for a job in the theatre. She liked the environment of commercial theatre production and looked for the same type of work, but with Broadway producers. Her only goal at the time ("I was no Eve Harrington") was to get to work with a director.

"If you're working around the industry or care or love the theatre, you read everything you can about it and learn what's going on. I read the trade papers and *Theatrical Index* [weekly listing of theatrical events; see Appendix B] and learned they were preparing the Broadway production of *Funny Girl*. I sent the producers a letter."

In case she got no reply from *Funny Girl's* producers, Maxine handpicked a list of people she wanted to work for and sent them letters too. She got a number of responses. One of them was from Garson Kanin, director and co-producer of *Funny Girl*.

"We hit it off in the interview. He offered me a job in his office as a receptionist and of course I took it. I worked for him and a little bit for Ruth Gordon [his wife]. I answered the phones, made calls, typed the next day's schedule. I got whatever work came down the line. It was second-level stuff because both Mr. Kanin and his general manager had personal secretaries. Those were the days when producers still maintained the exclusive services of a general manager. Today, general managers maintain their own office and work for several producers simultaneously. Once the work on the show began, Mr. Kanin asked me to do all the research and I got to work with the playwright. Because I didn't like going back and forth to the library I found ways to con information out of people on the phone. Once I had to get a description of roller skates in the 1920s for a lyric. I called the Sears catalogue and had them read the description to me over the phone. I had the information to the lyricist within the hour. My boss was impressed. But I did it that way because I was lazy. Lazy people are often the most successful because they find short cuts!"

When the show went into rehearsal, Maxine was given permission to watch. She was in that theatre every spare moment she had.

"I became friendly with Barbra Streisand. Because I wanted to learn as much as I could, I was always looking for ways to make myself useful. One day I noticed Barbra standing in the lobby of our office building. She had an appointment with Jule Styne, the composer of the show, and he was late. I asked if she wanted me to read lines with her while she waited. She thought it was a terrific idea. After that, whenever she had five minutes she'd call me and I'd come down and read lines with her."

Eventually, Barbra asked Maxine to help "professionalize" her life and become her personal secretary. (This was just the beginning of Barbra's "super-star" status.) Maxine was to be set up in a small room in Barbra's home.

"Going to work for Barbra Streisand was a fascinating part of my education. It was a lateral move for me but I picked up knowledge about the recording industry [Barbra recorded the "People" album while Maxine worked for her] and about a star's behavior and how to deal with it. Later on, when I least expected it, I used what I'd learned. She really needed someone older and more experienced than I was. I never was on top of the job. After six months and a lot of fun we parted amicably and I set out to get back into the theatre."

Maxine sent out another series of letters. She found a job with the Broadway producers of *Sweet Charity* and *Mame*. She believes she was offered the job because when asked why she wanted to work for these producers she answered honestly, "Because I respect your work."

"There I was at the receptionist desk again, loving my work. I asked a hundred million questions. The best thing about being in an active office is that you have people to ask questions of. And no question is a stupid question; you must ask or you'll never learn. I was moved up to executive secretary to one of the producers. I kind of hated to lose the phone because there's no better way to get to know people in the industry than to answer the phones in a theatrical office. I had regular secretarial duties and tried to become as familiar with everything as I could. Any file they would open up to me, I would read. If I could take care of a problem without bothering my boss, I did. When *Sweet Charity* opened, I helped with the gala and handled house seats [very good seats reserved and paid for by VIP's and people in the industry]. In that job I got a good idea of what it's like to produce a Broadway show from the producer's office point of view. There were investors to deal with, money to be raised, advertising suggestions to mull over, logos to choose."

The next show "up" was *Mame,* and Maxine was asked to be director Gene Saks' assistant. Whether to accept was a difficult decision because if she agreed she would have to give up her secure position of secretary in a busy production office for the insecure job of director's assistant, which would terminate once the show opened. "I chose the show. I loved it so much. I was your basic low man on the totem pole. I ran for coffee, I was a gofer; if there were changes in the script during rehearsals, I would type them. The office life was over except for the Xeroxing. I was there at the director's side throughout rehearsals. If he needed cigarettes, I made sure he had them; I'd carry around an extra pack of his brand at my own expense. If he needed somebody to yell at or a smiling face to look at, I was there. There was nothing too menial for me. But, oh, what I learned just sitting there. I watched the director and choreographer at work; I saw Gene shape the show, handle problems, work with Angela Lansbury. I saw the components of the show come together, the difference between the first run-through and the dress rehearsal; I saw if the director's notes were fulfilled or not fulfilled. When we went out of town [to try out] I'd sit at the director's side taking notes, for the tech and dress rehearsal and all performances. I'd get the script changes from the author and run back to my hotel room to type and mimeograph them. At each day's rehearsals I would give the director a typed copy of notes from the previous evening's performance and new scenes from the author. I watched it all happen.

"Angela Lansbury was said to be very difficult to work with on forthcoming shows. I was surprised to hear that because on *Mame* she was a pussy cat, a piece of cake, a lovely lovely woman. I came to realize it was because we had a strong producer and director. Even though her name was above the title, she could relax because she didn't feel she was carrying the burden by herself. On chaotic productions where the producers and directors aren't strong, the stars get frantic and insecure. It was a valuable lesson to learn, but of course, while I was running for coffee, I didn't realize I had learned it."

Maxine's job was over opening night. Again she made up her list and sent out letters. She found a job as Dore Schary's assistant on a musical called *A Joyful Noise*. Maxine was to be a director's assistant, do some minor casting, and serve as one of the ASMs (assistant stage managers). The play was a flop but Maxine turned it into a positive personal experience. Associated with that musical were two unknown people, Tommy Tune, then a dancer, and Michael Bennett, on his first choreography job. Had Maxine handled herself differently during this disaster, she never would have gained the relationship of mutual respect she did with these two masters of musical theatre. She also learned what the term "badly produced" meant, for that show was a classic example. In fact, the producer literally took over the director's job. From there she went on to assist the producers and cast the New York production of *You're a Good Man, Charlie Brown*. Once it opened, she managed a "sit-down company" of the play in Toronto.

Maxine never did any of her jobs long enough to become truly expert in them, yet she gained enough experience and knowledge so that, one day, she could supervise people who were experts. She had assisted producers, directors, choreographers, playwrights, packagers, and a star. She had propped a show, stage-managed a show, cast a show, and managed a company. She was, she believed, ready to produce on her own. She was in her late twenties.

"At that point I met my former partner [and husband] and we began talking about opening a producing office. A year and a half and some odd jobs later, we incorporated. We had no property. To get one, we actually took out an ad in *Variety*. Our first show came about indirectly because of that ad. An agent contacted us and suggested we see one of her properties in L.A. While we were out there we saw a production of *Fortune and Men's Eyes* directed by Sal Mineo. By coincidence, it was represented by the same agent. We optioned it with the little bit of money we had. Front money [the money that is spent before you capitalize a show] is hard to raise. We got money from other people as soon as we could. It's a bad idea to produce with your own money because costs in excess of what you raise are your responsibility, and if there are debts of the company, they are yours alone. Also, you need your money for options, and to keep your producing organization going, so you don't speculate if you can help it."

Maxine and her partner produced the play Off Broadway.

"We were not into doing big things right off the bat. We had a lot to learn and we knew it. We were just as happy to learn it in the smaller commercial arena of Off Broadway. We were setting up our organization at the same time we were putting together the show, so we had to hire a lawyer to negotiate options, a general manager to give us advice about each new step, and a press agent who would begin by announcing the project. It took us about six months, which is fast. We opened to generally bad reviews but ran a full season. We saved the show through our advertising and publicity campaign."

Next, Maxine and Ken co-produced a production of Paul Zindel's *And Miss Reardon Drinks a Little,* starring Julie Harris and Estelle Parsons. The other producer needed additional money to finance the production and asked Maxine and Ken to read the script and consider raising money for it. They agreed, so that they could have their first experience producing on Broadway.

The next show they produced was *Grease.*

"A dentist friend of Ken's called us from Chicago to say he had seen this community theatre group do a play and maybe it wasn't right for Broadway but boy, did he have a good time. When he called back a second time, we realized he was serious and went out to see it. It was indeed a community production, with teachers and sales clerks playing the parts. The show was ragged but it was like opening a cedar chest of 1950s memories. In the middle of all the roughness, we saw the embryo of something very special. We asked the authors (a lingerie salesman and advertising copywriter) to come to New York and rewrite the play. We wanted to professionalize it, but keep the rough edges. They were very gutsy and agreed to quit their jobs and come to New York. As soon as the play was in shape, we showed it to a director. Then we hired a choreographer, a musical director, orchestrator, designers, and a cast. We raised the money in a month and opened Off Broadway. We kept it there until the climate was right uptown [for five months] and brought it to Broadway, where it stayed eight years. It was our job throughout those eight years to keep the show physically fresh on the stage and in the public's mind."

Maxine has brought entertainment to millions of people, made a lot of money for her investors, and influenced the styles and fashions of people throughout the world by bringing back the fifties. She is a producer in the complete sense of the word.

She offers the following advice to those who wish to follow in her footsteps:

"The very first thing is to always assume that you're going to be able to do what you want to do. The minute you think you're not, you'll never accomplish it. If you get a job as a secretary—and people who turn their noses up at secretarial work are crazy, it's an excellent way to get into the business—and you sit around thinking you'll never get to be a producer, you probably won't. If you assume you will, you have a chance. And of course, you've got to deeply love theatre because it requires a total commitment.

"If you want to make a lot of money, don't go into theatre, because in the beginning you practically pay them. It's possible to make a lot of money, but not for a long time, and it certainly shouldn't be your reason for entering the business; there are much easier ways to make money.

"It's difficult to do all the things you need to do in order to learn the craft of producing. But it must be done, for producing is a craft, a skill, and a business, and it's dangerous to underestimate it. Theatre is called the 'diamond of the arts' for a good reason. You get one shot to succeed or fail with a show, and to succeed you need an enormous amount of skill.

"I've always found that if you keep your nose to the grindstone, inevitably, you're going to land where you belong and get what you deserve. The only thing that is ever important is the work itself. If you let your ego interfere, you'll never learn the business. The best way to learn is to be around people in the business you respect and can ask questions of and observe in action. I've learned half of what I know through osmosis.

"The watchwords of the industry are: 'You never know,' and, 'Never assume.' You must always do your best work. You never know who's watching or who is going to be watching later on, or how a relationship formed at one point in your career will influence the rest of it. That's true for behind-the-scenes people as well as performers. The only time you're safe is when you're home with the door closed. That's why it's called *show* business."

Sidney (Sid) Kiwitt, Executive Vice President
Warner Brothers Business Affairs Expert

It's the job of the business affairs person to look out for his studio's interests on all contractual agreements. Studio executives and lawyers look to their business affairs expert for advice and foresight with regard to business matters. Business affairs people get involved with a project when someone else in the company with authority to do so, be it production executive, acquisitions executive, or corporate officer, decides to make a deal. The business affairs person is brought in because he is expert in the requirements of acquisition and the complexities of deal making.

Business affairs, as a defined job title, is relatively new to the movie industry. Movie companies recognized the need for a business affairs point of view sometime in the 1960s when so many of them grew into giant conglomerates. Until that time, company lawyers handled business affairs. What was needed was a "dollars and cents" person, someone to take notice of what an executive's decision might cost the company in the long run. Today, with the advent of video cassette deals, cable TV deals, participation deals, and other complicated long-term deals, some made to cover periods of twenty years and more, people with business affairs savvy are crucial to the movie industry.

Sid Kiwitt was one of the first to become expert in the field.

"Business affairs people augment things," says Sid. "They make things work that other people want to do. I'm not the creator or initiator of deals. I structure them and get them into the system, maximize the company's potential from them.

"The way business affairs works is an executive of the company okays a project. He tells whomever he's dealing with to have his agent or lawyer or accountant or business affairs person or even the person himself call one of our business affairs people. So they call, or we call them, and we either make a deal or we don't. If we do, then one side writes a letter and sends it to the other side, stating what the deal is. The other side writes back saying this is okay or asks for

Merri Anne Milwee

SID KIWITT

changes. At that point the negotiator [whoever in the business affairs department has been assigned to handle the transaction] writes a memo to the legal department asking them to draw up a contract based on such-and-such terms. The contract is drafted; before it goes out, it's checked to see that the details are consistent with the deal. If both parties then agree that the terms are properly stated, the contract is signed.

"As the job of business affairs has evolved, it means getting involved in any negotiations to acquire anything in a [film] company. That means dealing for people, places and things: an actor [stars only, since casting directors generally negotiate contracts for non-leading roles], a writer, a director, buying a property, a screenplay. It sometimes includes buying a complete picture. It can include almost anything there is a business need for outside the physical production area. For example, I've had to analyze companies we wanted to acquire, acquire the movie rights (from the musical acts) in the film *Woodstock*, set up a French and English subsidiary to take advantage of those countries' aid rules, acquire rights to pictures such as *Superman* and several thousand others. For a short period of time I was even the general manager of a theatrical play we had invested money in. All these types of actions, depending on the size of a company, may be included in the business affairs function."

Sid Kiwitt began his career as an accountant with the public accounting firm of Peat Marwick Mitchell and Company. Realizing there was no room for advancement, he asked them to find him another job, which is something public accounting firms do. One of the jobs they found for Sid was with Seven Arts Associated Corporation, a small (five-person) newly formed TV distribution company that would ten years later become Warner Brothers Inc.

"I was hired specifically to be the comptroller of Seven Arts, to do the bookkeeping and accounting and to be the lackey and 'handler.' It was a small company, we had five guys and four of them were bosses. I was the one worker. Because it was a small company—and this is important—I did certain things that weren't necessarily the comptroller's job. In the course of the next few years I not only carried out the normal accounting functions, but also negotiated contracts, got involved with taxes, handled the insurance on pictures, and even ran the projector every now and then. Whenever something had to be done, I ended up doing it because it was just my way of life."

Seven Arts Corporation grew rapidly. First, Ray Stark joined the company, making it a producing company as well as a television distribution company, and with him they started making movies for other film companies to distribute. At the same time, they formed a London production company. Things were really happening and growing—and Sid Kiwitt grew along with them. He got involved with business affairs when Ray Stark joined the company. Ray had brought in a business affairs expert who remained mainly in the West Coast office. Sid worked with him and handled the New York business affairs.

"Elliott [Hyman, then president of Seven Arts] or Ray would make a deal with, let's say, MGM and would lay down the broad strokes of the deal. I would sit in New York and talk with MGM's lawyer, because in those days there were few business affairs people, and negotiate some of the details of the deal and iron out the contract problems. The first agreement I ever did business affairs on was a directorial contract with the director of the film *Rampage*. Nobody was around to look at the contract before it went out and nobody who was around wanted to sign it. Since I was the only one who would sign anything, they forwarded it to me. I wasn't about to sign anything I hadn't read first, so I read it. I came to a provision in the contract that said the director will be getting X number of dollars for X numbers of weeks at X rate. If he goes over X weeks, he gets X number of additional dollars. It then went on to say that if the start date was before a certain time, it was a 'flat' deal and he got no overtime no matter how long the picture took. I called our lawyer and told him to find out what day the picture would begin. It turned out it would be starting one day after the director was to start on the overtime portion of the contract. I asked our lawyer to change the date of the contract by one day so that we could use the flat portion of the contract. He did, and the director was on a 'flat' deal. After that, every contract that came through from production that had to be signed in New York was read by me."

In 1967, Seven Arts Corporation bought out Warner Brothers and Atlantic Records. In 1969, Kinney Inc. bought out Seven Arts. As the company grew into the entertainment conglomerate it is today, the number and kinds of business deals it was involved with grew as well. Sid Kiwitt was made an officer of the company and handled some of its complex deals.

"To some extent the most difficult problem of a business affairs person is to maintain a consistency in negotiations. A business affairs person is brought in because he is supposed to have knowledge of the inner workings of a deal, but also to maintain some kind of consistency of corporate policy. You always have to keep in mind that what you're doing today is going to relate to what you'll do tomorrow. Every time you open your mouth, you set a precedent. You have to be consistent, among other reasons, so that the deal can be administrated without a substantial increase in overhead. For example, for years the industry had a policy of accepting a five-year license for the use of music in a TV show. I saw that that was absolutely absurd. It meant that every five years we would be at the mercy of the publishers or would have to take the music out of the film. I made it a matter of corporate policy that we would not accept anything less than a perpetual license.

"An example of what happens when you make a deal and don't consider what the long-term effect will be is one I made in 1971. I thought it was an interesting deal and it satisfied the situation at the moment. One of our executives developed a program to hire a number of unknown writers to do original screenplays for us [out of which came *Blazing Saddles* and its screenwriter, Andy Bergman]. The deal was we'd pay them guild minimum and a bonus to make up for the low initial fee if we made the picture. The deal ran something like this [1971 prices]: $3,500 for a first draft, $5,000 to $7,000 for the next draft, and a $20,000 to $30,000 bonus if we made the picture. If he got joint screenplay credit, the writer got half the bonus. That was the kick. I made ten or twelve deals, and the next thing I knew, everyone—not just this group of unknowns— was asking for half a bonus if they got joint screen credit. They even started to ask for percentage points [of the movie's profit] and that wasn't even in my calculation. Being competitive we gave percentage points, but all of a sudden every deal we made came through with 2 percent of the profits and half the bonus for shared screen credit. What happened was we stopped thinking about why they were getting half the bonus originally. It didn't make sense to give a guy a percentage of the profits and half the bonus if we dropped him after the first draft, because if we dropped him it meant he failed, and if he failed why should he get a percentage of the profits? I needed to put the whole thing back in perspective and after that make each deal to fit the situation. The next deal I made, the writer got more cash but no points if we picked up the second draft, and so on and so forth. What I'm trying to say is that just because you create one deal with a half bonus didn't mean that every deal from then on should include half a bonus. So, the problem in business affairs is to relate what you do today with what may happen tomorrow."

On working within the bounds of a large corporation, he adds: "The problem is how to do more yet do it in such a manner that you don't make enemies; how to be a nice guy and still get the job done. One way to succeed is to ask people to teach you; the more you know, the better you'll be able to do your job. Of course, the better you do your job, the more you may be putting someone else's in jeopardy. So you must learn to tread the fine line between being pushy and not pushy. Find the line where you can learn from many people without interfering with those people in a negative way. If you think a co-worker has done something wrong and you say so to the president, you may get a little closer to the president but you've sure made an enemy of your co-worker. On the other hand, if you go directly to the guy and say: 'Can you help me with this—do you think it would have been better to do it this way?' you not only rectify the problem, you may end up with a friend. It's one word— politics. How to present yourself, learn, grow, and not be negative or have negative things said about you. Fifty percent of getting ahead in this business has to do with your ability to deal with people; the remaining fifty percent is your ability to do the job."

Looking at his particular business affairs career, Sid remarks:

"Nobody has had the opportunity to learn what I learned. I was in a unique position with a company that was extremely small that got involved in every facet of the entertainment business. I was in a growing company and I took responsibility and I was mostly right. I could have been mostly wrong, and if I was, I'd be long gone."

Sid offers the following advice to anyone eager to enter the field:

"You can get into business affairs from any place, depending on your ability, talent, and luck. But it's very hard. There are no business affairs beginners these days; you're expected to perform immediately and you'd better know what you're performing about because if you don't you're thrown to the wolves.

"Your problem is to put yourself in a position where you can get a job. It's almost a prerequisite that you've been to law school [all but two business affairs executives in the movie industry are lawyers; Sid Kiwitt is one of the two]. Business affairs requires an extensive knowledge of business, law, and accounting.

"Since the motion picture companies don't have apprenticeship programs, you've got to find something that's closely akin to business affairs or the industry. You could get an apprenticeship with a legal firm that has connections with the industry. Or, you could do as my assistant did: pick up the phone and find somebody like me who needs an assistant. Another way is to get a job close to the area, even if it's as a file clerk, and work your way in, or you could get a job with a small company and as positions open up in larger firms, work your way up.

"I think the biggest factor in success will be your ability to be creative about the job you're doing, no matter what it is, and at the same time to be bigger than the job you're doing. If you think in terms of doing a casting deal, you'll probably never do more than a casting deal. If you think in terms of being president of the company, you may not be president of the company but you'll be doing more than casting deals. You get restricted by your own restrictions."

Bob Moss, Producing Director of Playwrights Horizons

Producing directors at Off Off Broadway theatre companies are the backbone of those companies. They are responsible for keeping the company fiscally sound, artistically successful, and emotionally soothed.

According to Bob Moss, the job description for producing director is somewhat different in every institution, because it depends on the people.

"My job is to keep the whole machine going. I am the spokesman for the organization; I do the 'politicking'; I keep the artistic director on the right track and maintain an overview for everyone in the company. I create long-range policy, artistic and philosophical, and see that it's carried out. I make the whole thing happen and keep up everyone's morale. No one ever sees me depressed."

One of the unique things Bob has done as producing director of Playwrights Horizons is to change the face of the street on which Playwrights is located. Once one of New York's most distressed blocks, 42nd Street between 9th and 10th Avenues is now the home of Theatre Row, a cluster of nine theatre companies, restaurants, and cafés.

"The concept for 'The 42nd Street Gang' was a half-baked idea born when we first moved Playwrights in. When I get an idea for something, I find it helps to give it a name. I started marketing it

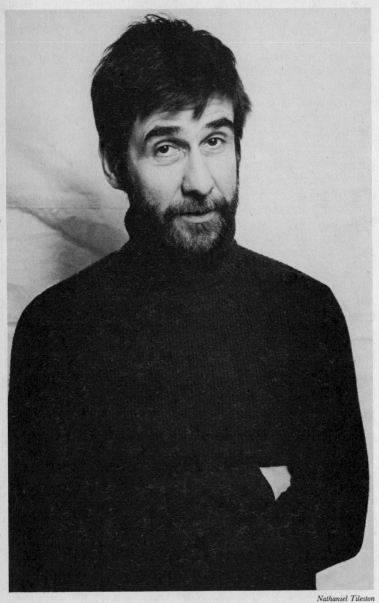

Nathaniel Tileston

BOB MOSS

around town, went to a lot of corporate lunches, and asked everyone I could think of for funds. Asking was the key. Asking is the key to everything; getting rejected is not so terrible. If you learn to live with rejection you can ask for everything. Eventually, the funds were raised by the 42nd Street Redevelopment Corporation and the concept became a reality."

When Bob came to New York in the late 1950s from Newark, New Jersey, he hadn't yet learned that "Asking is the key to everything."

"When I first came to New York to become an actor, I'd wander up and down 45th Street, stare at the theatres, and wonder how I'd get in. The simple solution of walking in hadn't occurred to me. As far as I was concerned, there was an invisible wall keeping me out and making it impossible for me to start my career. I knew I wanted to work in the theatre when I was nine years old. I wanted to be an actor because it was the only theatre job I could see. By the time I came to New York I had lots of experience; I acted in forty to fifty plays in high school, temple, the Y, and local stock companies, and each summer that I was in high school I went away to summer stock and worked props, or washed floors, or painted—whatever was necessary to stay there.

"When I got to New York, I enrolled in Queens College and immediately joined their student theatre group. Because of all my experience, I was made group director. As soon as I started to direct, I related to it more than to acting and moved toward directing."

While he was "waiting" to get to Broadway, Bob organized small productions of plays and acting classes all over town. There was no Off Off Broadway movement at that time, but what he was doing, without knowing it, was helping to start one.

"I was bursting with energy and nothing was going to stop me. I didn't know anything, so therefore I knew everything. I organized an acting class with forty students paying one dollar a session. I wouldn't dare do that today. I know enough to know I know nothing about teaching acting. I started a group, The Murray Hill Players, and produced and directed plays for them. Someone I knew from the group told me about a stage-managing job at a stock company on Nantucket. I was immediately interested, not for the reasons I should have been, like getting my Equity card and entering the profession, but because I could spend a summer in Nantucket and not go back to NBC, where I had a job as a gofer. As it turned out, I did the right thing; but I can't take credit for it."

Bob lied to get the job; he said he had his Equity card. He got the job and then he got the card.

"In five minutes on the job everyone knew I had lied and had never stage-managed before. I knew enough to paste up a script but did really dumb things like use a ballpoint [instead of an erasable pencil] to mark it. For two weeks it was a real disaster, but I bluffed my way through and learned. They never had to tell me the same thing twice. By the end of the season the same contact who had told me about this job told me about another, his. He was stage-managing a big Off Broadway play and was leaving it. I took the job immediately and found I was a natural stage manager. At the time, I didn't think of it as a career, but of course it's a wonderful career. Who knew that then? Stella Holt was the producer of the show and she was blind. One day she wanted coffee and I got it for her. The next week she again asked for coffee. I remembered she took it black with no sugar and on the strength of that she hired me as stage manager for a new musical she was producing with Dom DeLuise called *All in Love*."

Bob developed a reputation as stage manager extraordinaire and was always able to leave one show for another. He still thought that someday he'd go back to his "career" of directing, never realizing he had a good career in stage managing.

"Every fall, Gordon Davidson, then production stage manager of the Phoenix Theatre, would call me in for an interview for some job or another. I never did get those jobs. In 1963 he called, and I thought, one more futile interview with Gordon. This time, I got the job. Gordon was off to California to start his own small theatre group, which today, of course, is the Mark Taper Forum, and I was to be his replacement at the Phoenix. Shortly after I arrived, the APA [Company] came in, with Ellis Rabb. My relationship with that company was love at first sight. I worked with it for four years, the last two at the Lyceum [Theatre] on Broadway. There simply was no better stage-managing job. There was nowhere else for me to go. Having worked with Ellis, his wife Rosemary Harris, and Helen Hayes, I realized no one could offer me anything better."

After a ten-year career as a stage manager, Bob drew the line. "I needed to get myself emotionally ready for a change, so while I was still at APA I organized a group of the 'spear carriers' from our Broadway production of *War and Peace* and, in our spare time, directed them in a production of *Two Gentlemen of Verona*. They were getting $125 a week, could afford to work for free and were very restless. I was earning a good $300 a week and could afford to rent a theatre and pay for the flyers, so I thought, why not? We rehearsed in the costume shop for three weeks from 11:00 P.M. to 3:00 A.M. The hours didn't seem unusual to us; we'd have been out drinking anyway. I rented Theatre Four on West 55th Street for two weeks and played eight performances. Now you'd call it a 'showcase,' but then, no one knew about such things. I just did it because I emotionally needed to make myself a director and pull myself out of stage managing."

He didn't anticipate what happened next, but again, by following his instincts and making things move, Bob did the right thing. Two directing job offers came from that production he showcased. From those two came other offers, and for the next year and a half he traveled around the country earning a living directing plays for regional and dinner theatres.

"As part of my guest directing stints, I directed some new plays at the Playwrights Unit, an experimental theatre run by Edward Albee and Richard Barr. Richard and Edward asked me to be managing director of the Playwrights Unit. I was honored and of course said yes. It turned out to be a glorified stage management job, but I did run the theatre and functioned as a producer. I had never envisioned myself running a theatre or working by choice with new playwrights, but as soon as I started to do it I connected with it. It took eighteen hours of my day but I loved using my energy that way."

After a year the Playwrights Unit closed, leaving Bob unemployed but with a direction. He now knew that what he wanted to do was to work with new playwrights in his own theatre.

"I found that there was a whole other theatre going on in the world. I had been so busy hustling a career on Broadway and working from 8 A.M. to midnight for a repertory company that I let the sixties go right by me. It wasn't until the early seventies that I became aware of Off Off Broadway and the regional theatre movements."

Once aware, Bob acted. Because of his work with the Playwrights Unit, he was asked to suggest new playwrights for a project at the YMCA. Bob recognized this as an opportunity. He refused the request and asked instead for the room so that he might make a theatre out of it.

"We supported ourselves by holding up a shopping bag at the end of the show and asking people to donate. Slowly we took over the Y. They managed to find $50 in their budget for me. I supplemented this by producing fashion shows, but by the second year the New

York State Council on the Arts came in with my salary. The National Endowment for the Arts came in right after that."

That theatre at the Y and the funding Bob raised for it was the beginning of Playwrights Horizons, the birthplace of some of our most successful contemporary American plays: Albert Innaurato's *Gemini*, Jack Heifner's *Vanities*, Robert Patrick's *Kennedy's Children*, Wendy Wasserstein's *Uncommon Women and Others*.

In 1974, the Y underwent a fiscal crisis and was forced to sell some buildings, among them Bob's.

"I could have stayed there forever; I was as content as a cow in pasture. Playwrights knew their plays would be treated well; we used good actors, had professional management and working toilets. The plays poured in. Then suddenly in the summer of '74 we had no building."

Once again, Bob walked the streets of New York, staring at theatres, wondering what to do to get in. This time he had a possible $44,000 in grant money, an established theatre company, and twenty years of experience along with him.

"I wandered around the city for months. I didn't know what to do or where to go. One day it suddenly dawned on me, if I wanted something I could figure out a way to get it. Playwrights Horizons began on that day. I found the building on 42nd Street. Thirty days and a lot of grimy cleaning up later we opened our first play. At the same time I went to the Department of Cultural Affairs and told them they should help me because I was an asset to the city. A few days later they gave us a building in Queens to start another theatre in. It was madness, but we did it."

Today, new plays that mature successfully at Playwrights on 42nd Street go into a subscription season in the Queens theatre. This unique "theatre institution" came about because Bob Moss made it come about. He let people know who he was and what he was doing, and he asked. Bob manages both theatres, teaches at NYU, is on the advisory board of the International Theatre Institute and a production company known as Creation, has been an NEA and NYSCA panelist, on the board of TCG, and co-founder and president of OOBA. (See Appendix B for descriptions of these organizations.)

"I know myself well. My gift is energy and the ability to make full use of whatever intelligence I have. Most people use only a fraction of their abilities. I have good instincts. I'm willing to stay up all night to make things happen. I 'win' simply because I hang in there longer than most people will. If I want something I won't let anything stand in the way. You have one life; if you want to spend it drinking beer and watching television, terrific, but don't complain that everyone else is getting things. Most people are afraid that someone will say no, so they don't do much, they don't venture out. What I've learned is not to shrivel up into a pile of dust if someone rejects me. There's nothing wrong with being rejected."

Bob's day as producing director is filled with a variety of activities: attending rehearsals and performances at both theatres (he shows up regularly); meeting with funding organizations, staff, artistic directors, and the new playwrights being produced at Playwrights; along with the managing director, looking for new means of support for the theatre; speaking to his subscription audience in Queens; doing all the "politicking" necessary to keep a nonprofit theatre alive, and generally acting as the theatre's spokesman.

To would-be producers, institutional entrepreneurs, and theatre politicians, Bob says:

"If you want to get ahead in this business, you have to decide to be exceptional. Exceptional has nothing to do with brilliance or genius. It has to do with a person, even with ordinary skills, saying to himself, 'I'm going to be exceptional, I'm going to make a massive commitment to something.' It's all up to you. Most people are waiting for the curtain to go up. They think they're in rehearsal when they're in the second act. Off Off Broadway (and outside New York, community theatre) is an open door; it's very accessible to people. Our artistic director walked in here five years ago and ran for coffee and sharpened pencils. He voluntarily read plays from the huge pile that accumulates here and wrote reports on them. I created the job of literary manager for him. He made himself so indispensable I had to hire him. Last year he co-produced the season. When I hire someone, I look for energy, commitment and a good ego. Running for coffee is a shit job only if you look at it that way, but if it helps the actors act, it is an important job. When you get to be someone's assistant, do whatever you think has to be done and don't be afraid of stepping on toes, or going for your boss's job. If he's good, you can only push him up. Wherever you feel yourself going, go."

Peter Saphier, Production Executive
Production Vice President, Universal Pictures

Production executives at the major studios represent the studio and act on its behalf. They are not given screen credit but when the line reads, for example, Universal Pictures Presents, in a manner of speaking, the production executive *is* Universal Pictures.

Madeline Porter

PETER SAPHIER

Production executives are responsible for developing and acquiring new films for their studios to release. Peter Saphier has such a position. He is a production vice president with the film division of MCA, Inc., Universal Pictures.

"My job as a production executive is to create new films—to find something that seems to have promise and then figure out a way to bring it to fruition. I make it my business to find new business. What that means is finding talented people and attracting them to the studio."

Once Peter, or any production executive, finds a project he is particularly interested in he must sell it to his studio, which means selling it to the one person who can say yea or nay to a project and "release the vault"—the head of the film division.

"The way I try to get a new project going here is to find a writer whose work I like and get together with him and figure out a story to do. Once we get the story into a form that I think the studio should begin to invest money in, the two of us make a presentation to the head of the film division. If the project is approved, we get the script written and the project is born.

"Most of my projects haven't been assigned to me, they've come out of a relationship I've had with someone (a producer, writer, director). The relationships you develop are very important in terms of determining what projects you as an individual production vice president will be responsible for. I can't depend on script, book, and story submissions for material. Occasionally something like that will come in already made and ready to go but that really isn't my job."

An example of a promising idea that Peter was able to bring to fruition was the film *Resurrection*, starring Ellen Burstyn. The process took about three years and began with a one-line story idea.

"The project was brought to the studio by the young producing team Howard Rosenman and Renee Missel. It was a 'what if' idea. What if Jesus Christ came back in the form of a woman living in the San Fernando Valley? I thought it was a fascinating premise. Renee and Howard and I got together and tried to figure out what to do with it. We hired a writer living in Rome who had written quite a few books. We talked to him about the material, made a deal with him and eight months later we had a script. We agreed from the start that Ellen Burstyn was the perfect actress for the role and we had our eyes on a particular director. We sent Howard and Renee to Greece to speak with Ellen Burstyn, who was making another film there. She liked the premise and the producers but she wanted the script changed. We had already spent $180,000, but we hired another writer, Lewis John Carlino (*The Great Santini*), whose work we had all read and loved, and got Daniel Petrie to direct. The studio thought the script was marvelous and we went into production."

Once Peter brings a project through development it becomes his job to supervise it from a production executive's standpoint.

"I have to make sure there is fiscal control as well as qualitative control. At any given time I may have twenty projects at work but I usually don't have more than one film shooting at a time. When a film that I'm supervising is shooting, it takes precedence. I am totally involved. I try to get to the location once a week and I'm always on top of the figures. I deal with everybody involved with the film—producers, unit managers, everyone."

Peter is a kind of "generalist" production executive who stays involved with a project from inception through release. Once production activities are over he attends post-production activities such as dubbing, mixing, and scoring. If he has a strong stance he will also get involved in the distribution of a film. He did so with the film *Resurrection*.

"Once *Resurrection* was made there was a great deal of contention at the studio because nobody was sure how to handle it. It was a different kind of film. I personally felt it should have a kind of exclusive release in a major theatre in a major metropolis with a big ad to create audience notice and word of mouth. I was at odds with the studio sales department, who felt the film should be shown to a broad audience, especially in the Bible Belt states. So a release pattern was developed on two waves. The first wave would be in the Bible Belt, the second wave six weeks later in the metropolitan main city areas. The film was a failure at the box office even though we had marvelous reviews. Finally we were able to overcome resistance from the sales department and get our exclusive release in L.A. and New York and that worked out pretty well. I did the best I could for it. I was somewhat emotional about the whole thing."

There is no such thing as a typical day in Peter's schedule. He's always out there finding new projects and winning friends for Universal. He reads a script every day before he comes to work, has business lunches, and takes and makes hundreds of calls to producers and agents. Someone is always trying to bring him a new project and keep him apprised of the new "talent of the week." He supervises two to three films a year, so one is always in need of his attention, which means attending story meetings, running to location, and going to mixes and dubbing sessions. Although he admits there are some frustrating aspects to his job he's doing just what he always wanted to.

Peter came from a theatrical family. His grandfather was head of music at Paramount and MGM in the thirties and forties, his father was a prominent agent, and his mother was a movie actress. He grew up in Los Angeles but went to college in Ohio (Antioch) where he studied history and communications while participating in the college's work-study plan. One of the internships available was with Universal Studios for a three-month stint. He took it and after graduation came back and got a full-time job as an assistant television production coordinator. During the next sixteen years he moved up and over to the feature film area, was made a production executive and then a production vice president.

Peter believes production executives of the future will have to have the chemistry to attract people to their studio. When looking for an assistant he has that in mind.

"I'm looking for people to attract other people. I don't really care what their background is—I'm more interested in their intuition, whether they have a good sense of audience and that special quality that attracts talent. Getting books and scripts is easy. Sure we need to be aggressive and ahead of the pack there, too, but that's a mechanical thing. What we need to do is bring people to our studio by making them see that this is where it's going to happen. And that's the job of the production executive.

"A good production executive has to be somewhat schizophrenic in the sense that he has to separate his likes and personal tastes from those of audiences. Some people are lucky enough to be totally 'in sync' with the audience but most of us aren't, just because we aren't twenty-four years old. A production executive must have a good sense of story and a good sense of the kind of talent—writer through performer—necessary to realize a particular story, and of course, he must have the ability to sell. When I made a search for my last assistant I tried to find somebody I'd like to see try to take my job away. That's the kind of person I looked for."

PART III

PRODUCTION

The Production People

Production people make creative choices and transform ideas into entertainment. Their talent is their imagination and the way they communicate what they imagine to others.

Production people are the creators behind the scenes of theatre and film.

6 Production Job Descriptions

Artistic Director. This job, specific to noncommercial resident theatre, is without a neat description. Together with a business-oriented arts manager, the artistic director runs the theatre and is responsible for all artistic matters from play selection through casting. Depending on the theatre's raison d'être, the artistic director may spend most of his time functioning as a director, literary manager, or anything else needed to keep the theatre's artistic event happening. For additional information on an artistic director, see the profile of Vinnette Carroll on page 72.

Auteur. A term rather than a job title, this refers to film artists such as Woody Allen or Ingmar Bergman who maintain complete control over their work. Auteurs generally do all or most of the following on their films: write, direct, produce, and perform.

Casting Director. A casting director, in theatre and film, can be a nonpaid apprentice or highly paid specialist, depending on the medium, the budget, and the situation. At any rate, he is the person responsible for casting roles and maintaining an ongoing relationship with talent agents and managers for that purpose. A number of resident theatre companies employ on-staff casting people, and some film production companies maintain a casting assistant during production time to cast extras and handle casting phone calls from agents and actors. For the most part, however, films and commercial theatre productions are cast by highly paid independent casting consultants. *Casting consultants* are self-employed and hired on a project-to-project basis for a fee. In theatre, they cast all productions of a play—that is, Broadway, road companies, and sit-down companies. In film, they cast all the speaking roles. Casting consultants function as an actor clearinghouse for the director. In addition to seeking out and hiring actors, they negotiate for salary and billing with the actor's agent or manager, prepare contracts for all players, make the traditional first work call to actors, and in film hire actors to dub voices.

Choreographer. A choreographer creates dances and supervises all dance movements in a production. This can mean anything from doing incidental dance movements, directing a production (e.g., Bob

Fosse in *Dancin'*), integrating the dance movements into a production (Twyla Tharp in the film *Hair*), or creating an entire repertoire for a dance company. Most choreographers begin as dancers. All must understand dance movements. Contemporary choreographers will work in every medium: dance, theatre, and film. For a related job, see *Dance Supervisor* in Part IV.

Composer.   A composer, in theatre and film, writes music—anything from a musical comedy and film score to incidental music and a title song. In musical theatre, the composer works collaboratively with the lyricist and writer of the "book" (dialogue). In film, the composer works with the director in scoring the picture. Often two composers work on a film, one to score and the other to write a marketable title song. New film composers arrange and orchestrate their own work; established composers hire *arrangers*, *orchestrators*, *copyists*, and *contractors* when there is a need for them. *Arrangers* fill in a song from the composer's sketch; *orchestrators* assign parts, line by line, to sections of the orchestra (strings, woodwinds, brass, percussion); and the *copyist* actually copies each part onto a separate sheet of paper for the members of the orchestra. *Contractors* hire and supervise the members of the orchestra and make certain all union rules are adhered to.

Cuer.   Cueing is a job specific to films; in theatre, a second or third assistant stage manager has the responsibility of cueing the actors. The film cuer is responsible for the cue copy and for making it as visible to the actor as possible during shooting. The cuer sets up and takes down cueing apparatus, makes certain the actor gets the right cue for a particular scene, keeps up (from the script supervisor) with script changes, and tries to keep out of the director's, DP's, cameraman's, and electrician's way. This is a good entry-level job. On low budget films, the job is given to the third assistant director.

Dialogue Director.   The job of dialogue director is found almost exclusively in film, although a dialogue coach might be hired on special occasions for a theatrical production. The dialogue director assists the director in matters pertaining to dialogue. He goes over lines with actors prior to a take to make certain they have them memorized. He follows the takes to make sure the lines are delivered as written and informs the director of any mistakes during takes. If the director so instructs he coaches the actors in proper delivery of the lines, and if need be, in proper pronunciation of foreign languages and accents.

Director.   In both theatre and film, a director is responsible for translating the script into a form of entertainment. He has a staff of assistants and associates to help him with this arduous task. The jobs of film director, associate director, theatre director, assistant director, and director's assistant are all described below.

Film director. He has control over every function, from staffing and casting through editing; it is said that film is a director's medium. The film director plans his work to utilize as effectively as possible the elements of film (photography, lights, color, sound) and the talents of staff and cast, and to integrate these into a completed whole. He may be involved with the film's inception, having co-authored or consulted on the screenplay. If not, his first pre-production task is to read and reread the final script. He then casts the film and hires the key production staff members (director of photography, editor, production and costume designers, etc.). He surveys choice locations, breaks down the shooting script into individual scenes, plots the camera angles for each scene, arranges for and supervises all casting not completed, and confers with the production and costume designers to assure his requirements are being met. During production the director confers with the director of photography to assure proper lighting and mood, checks the action through the camera, rehearses actors, extras, and sound prior to each take, supervises the dialogue director, makes script changes as called for, supervises the action of the crew during rehearsal and shooting periods, and blocks and directs the action of the actors, extras, and cameras. Each day after shooting he views the dailies. His post-production activities include working with the editors and viewing the final cut to assure proper film and sound quality. For additional information on the job of film director, see the profile of Lewis Jackson on page 97.

Associate director. In both theatre and film, he is a director who takes over from or gives assistance to the original director and is of equal status to that director.

First assistant director (AD). In film, assists the director in his administrative and production responsibilities. The AD serves as an intermediary between the director and the production manager. He is an on-the-set facilitator and is responsible for maintaining the pace required by the shooting schedule. He times out the shooting script scene by scene, estimates final footage, prepares a script breakdown, follows the day-to-day shooting schedule as closely as possible, and roughs out the action of the actors prior to shooting each scene. He assists the director in handling and directing large groups, supervises the second and third AD's, cues cast and crew, informs the production manager of the shooting schedule for the next day, authorizes overtime for cast and crew, sees to it that only authorized people are on the set, and requests quiet prior to giving the order to roll sound. He assists the director in any way he can, including offering creative suggestions.

Second and *Third assistant director.*   Employed on films where the AD needs help. They maintain constant communication with the AD through a walkie-talkie and assist him in all his responsibilities. They help him direct mob scenes, hold back traffic when on location, keep quiet on the set, serve as clapper and cuer, and make sure that everyone and everything needed during production is on hand in the right place at the right time.

Theatre director.   This job is similar to a film director's, except that he has less control over final performance and script changes. In fact, theatre was born without the director; the stage manager told the actors where to move. Even today it is said that theatre is the actor's medium; film the director's. The difference is due to the nature of film production. The film director can alter a performance or storyline with camera angles and editing; the theatre director can guide, block, and comment on an actor's work during rehearsals, but at performance time the actor is on stage alone. Still, the theatre director is finally responsible for the entire presentation and for the joint efforts of everyone involved. His responsibilities are the same as the film director's, with the exception of camera, location, and editing-related activities. A great deal of his time is spent rehearsing and directing the actors; he blocks their physical movements, orchestrates their voice inflection, and fosters their emotional output. Theatre directors must be sensitive to the playwright's intent. This is particularly true of new plays, where the playwright often attends rehearsals. If the playwright is alive, the director must consult him before making any cuts or alterations in the script. The theatre director keeps a close watch on all technical progressions, has final design approval, and maintains control over backstage activities through the stage manager. Both theatre and film directors must have a strong ability to communicate their ideas, for they are the liaison to producers, cast, crew, designers, and finally to audiences.

For additional information on the job of theatre director, see the profiles of Robert Allan Ackerman (p. 89) and Vinnette Carroll (p. 72).

Assistant director. In theatre, serves the same function as his counterpart in film. He acts as an intermediary between the production office and the director in rehearsal, tries to keep everyone to the production schedule, assists the director in blocking large groups and mob scenes, and informs the stage manager of changes in scripts or blocking or schedules.

Director's assistant (not to be confused with an assistant director). In film and theatre, works for the director rather than for the production and is responsible for helping that director in every way. He handles personal matters, takes phone calls, sits by the director's side during casting and rehearsals taking notes, handles the director's appointments, makes his travel arrangements, and generally keeps the director's life in order.

Fight Director. A fight director, in film and theatre, choreographs violence of all sorts: prizefights, wrestling, duels. His responsibility is to make these fights appear authentic to the viewing audience without causing pain to the actors. While it's the fight director who works out the fight sequences, he does so according to the director's ideas.

Independent Filmmaker. A term, rather than a job title, it describes someone who comes up with an idea for a film, writes the script, seeks out and raises the funds to produce it and, depending on the budget and type of film (i.e., theatrical, documentary), might DP, star in, produce, arrange for distribution of, and/or release it. For additional information, see the profile of Lewis Jackson on page 97.

Location Scout. In film, a location scout finds suitable sites to shoot particular scenes. He takes direction from the production designer, who shows him a sketch and talks about the proposed site (a barren field, a Victorian house, or a place to build a yellow brick road). The scout then photographs eligible sites, reviews the photos with the production designer, and accompanies the designer to the places he is most interested in. Once a site is chosen, the scout makes arrangements (permits, fees, contracts, owners' agreements, etc.) to rent the site for the duration. On low budget films, an art director and/or production assistant might function as a scout for the production designer; at times, the production designer functions as his own scout. When no one on the production staff is familiar with the area, local *scout consultants* are employed to do the initial search. On films where many locations are required, a *location manager*, or *location designer*, is employed to oversee all scouting activities and decorating of sites; he serves as the production designer's right hand with regard to location shooting.

Lyricist. A lyricist is found anywhere original music is to be a part of a production, whether it be theatre or film. The lyricist writes the words to songs and has a close working relationship with the composer. In musical theatre, the lyricist, composer, and playwright collaborate on a play's creation. At times, the playwright will serve as the lyricist as well as author of the book. In film, a lyricist rarely works with the screenwriter; more often, he works with the composer of the score and/or title song.

Musical Director (Supervisor). Responsible for all musical aspects of a film or play from hiring the composers to hiring the conductor, they are employed on projects with extensive music. Some of the film studios maintain a staff of full-time music supervisors who function as producers' musical advisers.

Playwright. Playwrights write original plays for the theatre. Most write on a free-lance basis with the hope of getting their plays optioned and produced; a few work as *playwrights in residence* at universities and noncommercial theatre companies interested in nurturing the work of new playwrights and producing new plays. The latter are paid a weekly salary from grants, fellowships, stipends, and government support raised by the theatre companies for that purpose, and have their work read and produced. If their plays are then picked up by commercial producers, they earn additional income. Free-lance playwrights present their plays in manuscript form, staged readings, and even independently financed productions. Once their plays are produced, they share in the profits.

Production Assistant (PA). A production assistant, in both theatre and film, assists whoever he is assigned to in whatever capacity is needed. PA's are assigned to administrative, production, and technical personnel. The production assistant job has always been considered to be *the* entry-level job for most production and technical careers. Within the industry it is said that a production assistant's performance can make or break his career; enthusiastic workaholic types are recommended for more work, while those with any kind of negative attitude are blackballed forever.

Here are some of the potpourri responsibilities a production assistant might have: take notes during casting sessions, take and transcribe notes for the director's assistant, Xerox production material (scripts, prop lists, work calls), run errands, arrange meetings with the production staff, keep all production reports, help move props during rehearsals, fetch cabs for the stars, maintain quiet on the set for the third AD, help the food coordinator set up meals, answer the phone in the production office, and serve as the company gofer (that is, do anything asked, including picking up the producer's laundry, chauffeuring, getting coffee for the crew). It's safe to assume the production assistant does what no one else wants to. The job is one of the most difficult and competitive to come by even though many PA's work a twelve- to fifteen-hour underpaid day. The more skills (typing, shorthand, driving, cooking) you have, the better your chances of getting a job. It's probably the best learning experience available for the novice interested in a behind-the-scenes career. The job can be a nonsalaried or salaried position; often a volunteer can turn himself into a salaried PA by making himself indispensable to the company. NABET (see Appendix B) has a category for PA's, so at times it is a union job.

Screenwriter. A screenwriter writes the script (the dialogue and action) from which a film is made. The script may be based on his own idea (an original), a producer's idea (assigned material), his own or another writer's book (an adaptation), or another screenwriter's story (a rewrite). Often, novice screenwriters will prepare a treatment (an outline and synopsis of the proposed script written in the narrative) to test the interest of an original. He may then be asked to prepare a first draft, second draft, and so on, and get paid accordingly; this is called a step deal. Established screenwriters (those who have sold something) are hired by studios and independent producers to write scripts based on assigned material or adaptations, and to polish or rewrite someone else's work. The Writers Guild determines who is credited for multi-authored screenplays. For related jobs, see *Playwright;* and for additional information, see the profiles of Paul Monette (p. 77) and Lewis Jackson (p. 97).

7   Production Profiles

Vinnette Carroll, Artistic Director of the Urban Arts Corps Theatre and Creator of *Don't Bother Me, I Can't Cope*

Artistic directors keep all the "artistic events" in their theatre happening. It's their job to keep their theatres artistically interesting.

"It's an artistic director's job to maintain artistic control over her theatre. By artistic control I don't mean a dictatorship, I mean freedom. Freedom to surround oneself with artists, directors, choreographers, designers, stage managers, and actors whose talent, judgment, and maturity one respects. Freedom to choose people to work with who can help with artistic problems. Ultimately it's the artistic director who must make final decisions. But the team she chooses is so important. The artistic director must be concerned with all details of the company, from the very small—like the biographies in the program—to the essential."

Vinnette Carroll founded and has worked with the Urban Arts Corps Theatre for twelve years. She has conceived, directed, and brought three of its productions to Broadway (*Don't Bother Me, I Can't Cope; Your Arms Too Short to Box with God;* and *Never Jam Today*). She has directed all over the world, won an Obie, three Tony nominations, a New York Outer Critics award, and a Los Angeles Drama Critics award.

She originally planned on a career in psychology.

"I spent a lot of time pleasing my family and getting my education. My father was a dentist and wanted very much for all his daughters to be doctors. He was very upset that I wanted to go into the theatre. I majored in psychology in college and did all the work for my Ph.D. and went to work for the Bureau of Child Guidance. But then I decided I wanted to work in theatre. So, I practiced as a clinical psychologist by day and took acting classes by night. Those were very special days. So many of the actors my age who are working now were at the workshop then. Marlon Brando, Harry Belafonte, Ben Gazzara, Walter Matthau all were starting out."

Vinnette faced a difficult decision: to please her family and stay with the career she had spent so much time being educated for or to take up a career as an actress. The latter seemed unlikely for a black

Tom Brocato

VINNETTE CARROLL

woman approaching thirty, but she chose it anyhow.

"I don't regret that I didn't go straight into theatre. I don't think you can go to school, come out of that womb, and say, 'I want to be a director and have a theatre of my own.' I think you can come out and say, 'I want to be a theatre person,' and then you start to find out what. I'm a great believer in education. I wouldn't have changed a minute of mine. Studying psychology was a very wise thing for me to do. I think everyone should go to college if they can and study more than theatre. The more education you have the better off you are."

Vinnette was a good, strong actress. But there weren't many roles for strong black women actresses in the 1950s. To supplement her income she took a job teaching acting at the High School of Performing Arts in New York City. Her time at P.A. was productive and, in retrospect, a good place to discover herself and crystalize her career goals.

"I learned a lot about acting and directing while I was at P.A. When you try to teach it, you get a clarity that you wouldn't have any other way. At P.A. I learned for sure that I wanted most to direct and that I loved working with young people and I didn't want to act any more. Later on, I began to see that what I wanted was my own company. I didn't want to worry from job to job. I wanted it (theatre) to be a way of life. And I knew I couldn't spend my life always worried about what critics said or whether the phone would ring or whether the whims of some producer would interfere with my working. I knew than that I'd prefer making much less money and having my freedom."

The transition from acting teacher to artistic director of a not-for-profit company—and all the good things she wanted for herself—was a slow one for Vennette. The first step was leaving Performing Arts, which she did in 1964.

"Ellis Rabb asked me to direct a production of *The Flies* at the APA and it went very well, and because of it I was asked to go out to California and be associate director of an inner city repertory theatre. I did it and enjoyed it. By then, the New York State Council on the Arts was forming a ghetto program and they asked me to head it up. It was primarily an administrative job and I'm always more interested in doing something than talking about it, but I said yes. What we did was pilot programs. In the sixties, talents were emerging that had no direction, and there weren't enough black people who could be role models for the kids who were coming up. So we thought what we'd do with these young people was to form a theatre and do plays. All the black writers of the sixties were getting started, so we had material to work with. We'd meet at the Y or at night in my office in the council, and we'd read plays and work. There were a lot of talented people who could work on pieces they ordinarily couldn't work on because they were black, and we'd sit and talk about the philosophy of theatre and try to come up with some measure of success that didn't have to do with being discovered at Schwab's Drugstore or how many commercials you did. We were after some enduring values and theatre as a way of life so you could get up in the morning and come to the theatre because that's what you did, and anything else would be incidental."

That "grass roots" theatre was the beginning of the Urban Arts Corps Theatre. In 1969, the Corps moved into its own building and got its own funding, and what seemed like a hopeless dream became a reality: Vinnette had her theatre. In addition to the workshops and showcases, Corps productions have been seen all over the country, have been presented on the Public Broadcasting System, at Lincoln Center, on Broadway, at the Spoleto Festival in Italy, and in the Virgin Islands. Most important to Vinnette is that she has created a "home" for a company of young and talented minority actors and a place to develop good theatre.

"One of the advantages of having a theatre is to have the artistic freedom to develop your work. I can't work if I don't have that. I always start plays at the Corps, with the kids [actors], make a pattern, try it without pressure. I can't let the commercial market influence my work. I always let the commercial producers see the project once it's completed at the Corps, then they can decide if they're interested in moving it. But whenever they're breathing down my neck, I can't get any work done. If Off Off Broadway weren't there trying to experiment and putting all sorts of colors on the canvas, there wouldn't be any theatre. The economics of Broadway are so crazy, you can't create anything. It's scary time up there."

Early in her career, Vinnette realized that two things were important to her: one, that she wanted to be affiliated with a theatre that would not be judged entirely by financial success; and two, that she needed to "feel the pulse of the young." Today she has satisfied both. And she's never really given up her acting career, having played a West Indian doctor on *All in the Family* and performed in

the film *One Potato, Two Potato*. Besides directing and managing
the Corps, she teaches and directs at least once a year as a guest of a
university.

For a black woman to succeed at all these things is unusual, even
more so for one trained as a psychologist. Vinnette believes in hard
work and is a tough artistic director.

"My day begins at five when I get up and have phone meetings
with our managing director and my friend for thirty years, Anita
MacShane. We talk over what will happen that day, or a play I've
read, or a problem with the kids, or anything we might be negotiating. We talk till six-thirty. Then I watch the *Today Show*, and after
that I go to the gym and swim for at least an hour; I must swim
every day to get that oxygen to my brain. I get to the theatre by
twelve and meet with my assistant regarding phone messages and
with Anita regarding administrative things. I check out how all projects are going. For instance, if a new director is directing, I watch
rehearsals and talk to her or him about any problems she's having
with the cast.

"When the Corps first started, I directed all the plays, but now I
bring in new directors. I start my rehearsals at two o'clock. I rehearse for five hours, break for dinner, and at that break have more
meetings because if I take a dinner break all I want to do is go to
sleep or watch television. We come back to rehearsal and work till
ten or eleven. When we're preparing a program, like the one at
Lincoln Center, we start rehearsals at eleven when the choreographer will work with the dancers, and the musical director will work
with them on the music, and then I'll come in after and take them."

On making it as an artistic director, Vinnette gives this advice:

"Study. Out of high school is too young. Once you're out of college, get experience. Do bus and truck tours, work backstage, work
with costumes, act a while, direct, do all sorts of theatre jobs, all the
most unglamorous jobs. Do administrative work: learn how to raise
funds, how to do budgets, choose actors, rent space. You must learn
those things because they all go into being an artistic director. You
can't get into an ivory tower, because the job is sometimes cleaning
the john and getting toilet paper; answering the phone and making
up a budget when someone is busy; dealing with the actors' problems as well as your own; knowing if you can bring in a show at a
certain budget; knowing the kinds of actors that can survive a tour.
All those things are the artistic director's job to know.

"Stick-to-it-iveness. That's what you need most. That covers everything: the hurts, the disappointments, the not having money. Nobody promised you a rose garden; nobody promised you the opportunity to make money. You made that choice if you're in the theatre."

Paul Monette, Hollywood Screenwriter

Hollywood screenwriters write scripts based on their own ideas, producers' ideas, published novels, or any number of "provocateurs." It's the screenwriter's job to take the storyline and the characters and transform them into a titillating film script.

"A screenwriter in a sense creates the blueprints for a film. He sees the film in his head and tries to present it as a visualized whole where people say interesting things to each other," says Paul Monette, a writer currently working in Hollywood on his third script for Universal Pictures.

Occasionally, a script is conceived, written, and rewritten by one writer, but in Hollywood filmmaking this is rare. (New York writers on independent projects and "auteur" types tend to maintain tighter controls on their work.) In Hollywood, the usual practice is that a producer has an idea he thinks he can sell to a studio, a writer is hired to adapt that idea into a script, and another writer is brought in to polish, or doctor, the original draft.

"Screenwriting is job work. It's not like playwriting or writing novels. It's marvelous job work, but job work just the same. I don't mean to condemn it. It requires very very good writing and the better writer you are, the better job you can do. But writing for film is a collaborative effort, not a personal statement. I don't mind when a screenplay of mine is collaborated on. If they hire a big name to rewrite my script, in a way it becomes his or her movie, but that's how the game goes. If a script by *me* gets made, my clout is that much greater on the next deal. You can't get too tied down to anything you do. I know too many people who write a screenplay and then rewrite it and rewrite it again. You must have a broader view than that."

Paul Monette is a young (thirty-five) screenwriter who spent most of his twenties teaching high school and prep school English. As a young child he thought about becoming a writer, but it was "all in soft focus. I used to think: 'I'd love to be an actor, I'd love to be a writer.' What I meant was: 'I'd love to have an unusual lifestyle.'"

Paul's parents managed to get him a scholarship to a fine prep

Roger Horwitz

PAUL MONETTE

school in Andover, Massachusetts, where an English teacher encouraged him to write. He went on to Yale as an English major, but was more interested in plays and editing magazines than the courses he had registered for. Not knowing or even thinking about what he wanted to do with his life (a condition quite common among the young in the late 1960s), he "schlepped" from one teaching job to another. In his middle twenties he began writing poetry and novels; and as time went by, he began taking his writing more and more seriously. His "softly focused" career goal began to get clearer. By his late twenties he had turned himself into a working writer with two published books of poetry to his credit. As a kind of "hedge against inflation" he got together with a friend and wrote a screenplay.

"In 1975, in Boston, a friend and I got together and wrote a screenplay, a thriller, which took us four or five months. We sent it to a friend in L.A. who gave us a critique on it and then we did a rewrite. We were terribly naive and didn't know there were ten million people out there writing screenplays. Still, it was a beginning and a way to learn the form. Then we wrote a romantic comedy. We tried to place it with an agent but couldn't and were very depressed about that. I showed the screenplays to a producer I met in New York, and he said they were marvelous but told us to do more. He said we had to be able to show people our 'wares.' I realized that you've got to really want to be a writer and write, write, write if you intend to get anywhere. That's what most would-be writers don't do enough of. So I did a *third* screenplay—and when nothing happened, I started thinking, 'This movie business is so crazy, how does anyone ever get in?' "

Paul kept on writing. And not only screenplays. His first book of poetry (*The Carpenter at the Asylum*) had won him enough prize money so he could take a year off from teaching to write a novel. He finished the novel (*Taking Care of Mrs. Carroll*) in six months and sold it. He used that money to take another year off to write yet another novel (*The Gold Diggers*) and sold that. He began to feel "trapped" by Boston and considered moving to Hollywood.

"It was a year-long decision to move to Los Angeles. I came out here knowing I might never make it in the movies, but I loved the place and knew I wanted to write about it. At least I was a known writer. I had sold my first novel for $10,000 and my second for $20,000, and I had acquired an agent in Hollywood through my New York agent, which was, I thought, an incredible piece of good fortune. As it turned out, the L.A. agent did nothing to advance my career. She did send my novel and screenplays around, but it was a 'gay' novel and nobody was interested, and as for screenplays, so many are sent to so many people, nothing ever happens.

"I decided to change agents. The next one was even worse. I really didn't know how few this guy's contacts were. He was trying to make it as an agent with my properties. He got me a chance to work on a nightclub act. I did it, but it was a horrible experience for me. I guess I was just paying my dues. At that point I just wanted to get paid to do some entertainment writing."

Paul spent six months getting to know people socially. In Hollywood your social and business contacts tend to be one and the same and terribly important for your career. One of those people was a producer, Howard Rosenman, who together with his partner, Renee Missel, produced *The Main Event* and *Resurrection*.

"I met Howard a couple of times and we made a date to have lunch. I went to his office and he didn't show up, but his partner Renee Missel was there. She and I said hello to one another and I ended up having lunch with her instead. She pitched me an idea, I liked it, we talked more about it, and then I went away on vacation. Before I left, I called my agent and contacts back east and asked her to get me some kind of work with a Hollywood angle. I would have done anything—a novelization, a biography of a film star, *anything*."

Paul spent his entire vacation thinking about the possibility of Renee's film project and a possible book project, hoping one of them would come through. When he returned, he learned they both had.

"Avon offered me $4,000 to write a novelization of Werner Herzog's film *Nosferatu* in four weeks and it looked like Renee had made a 'development' deal with Universal Pictures to fund *No Contest*, our film project. I did the *Nosferatu* novelization because I felt it was somehow connected to film and I wanted to show them how good a writer I was. I never saw the film [*Nosferatu*]; I wrote the book from the screenplay—the film wasn't ready to see—and completed two hundred pages in twenty-eight days. Meanwhile, Renee and I met and met and met with executives at Universal. It took the autumn to negotiate a deal. When it went through, in December, I went to Houston to research the story. Renee met me there and we worked out a plot over a couple of weeks and went back to L.A. to present it to Thom Mount, the executive in charge of production at Universal. He read the summary, said I should do this, this, and this, watch that, and he gave me some hints and said, 'Go to first draft.'

"I completed the draft in three months, but when Renee read it she felt it was too long. We cut it down from 170 pages to 125, changed a couple of scenes, changed a couple more scenes, and gave it to Universal to type and turn in to the executives. They loved it. Because of that script Renee was able to get me a two-picture deal with them. I got $17,500 for the first script, which is low; not wildly low, but low. On my two-picture deal I'll get $46,000 and $66,000 for the first drafts. On the strength of having done a screenplay they liked, I apparently will work for a couple of years. None of my scripts might ever get done, of course. Very few projects are actually produced, but marvelous projects do get funded. The first script, *No Contest*, is in the packaging stage now [two years later]. They're looking for a director. It's gotten quite close to being assigned but still no cigar."

Paul's success came about for a number of reasons. He never stopped writing or believing in himself as a writer, and he didn't sit back and let his agents do the work. When he felt he wasn't getting the attention he deserved, he moved on. As it happens, the producers who eventually hired him received his novels from an agent (one he didn't remain with), but had he not kept a "high social profile," he never would have met those producers personally. Once hired, he took the responsibility to ensure that his script would have priority with his producers and the studio.

"At any given time, Renee and Howard are developing a dozen projects. Only one may ever see the screen. When I started with my project, it was number eleven on their list. I had to make sure it was good enough to go to the top of their list. I did. And it did."

Paul has this to say about surviving in Hollywood and finding an agent, an absolute must if you expect to be taken seriously as a screenwriter.

"Who knows if you can orchestrate a career or not? Writing and finding an agent are very different things. Everyone is so swamped with things to read, no one has a chance to read anything. You end up giving your work to all these agents who six weeks later will give it back to you unread. You have to get used to that. You have to be lucky. You have to be good. And, you have to articulate. When you get shown in to an office to hand your work in, you must articulate. When you go back to pick it up, you must articulate. You have to make people aware of you. If you can convince somebody to read your work, something might happen. The truth is, it's a one-in-a-million proposition, yet it's a very big thing to go for. It's an extraordinary thing to be paid to tell stories."

On the subject of screenwriting, he adds:

"If you want to be a screenwriter, then write screenplays. Write a few knowing they will never get made. I know how hard a task that is, but the bottom line is, it's tough! A writer I knew used to tell his students in a UCLA screenwriting course that if they want to be a screenwriter, they'd better be prepared to eat spaghetti for ten years.

"I know some people who've made it into screenwriting by doing a little work in television (series and situation comedies); that way you can get into the guild at least. But of course that's tough too.

"You can learn the form of screenwriting by reading a few screenplays. There are books that teach you; I didn't happen to learn that way. I went to the library and looked at a few screenplays. Remember, *anyone* can write a screenplay; all the waiters in Los Angeles do. Some are good at it and some aren't, but it's certainly not like writing a sonnet or a novel. You just make up conversation that takes place scene after scene. One of the difficult things about screenwriting is that because it's so easy to learn, it's hard to know how good you are at it. A lot of people are deluded about how good they are.

"You must keep writing. You can't roll the snake eyes if you don't roll the dice . . . so roll the dice. Write! And once you do sit down you must write every line as if it's going to be spoken by Katharine Hepburn and be remembered like Bette Davis's 'Oh Jerry, why ask for the moon . . . we have the stars.' Everything's got to resonate like that in your head. You have to have dreams like that and you have to be able to deal with the fact that those dreams are dreams, but believe me, they are what keep you going."

Richard Fischoff, Associate Producer of
Kramer vs. Kramer

Associate producers help executive producers produce. This can mean anything from giving emotional and/or financial support to complete involvement with pre-production, production, and post-production activities. A lot depends on how they got the job. Some are hired by studio or production company executives on a free-lance basis, some help finance the film, some have friends or relatives in the right places, and some, like Richard Fischoff, come up

David Lustig

RICHARD FISCHOFF

with the idea for the film and/or work for the studio or production company making it.

Richard Fischoff is vice president of Stanley Jaffe Productions, a small production company now affiliated with Twentieth Century-Fox. Vice presidents at small production companies do a little of everything and often function as creative filters for their "boss," keeping an eye out for properties, talent, directors, ideas. Richard Fischoff found *Kramer vs. Kramer* for his boss Stanley Jaffe, who in turn produced the film and offered Richard the job of associate producer.

"Once I started working for Stanley, I let people in New York [publishing companies] know I was looking for material for him. An editor at a paperback house told me about *Kramer vs. Kramer*, which was to be published by Random House the following fall. I asked her to get a copy of the manuscript to me, which she did. I liked it a lot and gave it to Stanley. I said to him . . . you'll either love it or hate it, but please read it quickly. That was on Thursday. I went away to Palm Springs for the weekend, and when I got home on Sunday he called to say he had read it, loved it, and wanted to buy it. I thought he was just being nice, but we negotiated the deal and owned the property by the end of the week."

Working on *Kramer vs. Kramer* as associate producer was Richard's first production experience. In a sense, he began his film career as both executive and apprentice. He managed that by changing careers after he had gained skills and contacts in a business important to the film industry—publishing.

"It all begins with the material, with the word. It's the ability to find material and recognize what it is both artistically and commercially, the ability to help a writer improve his work. That's what an editor in publishing does and what anybody in the creative end of film does. In both fields you need a willingness to be open to new material, to make the imaginative leap between what is presented and what could be. It's rare that something comes in and you can say, This is a movie because what's on the page is a movie."

And so Richard, like many others in publishing, made himself useful to the film industry.

"In retrospect it was a step-by-step process, but it was no master plan I had at twenty-one. I never thought I'd wind up living in California working in film. I didn't think you could make a career out of it. I was supposed to have a profession or go into business. But there were always two things I was interested in, books and film.

Those interests were threads that have remained intertwined throughout my life. I just followed my instincts and made decisions that made sense for me. And each one sort of led to the next."

In college [the University of Rochester] Richard was a pre-law student with a double major in English and history. He managed also to minor in film.

"I first got interested in film because of the Eastman House and the Eastman Archives and the film courses I took there. Because of Kodak, Eastman had the second-best film archives in the country. The curator at Eastman House taught film courses at the school—primarily history and aesthetics, not production. Because I studied with him, I had access to the archives. I could book time at the theatre and see movies: silent, sound, particular directors or genre forms. I got a terrific knowledge of film as an art form and of the evolution of film. I did not get technical background but I developed a love and a knowledge of film—a real matrix.

"From there I went to NYU law school. I hated it. I took a leave of absence, knowing it was going to be permanent, and it was. Every summer, through high school, I had worked in publishing as a reader and editorial assistant. The natural step in getting myself employed when I left NYU was to look in publishing. I went to work for Saturday Review Press as an editorial assistant and stayed for about a year and a half. I was going through things I suppose everyone goes through in their early twenties and I wasn't thrilled with the way things were working out, so I left and began free-lancing. I read manuscripts for publishing companies and film companies, including United Artists, Warner Brothers, and Paramount. A lot of people who want to break into film go that route. It's a good way of making yourself aware of the kind of material that's out there and of seeing if you're able to recognize the commercial and artistic possibilities of a piece of writing. It's your job to screen submissions for either the house reader, the story editor or the producer. Most of the work that comes to film companies is free-lanced out. I did that for about a year. Ultimately it's sort of grueling work, but it's a good way to get your foot in the door."

Because of his work as a reader, Richard was offered and accepted a full-time job as an acquisitions editor with Warner Communications' publishing division. About that time (1972) the tie-in novelization was becoming popular. Publishing companies were creating books based on successful movies. Richard was a regular acquisitions editor in the sense that he covered hard-cover publishing houses and dealt with originals, but motion picture and television-related acquisitions were his specialty.

"Initially, I dealt primarily with Warner Brothers [film division], but it became clear to me early on that there was no reason why we had to work only with their products. I established relationships with other major studios and television suppliers. I would go to California a couple of times a year and I'd meet with the Hollywood people when they came to New York. My job was to read a lot of scripts, negotiate the publishing rights, hire writers to novelize, supervise the novelization, work on the promotion, and coordinate our book with the film company."

Richard remained with Warner Books for four years. He was, in a sense, a pioneer in the tie-in field. In the summer of 1976 he was offered the job of vice president of MCA Publishing, which is a division of MCA Universal.

"I had worked with MCA on a number of tie-ins and projects. The head of their publishing division came to me and asked me [for the second time; Richard had been approached by MCA a year earlier] to work for him. I guess I was ripe, and I certainly was curious about the film business and California and I felt it was time to make some changes in my life. This was a natural evolution. There was nobody's job in publishing that I wanted, so I felt it was time to learn another business. My job was to set up a network of foreign agents and to handle world rights in the English language and in translations for all books that were created by or licensed by or tied into a Universal product—either television or theatrical. I was to straddle the book, television, and film divisions at Universal in terms of generating projects, and in so doing, make the most of the symbiotic relationship that existed among them. Basically, I was responsible for creating and licensing books based on MCA feature and TV films. I traveled to the Frankfurt Book Fair and to London. I was involved in some serialization. I supervised and edited the *Jaws II* book."

Richard stayed at MCA for only eight months. He was not happy with his job and faced it early on. "The move to Universal [MCA] was a terrible experience for me but it makes sense that I made it. It did crystallize in my head a lot of things: what I wanted to do, what I was good at, what I was willing to trade off to work in this industry and what I wasn't. I felt I had given up work that had given me great satisfaction and a life [in New York] that was very nice. It was clear that the way Universal was set up I was not going to get to do what I wanted to. The best that the job would ever be was tolerable. I wasn't ready to quit without something to go to because I was out here [in L.A.] and it was really like starting all over again."

He let his friends and former associates in New York and L.A. know that he was unhappy at Universal and open to suggestions. At about this time Stanley Jaffe, the producer of *Goodbye, Columbus, The Bad News Bears,* and *Bad Company* and the one-time head of production at Paramount, was setting up his independent production company at Columbia Pictures and was looking for someone to work with him. Richard's name was mentioned by several different people (always a good sign). He was told of Richard's good reputation and current predicament. Stanley Jaffe called Richard. They spoke, met, and Richard was offered the job of vice president of Stanley Jaffe Productions. He accepted and began work in April of 1977.

"Initially I came in to find properties and to work in development and acquisitions. I'd meet with editors, agents, writers. Then I began working closely with Stanley on all aspects of the company's operations. I became responsible for looking at the work of directors and talent, to let him know what was out there. I worked with screenwriters assigned to projects. And, because it was a small organization, I was involved in the day-to-day running of the office."

Once production of *Kramer vs. Kramer* began, Richard's responsibilities included those of associate producer on the film.

"I worked intimately with Stanley and Robert Benton, the screenwriter, on the script. Dustin Hoffman was always Stanley's first choice, and once he came to the part he worked on the script as well. I brought Meryl Streep to Stanley's attention. Kate Jackson was everyone's choice but she couldn't get out of her ABC contract. No one had seen Meryl do much and thought she wasn't right for the role. I had seen her on stage and knew differently. I ran *Holocaust* and *Deer Hunter* for Stanley [Meryl was in both] and he and Robert Benton decided to go with her. I was there when we looked for kids. We hired a casting director, Shirley Rich, to go out and look in schools. I would see the best of them. While we were casting, we were doing budget breakdowns and crew assignments with Columbia and with a production manager we hired. We did storyboards, figuring out days and nights, interiors and exteriors, the call sheets, all those production things that were new for me. Then, when the film began shooting in New York, I was there on the set and at the production meetings. I remained in New York during most of the shooting but not all the time because as a vice president I was responsible for other projects back in L.A. I went back and forth. Stanley remained in New York.

"Then I was involved in editing. Stanley, the director, the editor, and myself looked at the dailies and rough cut. We kept the studio [Columbia Pictures] informed; we showed them the dailies and went back to L.A. to show them the first cut. I was allowed to attend and learn about the scoring, the mixing of the soundtrack, and the color correction. I sat while we went through the film scene by scene adjusting the colors—sometimes it's too hot or too cold or too red or blue and can interfere with the emotional quality of a scene. I met with the advertising agencies on the marketing and advertising strategy for the trailers and print campaign." Richard's experience on *Kramer* taught him the production process and gave him a clear idea of the producer's role. It provided him with a good view of the film industry in general.

"You see something that you think is special, something that's worth spending two years of your life, several million dollars, and a lot of aggravation on. A strong producer, which is what Stanley is, in a sense imposes his vision. He's responsible for hiring the key people and for making them all see the film in a certain way. He works with them, supervises them, and serves as that buffer, that interface for the problems that will invariably arise when you have clearly talented, intelligent, strong-willed people working together. Film, to be successful, must be a collaborative effort."

For those interested in pursuing his kind of work, Richard suggests:

"What you have to do is develop skills and use them as a card of entry. Make use of what you know to get in the door. Be willing to do a certain amount of 'shit' work but do it in a place that gives you access to people who are doing what you want to do. Ask lots of questions. Show them you're interested in getting into whatever it is you want, while you're performing the functions you were hired to do. Be at those meetings; offer to help even if it's not your responsibility. Recognize and try to work for the people in authority who won't be threatened by you, who'll delegate responsibility, teach you, and allow you to grow. Finding a mentor is most important. Once you find one, talk to him about movies that you have seen, the writers, the directors, whatever; be a source of input, and a sounding board.

"To get your foot in the door, well that's a tricky matter and unfortunately different for men and women. A man has to come in with some kind of skill that will be of immediate value, be it marketing, editing, business affairs—some skill. Women can start as a secretary but must watch not to be slotted as such.

"Publishing is still a very good way to break in. A new field that is opening up is cable TV. It is becoming one of the major program acquirers and outlets, and the capacity for growth is enormous. You can be involved with acquisitions from the studios, or in business affairs, licensing, distribution, or the creative side. Public Television is doing good and original material.

"Another way is agenting. A lot of people come into this business through agenting.

"The first thing I would ask someone who wants to get involved in this business is why. You shouldn't spend a good part of your life trying to do something unless you really, really care about it . . . unless it gives you something beyond just a place to go and a way to earn a living. And I would tell them to remember that the second word in show business is business and that that is what it is. So, I would say, be pragmatic."

Robert (Bob) Allan Ackerman, Director of the Broadway Production of *Bent*

The theatre director envisions a production and guides all those involved so that his vision becomes an entertaining theatrical event. He is responsible for the entire presentation. It is part of his job to gather a cast and crew that will be compatible and think along the same lines so that each production element complements another. He must communicate to the designers, technicians, stage managers, actors and, ultimately, the audience. He needs to understand and sometimes converse with the playwright. He must be someone who is able to turn a dream into a reality; to be both dreamer and doer.

Robert Allan Ackerman explains the process this way: "When I'm handed a script, it's essentially a piece of literature, a collection of words on a collection of pages. It's my job to take this piece of literature and turn it into something that's theatrical—to give it a stage life. What I actually do is take something that exists in one form and transform it into another form. The physical staging of a play must be a metaphor for the written script.

"The process begins as soon as I start to read—in my imagination. I get a vision and hopefully it grows. For a long while it's a part of

ROBERT ALLAN ACKERMAN

my subconscious, just like a dream that stays in your head all the time. I carry it around with me. I may be in a room and notice a lamp and think to myself that the color coming from that lampshade is exactly the color the lighting of a particular moment in the script I'm working on should look like. Or I'll see two people arguing on the street, and I'll think that so and so in the play should look like the woman in the street. I subconsciously deal with a play long before I go into rehearsals."

Bob Ackerman, native New Yorker, did not begin directing professional theatre until he was thirty years old. He is now only thirty-six and has directed some of this country's finest actors, including Jason Robards, Colleen Dewhurst, Fred Gwynne, Richard Chamberlain, Richard Gere, and Meryl Streep. Our most prominent contemporary playwrights, among them Thomas Babe, Israel Horovitz, David Mamet, and Martin Sherman, have asked Bob to direct their plays. He's one of the few directors who have been invited to spend a season as a director in residence at the New York Shakespeare Festival. He's won an Obie Award. He knew since age six that he wanted a career in theatre, yet it took him years before he could admit it to himself. The idea was too frightening to deal with.

Bob spent his childhood summers at his family's New Jersey hotel. One summer a drama counselor was hired to direct the Ackerman's Hotel's guests in a play. It was a production of *Death of a Salesman* and ten-year-old Bob was cast as the middle-aged Willie Loman! This auspicious if somewhat precocious beginning gave him a taste of theatre and whetted his appetite for further experience.

"They didn't hire a drama counselor the following summer, but I really wanted to be in another show, so from then on, each year I'd get all the kids together and direct them myself. We'd do whatever musical was popular on Broadway. I didn't even know then that what I was doing was called directing. Somebody had to put the people on the stage and tell them where to go, that much I knew, and somebody had to decide what costumes they should wear and what props were needed and what kind of scenery should be used. I made all those decisions and I did all the things a director does, but I had no idea I was a director. I did the same thing in high school. I directed because no one else would. At college [Adelphi University] I was intimidated by the whole idea. I couldn't commit myself to it. I didn't have the nerve. I'd go to an acting class once and drop out the next day. I studied speech therapy instead."

None of Bob's relatives had been involved in theatre and he got no encouragement to participate until he met Judy Zarin, who a few years later would become his wife. She thought he should at least try it and told him so. When a college friend asked Bob to act in a scene she was directing, he agreed to try. It went well. Everyone in the class asked him to be in their scenes. He became friendly with this group and told them of his experiences directing at Ackerman's Hotel. When they needed someone to direct them in an all-student musical, they asked Bob. He accepted and the production turned out to be the talk of the campus. After seeing it, the head of the drama department took Bob out to lunch and said something she never said to any of her students; she suggested that he pursue a career in theatre.

"That's all I needed to hear. I threw up and became a teacher. It was too frightening. Also, at the time, the Vietnam War was on and I had to do something so that I wouldn't get drafted, and teaching kept you out."

Bob taught for five years; he never committed himself to it, he always took cluster assignments and temporary jobs. One day he said to himself, "Enough of this," and went out and bought *Back Stage*. In it he found an ad for actors to audition for an Off Off Broadway theatre called C.S.C.

"I was twenty-seven or twenty-eight then. They were doing a big epic and needed a lot of guys. I auditioned and they gave me the job, for no pay. I was thrilled. I was so excited. It was the first audition I had gone on and I got the part. We rehearsed forever, for four months. The thing that was rewarding was that the group of people in the company were all bright, talented, and interesting. We were dissatisfied with the way we were being managed and I suggested we form our own company."

In a sense, Bob simply repeated his hotel experience.

"My whole career is based on what I did at Ackerman's. I wanted to do a show, so I directed it. When I decided I wanted to be in the professional theatre, I did the same thing. I knew no one would hire me; I was going on thirty years old and had no background, experience, or connections. The only way I'd get a job would be to do it myself, so I started my own theatre company."

The company, NRC (New Repertory Company), was made up of ten moonlighting teachers from C.S.C. and the $250 they put together for expenses. They'd teach school by day and rehearse by night and give weekend performances. This continued for a couple of years. No one made a dime; they all volunteered their services.

The group found a YMCA with some suitable space and moved in. The Y took 10 percent of their box-office. The arrangement was ideal except that they shared the space with a cooking teacher and had to reconvert the space into a theatre every weekend. They continued this off-with-the-bouillabaisse-on-with-the-show routine throughout one summer and managed to pull together a repertory for the following fall. One of the plays was a production of *The Visit* directed by Robert Allan Ackerman.

"It was the first time anything I had directed got reviewed, and the reviews were fabulous. It scared me to death. I immediately enrolled in all the directing classes New York had to offer. I had no background in directing except Ackerman's and I thought, 'If the reviewers are right and I do know what I'm doing, then I'd better really find out what it is because I don't know if I'll ever be able to do it again.' As it turned out, the classes and the books I read were useless. All they did was intimidate me. I tried to learn what I already knew, but didn't know that I knew. Eventually, I developed my own way of working."

Encouraged by the positive reaction to his work on *The Visit,* Bob directed another piece for the company. It too was well received and the company named Bob artistic director. In order to kill some time between two productions, he decided to produce a collection of one-act plays. He went to the Drama Book Store and browsed around until he came to three very short Ionesco plays. He got the idea to put them together, add music, and present them as vaudeville.

"It was a beautiful production we called *Ionescopade* that was to run for four weekends at our theatre [by this time they had earned enough money to lease a theatre on West 43rd Street]. The reviews were so good, one would think they were written by my mother. In one after another I was called a genius and the production the best of an Ionesco play in the country. I took all the reviews and went around to producers' offices and tried to convince one to move the production to Broadway and make us all stars."

One of the many producers Bob approached was the late Kermit Bloomgarden. He optioned *Ionescopade* and sent Bob to Paris to meet with Ionesco and to gather more material.

"Kermit did the show because he felt I was going somewhere and he wanted to be part of it. That's what the theatre is all about. You play hunches and bet on people and plays. So, Kermit did this show. Unfortunately, he never really understood it and it ended up being overproduced. We turned a charming fifty-minute piece of work into a two-hour flop. I didn't know what I was doing either. I had never done anything involving unions or designers. I didn't even know how to talk to designers and the production did not come out looking at all like what I wanted. One way of knowing you're getting better as a director is when your vision at the beginning is very close to what you eventually end up with. In this case my vision and the actual production were very far apart. I didn't know how to cast or relate to a stage manager. I didn't have experience saying no."

The play closed in two weeks, but what came out of it for Bob was more important than a long run. He finally decided to commit himself to a life in the theatre; he was thirty years old at the time.

"I discussed it with my [then] wife Judy and decided I would quit teaching. This is what I was—a director. I had no idea of how to go about finding work but I did have all these wonderful reviews, an Off Broadway credit, and an agent, Clifford Stephens, who had come to see *Ionescopade* and taken me on as a client, and I was a member of the union SSD&C. I had some foothold but no connections."

Bob spent the next five months looking for work. He sent letters and résumés to summer theatres, dinner theatres, regional theatres. Nothing came of it. Then, a friend who had seen *Ionescopade* recommended Bob for a job at an Off Off Broadway company. Bob met with the artistic director and got the job to direct a rock musical, *Joe's Opera*. The production was well received and got Bob another job offer, at the University of Texas, where Lloyd Richards, artistic director of the Eugene O'Neill Memorial Playwrights Conference, saw his work. He liked what he saw and told Bob. Bob followed up and wrote him a letter asking for a "stint." A reply stated that as soon as a job was available, Bob would be considered. Despite all the promise, Bob remained an unemployed director for the next year and a half.

"I was right out there. I kept sending résumés. I kept meeting people and I always believed it was going to happen. I continued to believe I was going to be a success. I knew I'd have to put in some time [waiting it out].

"I was finally offered a job directing an Off Broadway production of a new play, *Memphis Is Gone*. It was a flop but I got good reviews. Had my wife not been working [she was a psychologist] I couldn't have afforded to wait it out. Then all of a sudden, out of the blue, on the basis of my past work and recent reviews from

Memphis I was offered three very good jobs with the best summer theatres in the country: the O'Neill Playwrights Conference, the Berkshire Theatre Festival, and the Williamstown Playhouse."

Bob went first to the Berkshire Theatre Festival to direct a play entitled *Broadway*.

"I began to see there was a whole other way of being in show business—successfully; that it's not all sitting around and being miserable and asking yourself when, when, when? I was convinced I was good enough to have a career so I made a decision to call attention to this production of *Broadway*. The theatre had some money to spend and I knew that the best way to attract attention was to cast well-known people. I asked for and got Gilda Radner, Chris Sarandon, and William Atherton. The play was a success and it was optioned for Broadway."

Perhaps more critical to Bob's career development than the success of *Broadway* was the relationship that grew between Gilda, Chris, and himself.

"A lot of this business is social. A lot of it is who you know, although you don't get to know anyone until you start doing things. Gilda and Chris were very helpful to me and through them I met a number of people I later worked with. I feel particularly indebted to Gilda, Joe Papp, and Lloyd Richards."

A week after *Broadway* closed, Bob was off to the O'Neill to direct Thomas Babe's *A Prayer for My Daughter*. It was a success and Joe Papp invited Bob to direct it in New York that fall. During his period of unemployment Bob had been a reader at the Public Theatre and it was particularly satisfying to be asked back as a director. From that point on, Bob's career was a successful one. His New York production of *A Prayer for My Daughter* won him an Obie and he was invited, along with Andrei Serban, to serve as a director in residence at the Public Theatre for the following season. He was also invited to return to the O'Neill, where he met Martin Sherman, author of *Bent*. Although Bob did not direct *Bent* that summer, Martin was so impressed with his work that he asked Bob to direct it if and when it was picked up by a commercial producer.

In the past couple of years Bob's reputation has grown to the point where he is offered scripts from the very top playwrights, producers, and actors.

"The trend in the theatre seems to be that the writer and director are a package [for instance, Bob directs all of Thomas Babe's plays] so I get a lot of scripts through writers. Once I read a play and decide to do it, I reread it quite often until I know what I'm looking for in terms of designers and actors. The rest of the people are hired by the producers with my approval.

"I don't do a lot of research but I do look at photographs and paintings. Visuals help me to absorb an environment, an experience, and an emotional climate.

"Casting is sometimes complicated and sometimes easy. I like to work with the same people, so the first thing I do is think of actors I've worked with and see if there's anything in it for them. If not, I work with a casting director in trying to zero in on just the right personality for a role. Casting directors make up lists, look through the *Players Guide,* go through their files. The producer generally doesn't get involved with the casting until the very end, and then only with the leads.

"Once you narrow the casting list down, you have auditions, which are horrible for all concerned. The actor only has five or ten minutes to show what he can do and the director has to see the same scenes over and over again for hours at a time. It's an exhausting and embarrassing process. I've been forced to do four, five, even six call backs. A tremendous amount of thought goes into casting a play.

"On the first day of rehearsals I generally call the cast together and the stage manager takes care of union business. Then we sit around a table and read the play, with the stage manager reading stage directions. We break for lunch, and when we return we read it again, this time without stage directions.

"I invite the designers to present their sketches and models to the cast on the first or second day. The show is designed in pre-production and ready to be executed by rehearsal time.

"I do very little talking during rehearsals. I talk to actors through the working through of a scene. My feeling is, if I stage it correctly with them, a minimal amount of conversation is needed for them to know what I want. I let them improvise for a long time because their initial impulses are very interesting to me and it helps to break the ice. It's my responsibility to make the actors feel comfortable and flow freely. A good part of my technique is designed to make me feel comfortable so that I, in turn, can make them feel comfortable.

"Directing takes much concentration. I've been told I look as though I'm in a trance when I'm working.

"I generally rehearse three or four weeks, then go into previews.

When a play is running and I'm in New York, I stop by the theatre three or four nights a week. I don't actually watch a production that's running more than once every other week."

For those interested in pursuing a career as a director, Bob offers the following:

"Read plays—good plays—and see how they're put together. And trust your imagination, assuming you have one; if you don't, don't become a director. See a lot of theatre and movies and get to know and appreciate actors. A director's greatest friend is an actor; they are the people who make what you do wonderful or horrible. Learn how they work. Learn about every aspect of the theatre. Observe as much as you can and then do it—Direct!"

Lewis Jackson, a New York Independent Filmmaker

It's the independent filmmaker's job to get his film made and released. Generally, this takes years of writing, rewriting, sweet talking, coaxing, selling, raising money, compromising, and struggling. Through it all, the independent strives to maintain control over his film, and *his* film it is, as more often than not he has written, directed, and produced it.

Lewis Jackson wouldn't want to make films any other way.

"I have a specific notion of how I want to present the world to people through film. Unless one is very successful as a Hollywood director, one can't do that. Being an independent means that I can. I go after independent financing so I won't have a studio dictating parameters. I set my own parameters by the nature of my budget. And my aesthetics can basically hold to what I believe.

"To be perfectly honest, the days before I was assured of that financing, I was just another lunatic walking around the streets in search of backers, with all my friends saying, 'You're still doing this? Are you crazy? How can you still be doing this?' What makes the difference is being in the right place at the right time, which translates into being everywhere, being out there all the time."

Lewis Jackson, thirty-four-year-old native New Yorker, had an idea to make a film about a self-styled "Santa" obsessed with morality, with a compulsion to deal out violent punishment to those he knew to be bad ("Santa knows when you've been good or bad . . ."). It took him ten years to get the project off the ground. In between

© *Judy Lynn*

LEWIS JACKSON

there were a number of aborted attempts, other projects, porn films, and several odd production jobs. Before that, there was a life obsessed with film.

"I grew up in the movies. I lived my childhood in the movies. While in school I'd cut classes to go to the movies. My whole orientation about life is from the movies.

"Until a certain point I had no life except the movies. There are not many American films I have not seen. I spent some time at the University of Pittsburgh and at NYU film school, but mostly I learned from experience. My first job was for Pathé News. It was a nothing job but a way to break in. Then I lied about my experience and got a job with a company that made industrial films for a real estate company in Florida and Arizona. I told them I knew how to do what they needed and then learned by experience. I cut negative and other technical things. It turned out that the land they were making movies about was under water so my first editing job was to cut three lies out of the film. Soon after I was hired, the company was prohibited from selling the land, but not before I got some experience, a few location trips to Florida and Arizona, and a few contacts. One of those was a pharmacist who wanted to get into the film business and had optioned the rights to a Brazilian novel for that purpose. We made a deal. I was to write and direct, he was to produce. It took me four months to complete the screenplay: three months and twenty-nine days to write sixty pages and the last thirty pages in twenty-four hours. The script is amusing to look at. I wrote it shot to shot, seven hundred shots in all. But I learned from the experience. We spent a year trying to do the film; I would pick up odd production jobs along the way. I lived a hand-to-mouth existence."

In an attempt to raise money for the Brazilian novel adaptation, Lewis met someone who had raised $13,000 to make a soft-core comedy. As is often the case with independent filmmakers, Lewis hooked up with the "money man" and agreed to write, direct, and produce the film for him. The film Lewis turned out—in five days—was good but had no soft-core sex scenes and was $5,000 over budget. When Lewis presented the man with a budget for these remaining scenes and included a small salary for himself, the guy was incensed and accused Lewis of pocketing the money. He gave Lewis an ultimatum—come up with enough money to buy the film from him or relinquish all rights.

"I was only twenty-four when I began that project and although it was a lot of responsibility, I always believed I was a movie director and could do it, which was true, but the accusation really shook me up and I didn't know how to deal with it so I ran off [to San Francisco]. My home phone got shut off because of a $700 unpaid bill and no one could reach me, including a friend who had managed to raise enough money for me to buy back the film. I blew the deal. The money guy added some scenes, made it a 'hotter' film, released it, and made a lot of money."

Once Lewis managed to get himself together and back to New York, he was offered another soft-core film to direct, but he didn't want to repeat his past experience and refused the job. Someone he met while working on the previous film—again those contacts— knew the editor of *The Independent Trade Journal*, a trade journal that reviewed films for exhibitors. Lewis asked to be introduced to the editor, applied for a job, was tested, and got hired as a reviewer.

"I had always had a fantasy about being a movie critic. I spent over two years reviewing for this trade journal. They paid $10 a review. One year I saw 290 movies and reviewed 170 of them in order to earn enough money to stay alive. [This was not a part of his fantasy.] Another two years of madness. I was blitzed. I was out of my mind and I hated movies. Just at that point I got a phone call from someone I had known from years past who had raised money to make a porn movie and wanted me to produce it for him. Basically, I line-produced the film, that is, I handled the production, hired all the people, and made sure the film got made. He was the executive producer, which in this case meant he raised the money [in film the title executive producer is awarded for any number of different reasons]. We continued an association after the porn film was made."

The association led to a deal to make what Lewis had originally wanted to make: a straight theatrical feature, specifically, a sci-fi picture. At the end, the deal fell through ["the deal fell through" are words the independent filmmaker gets used to hearing] and Lewis and his associate made another porn film. This time Lewis convinced his associate to allow him to direct the film. Again his aesthetics got in the way of his mandate; the film had only three minutes of sex. When the distributor got the film, he cut out the three minutes so he could release the film as R rated. But an unforeseen problem arose. The executive producer, in debt because of an unsuccessful nightclub venture, never paid the "blow-up people" the $10,000 he owed them for blowing the 16mm print up to 35mm.

The lab refused to release the negative and the film got buried.

"It was a tacky movie and I'm just as glad it got buried but it was a good experience. I learned a lot from the mistakes I made during the production of that film."

For the next six months Lewis did nothing. Then he began writing scripts on spec with the hope of making a deal and getting to direct the film. It was at this time that he wrote the first draft of the *Santa* movie. Convinced by friends that L.A. was the only place to be if he intended to direct a film, Lewis took a trip to Hollywood. He rewrote *Santa* as a big budget Hollywood film and showed it around. He had lots of "good" meetings with agents and he made some contacts through friends who had just "broken ground" out there, but he had no job offers, no deal. He learned what Pauline Kael meant when she said, "Hollywood is the only place where you can die of encouragement," and returned to New York. He took whatever production jobs he could get (production manager, line producer) on New York–based films and hooked up with a writing partner. Together they pounded away on the typewriter. A Hollywood screenwriter friend of both of them called to say he could get Lewis and partner a writing gig if they could come up with an original idea in twenty-four hours. A Beverly Hills plastic surgeon turned independent producer was looking for original screenplays and he could arrange a meeting for Lewis.

"We got a call on a Thursday evening and were told we had twenty-four hours to come up with a sci-fi idea. If we did, we could have a deal the next day. I had spent years trying to get a deal and it came down to this. We were to meet the guy at ten o'clock on Saturday. We stayed up all night brainstorming for an idea. When we'd come up with one, we'd call our Hollywood friend and he'd say, 'Go back to work.' At five o'clock in the morning my partner went to sleep. Two hours later he woke and said, 'I'm freezing, let's write something about cold.' I thought it was a ridiculous suggestion but we worked out an idea, called Hollywood, and our friend there said it was great, profound, he'll give us a deal. He was right. We pitched the idea and ten minutes later had our deal. We joined the Writers Guild, the whole number."

Once again, "the deal fell through," but this time after a contract was signed, several drafts were written, a year and a half was spent in Hollywood, a lawsuit was filed, and much emotional distress was suffered.

"My partner was on the verge of a nervous breakdown. I was

learning lessons left and right. If you want to be a Hollywood screenwriter or director and fit into the system, then you have to go along with the 'collectivism' of the dream. I went to Hollywood with the best script I had ever been involved with, a great potential film. It became everyone's film, the director's, the producer's. At one point my producer actually believed the idea for the script was his. He made us take everything out of the script and then decided not to go ahead with it. I didn't know what to do. Should I stay in Hollywood and be on the low end of the totem pole and work my way up to screenwriter and eventually director? The stories I had heard discouraged that idea. Guys that had made it big as screenwriters and then moved on to director were changed so much by the experience that their whole aesthetic was different. In Hollywood, it's a matter of attrition; if you can hold out, you will eventually get a gig. But for me that would have meant at least two years with no means of financial support. New York would also be difficult. I went through a real crisis as far as what I was going to do was concerned. I had all this experience having made films and having not made films, and still I had few options. Nothing had opened up to me."

Lewis returned to New York.

"I floated. I was very broke and beaten down by the system. I went up to a friend's 'hut' in Vermont with the woman I lived with. I brought the *Santa* script with me. When I was in Hollywood I had tried to sell it, but the reaction I got was that you can't make a multi-million-dollar film about this weird Santa (that was pre-horror genre fever) and I hadn't done anything with the script since then. In the course of the week in Vermont my friend read the script and told me she thought it was great. She suggested I try to do it. I had nothing else to do and I thought I might as well try to raise money to do it myself. It meant rewriting it (again) as a low budget film."

Lewis worked on the script for a year. When he needed money, he line-produced and took other free-lance jobs. More important, he got out there and hustled. He hired a lawyer and formed a company, Azure Productions. He managed to interest an old fraternity brother (now a successful root canal specialist) in investing $10,000 seed money, which gave him "a little bit of credibility and a lot of confidence." With the help of a business-oriented friend, he organized his fundraising efforts, and with the help of other friends kept a high social profile—two elements crucial to putting together a successful "indie" project.

"I was out there pitching. I bought an index file and kept records of who I gave the script to and what their reaction was. A friend of mine had some contacts so I started going to more interesting parties with 'better' people. As strange as that may seem, it's very important."

At one of those parties, Lewis met an "investment guy" who was impressed with the idea for the *Santa* film, enough so to introduce Lewis to "financier-type" producer Burt Kleiner. Burt had read Lewis's aborted sci-fi script in L.A. and liked it. These "cross references" are usually a good sign to producers, and they were in Lewis's case. Burt was associated with independent producer Ed Pressman (*Badlands*, *Heart Beat*), and after meeting with Lewis and reading *Santa*, he decided to pass the script along to Ed.

"I had heard of Ed Pressman and always believed he was the perfect executive producer for *Santa*; besides being a good producer, his family owns a toy factory exactly like the one I had in mind when I wrote the script. [As it turned out, the film was shot on location at Pressman's toy factory.] I did not have a direct line to Ed and didn't want the script to get lost in a pile in his office so I never attempted to give it to him. When Burt said he would give it to him I thought it sounded good but, like everything else, could be one more drop in the bucket. Ten days later Pressman and Kleiner agreed to raise the money for *Santa*. I could have fallen over. Suddenly I had a deal. The projected budget was $400,000 and they put on an additional $50,000 producer's fee. No studio money was involved; it was all independent money raised in units of $50,000. The budget was so low it was ridiculous [the final budget was over the projected budget although still much lower than for a Hollywood film] but it allowed me to keep control and not have studio interference. They started providing money immediately."

On the actual experience of making an independent low budget film, Lewis has this to say:

"My typical day was a fifteen-to-sixteen-hour work day. I always wanted to be in that position so I had no hesitations. But the pressures that went with making a film were much greater than I had imagined and the problems were much more involved. I learned it was very important to keep some distance from what I was doing, so that I could have some perspective. Everything is at such a whirlwind pace it's hard to do that. During pre-production I would stay an hour or two after everyone left to reevaluate the day. Because this was a low budget film, we had no leeway; one catastrophe and I would be over budget. While working on other low budget films I learned that careful planning at early stages can compensate a little for lack of money, so I did a lot of that on *Santa*. By the time we got on the set, everyone knew what was to happen. I hired an artist to storyboard the movie so that it was completely laid out, frame by frame. I hired a friend with film experience as my associate producer and brought him in from the beginning. Together we hired a production manager who hired the crew and office staff. I wanted a particular cinematographer who had always been my favorite, Ricardo Aronovitch (*Providence*), so I sent him a fan letter and a script. He said he was interested and I flew to Vienna for a weekend to convince him to come over and do it. I took the casting as far as I could; I waited till the last minute to find the right people. Once I began directing, I tried to get out of my role as overseer. The hardest thing about directing is to get everyone to go along with your vision. You can't just tell people to do something and expect to get it done your way; maybe if you're Stanley Kubrick you can, but if you're just starting out you have to con, finagle, cajole, love, and go through a lot of numbers before you get what you want."

Once his directing duties were over Lewis oversaw all post-production activities and then went on to what is perhaps the most difficult part of being an independent filmmaker: finding a distributor. Lewis was fortunate that he did find one, for there are many independent projects made that never get released.

Lewis offers this advice to would-be independent filmmakers: "If you have written a script, you have a couple of options. You can try to sell it off, you can raise the money yourself or you can use it as a vehicle to integrate into the industry. If you're going to do it yourself, there are many ways of going about it. I know of an independent filmmaker who worked for years making commercials and trailers and then used the money he earned to make his feature. Whatever way you do it, be prepared to put in a lot of time. It's just the nature of the business that things don't move quickly. Perseverance is the key. You'd better be out there all the time and never give up.

"You have to get into crazy belief. You have to be obsessed. You have to be able to take a lot of abuse and have the ability to bounce back. To be able to spend years on a project, rewrite it over and over again, listen to people give you a hard time, and still be enthusiastic . . . what is there to say but that you've got to be nuts. There are lots of people that would say I am. I've had personal relationships that broke up because of my career. My personal life has been shattered. I've been broke and in debt for a long time. Once you succeed it takes on a romantic quality, but it's a very painful process.

"You must learn how to make connections. Every successful experience I've ever had came about through someone I knew. You must meet a lot of people. I started out knowing nobody. People put you on to other people. It took years to develop a social side. I was always shy, but you have to be able to project because you're in a world where thousands of others who want what you want are projecting.

"It's about ingenuity. You can do almost anything if you have the chutzpah and temerity to do it. You must be willing to hold out to that very end line, which means you risk stepping over the line."

PART IV

PRODUCTION CRAFTS

The Production Artisans

Production artisans interpret, design, and implement the production elements. They translate the director's vision into action.

Production artisans are the architects behind the scenes of theatre and film.

8 Production Crafts Job Descriptions

Animator. Animators work on cartoons, features, film titles, and special effects. For years animation was achieved by the "cel" method; however, with advanced technology came computer and other forms of animation. Described below are the traditional and existing animation job categories; this is a field where innovators are welcome.

Animation cameraman. He shoots the animation and is responsible for the photographic quality of the image on screen. He operates and maintains the animation camera, lights, and associated equipment, checking the placing and proper registration of the cels, objects, or aerial images in the field of view. He determines and sets the F-stop, focus, and position of the camera with each exposure and keeps a camera log.

Animation designer. He creates the picture or graphic in the first place and makes it come to life on the screen, using cel, computer, object, collage, or other (innovative) methods of animation.

Animation director. He controls the production and serves the same function as do live-action film directors. He is experienced in the techniques of animation as well as film directing.

Animation editor. He edits the sound and picture track, prepares orders for lab work, supplies, stock footage, and titles. He is in charge of dubbing sessions and quality control of the answer print (the first print, which sets the standard for all following release prints).

Background artist. He is responsible for drawing all background scenes.

Checker. Before the animation is photographed, he "checks" the ink and painting for imperfections.

In-betweener. In cel animation, the designer may only design the "key frames," in which case an in-betweener draws the frames that will make up the entire sequence.

Inker. In cel animation, the designer draws fine pencil drawings, and the inker traces these drawings onto cels (transparent sheets). A machine called a photocopier performs the same function. The *photocopying machine operator* places the drawings on the machine to prepare the cels.

Matte artist. These extremely skilled artists produce "matte paintings" for special effects. They often work in oil paints and create pictures which when re-photographed look exactly like a photograph or live-action shot.

Opaquer. He fills in the characters or graphics with color, tones, etc.

Art Director. A job specific to film, an art director is the head of a film's art department. He supervises all artwork associated with a production and is responsible for maintaining consistency and accuracy in the renderings of the art elements. Together with his staff of *assistant art directors, scenic artists,* and *draftsmen* he transforms the production designer's various concepts into roughs, sketches, working drawings, storyboards, construction drawings, floor plans, and costume sketches. He is sometimes called on by the production designer to have design and concept input on the artwork he prepares, and in those cases functions as an assistant production designer. For related jobs and additional information see *Production Designer,* and the profile of Mel Bourne on page 137.

Artist/Draftsman. In both theatre and film, the artist's job is to render the designs of his superior. In theatre, busy designers (costume and set) will conceptualize their designs and then hand them over to an artist (*sketcher*) to render and color. In film, the artist answers to either the art director or designers and pretty much serves the same function as the theatrical artist does. He assists his superior, details and colors storyboards, prepares and revises costumes and set sketches, and generally executes all other renderings. The *draftsman's* job is somewhat more technical in that he prepares plan and elevation drawings for the construction of the sets, scenery, and furniture. The duties of the artist and the draftsman are frequently handled by the same person. This is a good entry-level position for would-be designers and art directors with skills.

Camera Operator. The camera operator operates the camera for the director of photography. He informs the DP if a particular take is up to par or if it is faulty in any way: camera moves, focus, composition, encroachment(s) in the camera frames. The DP determines the composition and the camera operator maintains it. Some of the operator's duties are to line up the camera, adjust the ocular to proper focus for his eyes, check that the film has been properly threaded, and the shutter position and camera speed are correct prior to each take, see that the lenses are correctly positioned, operate the camera, properly compose and frame each shot as per the DP's direction, give the boom operator safe limits on microphone positioning, and give the camera assistant(s) the signal to mark a good take. Camera operators know and feel comfortable with their equipment, keep up with technical innovations, and communicate with the director of photography and crew. Within the union structure, the DP is considered the head camera person and the camera operator is next in line; the first and second assistant camera operators follow.

> *First assistant (a.k.a. Follow-focus).* He assists in the technical operation of the camera, maintains, unpacks, and assembles the camera and equipment, sets up the appropriate camera and equipment for each take, sets the F-stop and focus, loads the film stock if a second assistant is not employed, marks floor positions of actors, keeps accurate records of scene takes and expended footage, takes inventory, and "follows focus" during rehearsals and takes.

> *Second assistant (Loader).* He is employed on multi-camera productions to assist the first assistant cameraman. He is responsible for loading and unloading the film magazines, for labeling all loaded magazines and cans of exposed and unexposed film stock, for carrying the camera to nearby set-ups, and for preparing the exposed film for shipment. The loader sometimes prepares the slate and slates scenes for the camera (see *Clapper*). For related jobs and additional information, see *Director of Photography*, and the profile of Fred Schuler on page 147.

Carpenter. In both film and theatre, carpenters are responsible for set construction and movement. There are several kinds of carpentry jobs and titles to be found in each field. The jobs of master carpenter, production carpenter, carpenter, assistant carpenter, flyer, and rigger are found in theatre; those of key carpenter, carpenter, assistant carpenter, rigger, in film; and the job of construction manager in shops that build sets.

> *Master carpenter.* He is found on the staff of all commercial theatres. He shares the responsibilities with each production carpenter who comes into his theatre with a show, and is responsible for solving all house problems (e.g., faulty stage) as well.

> *Production carpenter.* He executes the work of the theatre's

set designer. He is hired on a show-to-show basis, and is responsible for hiring and supervising his crew of stage carpenters in the construction of the scenery and sets. He orders all construction materials and maintains communications with the set designer. He is in charge of the shifting, on-stage rigging assembling, and the general condition of the scenery, and for preparing the stage prior to performance for any special effect required.

Carpenter.   He is the skilled assistant of the head of the carpentry team; in theatre, usually the production carpenter; in film, he assists the key carpenter.

Flyer.   A flyer is a stage carpenter responsible for "flying" (raising and lowering) scenery, flats, etc., from the flyfloor (the area above the stage) during a performance for effect and after a performance for storage.

Rigger.   He installs the equipment used to lower, raise, or support scenery, props, and so on. In film, he erects scaffolding, "hangs" lights, builds camera towers, and erects rostrums on wheels for the painters' and scenic artists' use.

Key carpenter.   Acts as the head of a film carpentry crew. He executes the work of the production designer, being responsible for the construction of the sets, furniture, and set dressings, and for the supervision of the carpentry crew. He constructs the required sets from approved renderings and plan and elevation drawings, ordering construction material and equipment. In addition to the building of sets, he constructs scaffolding for production purposes.

Assistant carpenter.   In theatre and film, he assists the other carpenters in setting up shop equipment, ordering material, taking stock of existing materials, loading and unloading sets, delivering completed pieces from a scenic shop, and acting as gofer for the carpentry team. A good entry-level carpentry job.

Construction manager.   He is the head of the scenic shops crew. In both theatre and film, large parts of the set are built in scenic shops and reassembled on the stage. The construction manager's job is to act as liaison between the shop and the key and production carpenters; estimate budgets and time for bidding purposes; supervise the construction of the sets; and keep a close eye on the budget, carpenters' time sheets, and all labor.

Cinematographer. Cinematographer is more a term than a specific job title. Some people use it when referring to a director of photography, some as a generic term for all camera personnel, and others again when referring to a DP who operates his own camera (as many Europeans do). See *Director of Photography* for additional information.

Clapper. A film job, the clapper holds the clapboard (a.k.a. slate and "sticks") in front of the camera at the beginning of each scene and speaks the scene number and take number while he brings the hinged portion of the clapper onto the slate with a sharp sound. He does this at the beginning of each scene. A clapper operator is often a third assistant cameraman or production assistant, or someone else on staff, as this is not a full-time job.

Costume Designer. A costume designer's job—in both film and theatre—is to plan, design, and oversee the execution of costumes for the director. The designer is responsible for the total appearance of all performers, from stars to extras. Although the job is similar in film and theatre, one difference is that film designers "pull" (purchase readymade) their costumes more often than theatre designers do. Costume designers can work in both fields once they acquire the unique skills necessary to do so (which include, for example, predicting how a costume will "read" on camera, or designing a costume for a quick change).

The designer does much research. He reads and rereads the script until he knows each character intimately, he studies the period the play takes place in to assure authenticity of clothing and accessories, and familiarizes himself with any variable, such as country, time of year, etc., that might influence the characters' appearance. He then prepares (or has prepared) line drawings and sketches for the director, production designer (in film) and scenic designer (in theatre); if the producer is a "creative type," he too will be advised. The initial sketch conveys the designer's concepts and confirms that all involved are thinking along the same lines. Once they are altered accordingly, final color drawings are prepared, approved, and then implemented.

The pulling and building of costumes are closely supervised by the designer. He attends all fittings and dress parades (preliminary showing of costumes on stage) to ensure that the costumes work for the performers, move well on stage, and photograph properly. Often a designer will employ an *assistant costume designer*. If the assistant is a member of the union (United Scenic Artists), he is credited as an assistant costume designer; if not, he is credited as being so and so's assistant or secretary. The assistant acts as a sounding board and confidant to the designer. He might be asked to prepare line drawings, sketches, do research, "shop" for fabrics and garments, and help the designer in any way he can. For related jobs, see *Costumer, Costume Supervisor*, and *Costume Technician;* for additional information, see the profile of A. Christina Giannini on page 153.

Costumer.   A costumer is an assistant to the film wardrobe supervisor. The term is sometimes used in theatre to refer to the costume supervisor. Some of his responsibilities are to make minor repairs and alterations on costumes, to pick up and return wardrobe items during shooting, to take wardrobe to be cleaned and/or washed, and to supervise the dresses should the wardrobe supervisor ask. For related jobs, see *Dresser, Costume Supervisor, and Wardrobe Supervisor*.

Costume Supervisor (Costumer).   This theatre position is exclusive to theatre, dance, and opera companies that maintain their own costume shops (i.e., the place where old costumes are stored and new ones built). The costume supervisor functions as resident designer, head of shop, and wardrobe supervisor for resident theatre companies. The job is a fusion of responsibilities. Sometimes it means executing the designs of highly paid guest designers; on other productions it means designing and executing; and on productions with a shoestring budget it means pulling and/or selecting from the house stock of costumes. The costume supervisor is also responsible for maintaining all costumes stored in the theatre's shop. This is a good transitional job for costume technicians ready to take on design assignments and eager to learn from guest designers at the same time. Most regional (and resident) theatre companies employ an on-staff costume supervisor.

Costume Technician.   Costume technicians construct costumes based on a designer's idea. They work for costume shops that build for theatre and film productions and for resident theatre companies with their own shops. There are several kinds of costume technician jobs. *Buyers (Shoppers)* learn from the designer what fabrics are needed, seek them out at fabric houses, and buy those that will enhance the design, move well on the performers, say the right thing about the character, and photograph properly. Buyers are fabric experts and must know how much fabric is needed to complete a costume as well as what the best price is. *Dyers* change the fabric color to correspond to the designer's color samples. *Fabric cutters* draft the pattern for the costume, duplicating the designer's rendering. A *seamstress* puts the costume pieces together, and a *fitter* fits it on the performer. *Finishers* and *trimmers* add the remaining touches on the garment and do any hand sewing or decorating required. *Cobblers* build footwear and belts and *milliners* make the hats. The job of costume technician is a good entry-level one for would-be costume designers.

Crafts Service Person (Utility Man). A job exclusive to film, a crafts service person is responsible for keeping the shooting area and surrounding areas clean, performing all manual labor required, guarding the premises, assisting the carpenters, running errands and doing anything else he can to help during production time. The crafts service job is a good entry-level position, and the L.A. local (I.A. 727) is one of the easier unions to get into. The union wage is surprisingly high for this type of job.

Curtain Operator. A job specific to theatre, the curtain person operates the curtain at intermission or whenever a scene change requires that curtains be opened or closed. In noncommercial theatre, this responsibility is generally given to a stagehand, carpenter, assistant stage manager, and/or a volunteer apprentice. In commercial theatre, the curtain operator is a member of the house staff.

Dance Supervisor. In musical theatre, a dance supervisor is employed to oversee the dance members, keep the company up to muster, train cast replacements, and make certain the dance numbers are performed the way they were originally choreographed. He is sometimes assisted in his job by a *dance captain* (a member of the cast who analyzes performances, supervises rehearsals, casts and trains understudies, and performs in the show) and by a *dance master* (someone whose role is the same as that of dance captain with the exception of performing).

Ballet companies employ a *ballet master* and/or *regisseur* to supervise ballet rehearsals, cast and coach, oversee a production from the front, keep an eye on lighting and scenery, and do everything to keep the ballet the way the choreographer originally envisioned it. For a related job, see *Choreographer*.

Director of Photography (DP, Cinematographer, and Cameraman). A director of photography translates the screenplay into visual images. He more than anyone else is responsible for the way a film looks. Although the DP may operate the camera whenever he elects to do so, his primary responsibility is to maintain optimum photographic quality. He frames each shot for the director, creates lighting, controls color, and makes technical decisions to obtain the director's desired photographic effects.

The DP attends all pre-production consultations and location scouting trips, selects all equipment and film stock, checks the sets and costumes and make-up for photographic acceptability, supervises the camera crew(s), works with the director and cameraman to determine the camera positions, angles, and moves, determines exposure, selects the lens for each take, sets the composition of each take for the camera operator, and views all rushes for quality control. For related jobs, see *Camera Operator*, and the profile of Fred Schuler on page 142.

Draper. A draper works under the scenic artist on film crews and is responsible for the creative arrangement of draping material. His duties are to execute, arrange, hang, and sew all curtains, draperies, cascades, netting, and canvas backing, and to install any upholstery on furniture, sets, and props that might be called for in the design. There is also the job of *costume draper* (or *fitter*); see *Costume Technician* for more on that. For related jobs, see *Carpenter*, *Scenic Artist*, and *Set Decorator*.

Dresser. A dresser is found working in both theatre and film, although the job responsibilities change somewhat. In theatre, the dresser is assigned to specific performers and helps those performers make costume changes smoothly, properly, quietly, and quickly during performance times. He also checks and double checks the costume before each use to assure it has been properly maintained—cleaned, pressed, and if necessary mended. In film, quick changes and "pull-aparts" aren't necessary, so the film dresser assists the performer and wardrobe supervisor with repairs, alterations, spot cleaning, and pressing of the costumes. Noncommercial theatre companies and low budget film companies will often hire inexperienced people (for low or no salary) to work as dressers. This is a good entry-level job, particularly for those with sewing skills.

Editor. In film work, there are several types of editing jobs. The number and type of editors to be employed on each film is determined by the nature of the film to be edited, the amount of footage shot, the estimated total length of the completed film, the number of "tracks" required, whether the music is live or canned, and the time available to cut the film.

Generally, a feature film is put together by one editor working with an assistant and an apprentice. As the picture editing approaches completion, the picture editor is joined by one or more sound editors, each with an assistant sound editor, and, if the musical score is extensive, a separate music editor and his assistant. Once the picture is "locked" (it has been decided that no more picture changes will be made), the negative cutter and breakdown operator begin matching the negative to a marked work print, creating a single strand from which release prints may ultimately be struck.

If the editing team has to expand to cope with an enormous amount of footage or a tight editing schedule, the original editor may find himself acting as the "supervising editor" of a larger staff, assigning individual scenes or entire reels to different editors while attempting to coordinate their efforts so that the film will still appear to flow smoothly and retain a single editorial style. On some films, a consulting editor is brought in to provide an objective eye and a new creative voice. He is not in charge of the editing of the film, but rather serves as an outside adviser.

An editing team for a feature film might include a consulting editor, supervising editor, picture editor, sound editor, music editor, assistant editor(s), apprentice editor, negative cutter, and breakdown operator. Each of these titles and that of documentary editor are described below. For additional information, see the profile of Susan (Sandy) E. Morse on page 131.

Consulting editor. Hired to "look over" a project. He is not involved with the film on a daily basis, but will come in periodically to see how the film is shaping up. The consultant makes creative suggestions on the overall structuring of a film, helps make problem scenes work, and will ensure that all editing personnel are working up to par. The consultant job is given to editors of the highest standing.

Supervising editor. Hired on films where the coordination of two or more editors is required on the same film at the same time. This person is then responsible for supervising and scheduling the work of all editing personnel and for encouraging excellence in their editing performance. He is also responsible for the overall structuring of the film, the scene selection (along with the director), and the tempo and rhythm.

The supervising and picture editor job may be filled by the same person on some films. The head editor (be it supervising or picture) is ultimately responsible for realizing the director's intention.

Picture editor. He cuts the film for the director, and also coordinates and supervises other editing personnel if there is no supervising editor on staff. The picture editor can work in one of two ways. He usually views the dailies with the director and cuts during the shooting period; but on some films he begins editing only once the shooting is completed. In any case, he views the footage, contributes to selection of takes, cuts picture and voice tracks, plans scheduling and supervises all dubbing sessions, and is responsible for the quality control of the answer prints.

Sound editor.   Responsible for editing music and sound effects, although on large, complicated productions, he surrenders the responsibility for music editing to a separate music editor. The sound editor cleans up or smooths out the dialogue tracks, selects and positions the sound effects, and cuts the music tracks. He either selects appropriate sound effects from available stock or records appropriate effects, builds the sound effects and music tracks for an approved work print, prepares cue sheets for dubbing, records and sometimes performs "foleys" (sound effects, such as footsteps, not previously recorded), prepares music cue sheets for use by the music composer if original music is to be composed to score the picture, and selects appropriate music cues when canned music is used.

Music editor.   Works on films where extensive music is selected, transferred, and edited.

Documentary film editor.   Due to budgetary considerations, he often serves as picture, sound, and music editor in one. He performs all the editing procedures described above, selecting appropriate scenes, editing all tracks, ordering all lab work, supplies used in editing, stock footage, and titles, and conducting all dubbing sessions.

Assistant editor.   Assists the supervising and/or picture editor with his responsibilities. Some of his duties are to organize the cutting room, break down the dailies, synchronize live dialogue dailies, prepare dailies for "rush" viewing, catalogue and file all scenes and takes, measure incoming and outgoing footage, prepare orders for and take charge of lab work, order supplies, stock footage, and titles. In addition, he will mark, order, cut in optical work prints, clean and maintain all film tracks and editing equipment, and splice picture and tracks.

Apprentice editor.   Assists either the editor or assistant editor or whoever he is assigned to. He does not edit film unless he is strictly supervised. He does clean equipment, run errands, file "trims" and "out-takes," maintain the editing room, and assist his immediate supervisor with his duties.

Negative cutter. He works under the supervision of the editor and for the assistant, being responsible for cutting the negative to the editor's specifications. His duties are to cut, match, assemble, and splice the negative as necessary, send it to the lab for duping and/or additional prints, cleaning or treatment, record and catalogue edge numbers of the final work prints and clean and repair the negative. The negative cutter works on the final cut; consequently, his work begins once all other editing is completed.

Breakdown operator. Assists the negative cutter. His prime duties are to catalogue and break down, and splice the negative.

Electrician. There are several types of jobs for electricians in theatre and film. The number of electricians hired on a production is determined by the quantity, weight, and type of equipment used, the complexity of the lighting set-ups, and the duration and pace of the production schedule. Generally, on theatrical productions, there is a master electrician, a production electrician, and as many operators as need be; on film productions, there is a gaffer, best boy, generator operator, and as many operators as need be. Each of these jobs is described below.

Master electrician (a.k.a. House electrician). In commercial theatre, the house maintains a staff that works for the theatre owner; the master electrician is a part of that staff. His responsibilities are to hire the necessary lighting crew for the productions mounted in "his" theatre, to oversee lighting crews during production periods, maintain the house lights, and co-supervise lighting procedures with the production electrician. Noncommercial resident theatres generally employ at least one full-time electrician to hire and supervise the lighting crews and execute the lighting designer's work. He may be called master electrician, house electrician, or chief electrician.

Production electrician. A production electrician is brought in with a show and is responsible for lighting that show. Production electricians work on a show-to-show basis; they travel with the show when it tours and co-supervise (along with the house electrician) the lighting crew in all procedures—for example, a production electrician determines the amount of people needed on crew and the house electrician hires them.

Production electricians take direction from the lighting designer: it's their job to create the moods and effects for the designer. A production electrician's knowledge and manipulations
make the designs come into being. Working a crew of *"front
men,"* *operators*, and *assistants*, he arranges and focuses the
lighting instruments, maintains the electrical equipment, operates the switchboard for lighting cues, moves lighting when
necessary, and prepares the stage before the show by clearing
excess lighting equipment and running cables as needed, sets
and strikes lamps, changes gels (colors), and runs the spots and
all other lighting procedures from the booth.

Gaffer.   A chief electrician in film is called a gaffer. It is his
job to supervise the other electricians and to light the set to the
director of photography's specifications. He confers with the
DP early on to determine the type and amount of electrical
equipment needed to handle a production; he then orders
whatever is required.

He prepares instrument schedules and light plots for the job
he "gaffs." At the time of production the gaffer supervises all
lighting procedures and the loading, transporting, rigging, and
striking of the equipment. He operates the dimmer board, sees
that the lamps are cooled when not in use, maintains and repairs all cables and, most important, is responsible for the safety of himself and his crew. The gaffer is aware of any
violations to fire and safety regulations and corrects anything
that might interfere with safe conditions on the set.

Best boy.   The first assistant electrician, in film, is known as a
best boy. He assists the gaffer to light the set(s). Depending on
the complexity of the lighting set-ups, the best boy may be
called upon to do any number of things. Generally, he operates mobile lights and wind machines, sees that all unused
lights are stored clear of the set, and assists the gaffer at all
times.

Generator operator.   A film job, the generator operator is an
electrician responsible for maintaining the generator on location during all photography. He takes orders from the gaffer.
His responsibilities include maintaining, refueling, operating,
and servicing portable electrical generating equipment, and
observing proper safety precautions for the equipment.

Electrical operator.   In both theatre and film lighting crews,
the low man on the totem pole is called the operator. It's his
job to assist all other electricians in their duties, which could

mean anything from operating lamps and equipment, rigging, dressing and striking lamps and cable, to loading and storing equipment. Most electricians (and some lighting designers) began their careers as operators; it's the best way to learn the switchboard and familiarize oneself with the lighting equipment.

Fabricator. In film, the fabricator works with the set decorator and prop buyer (or outside prop man). His expertise is in searching out materials and fabrics to be used in the decorating of the sets. For related jobs, see *Property Master* and *Set Decorator*.

Grip. A grip, in theatre and film, is a stagehand. In theatre, grips work under the supervision of the stage carpenter, move scenery, and assist in the building of the sets and the rigging of machinery. In film, the number of grips employed depends on the quantity, weight, and type of equipment and material to be used. The first grip to be employed is the *key grip*. He works with the DP and gaffer, and is responsible for supervising the grip crew in their duties. Some of the grip's duties are to load, unload, and place equipment and scenery; to erect dressing tents, portable dressing rooms, and comfort stations; and to assist all other crews (wardrobe, carpentry, property, electrician, camera) in moving their equipment and materials. Frequently a grip will be assigned to work with the camera operator in coordinating moving shots; it's his job to operate the mobile camera smoothly to help make the take as technically perfect as possible. Although a grip is basically a manual laborer, the work requires special skills and knowledge germane to theatre and film. It's a good entry-level job (particularly on nonunion films and in noncommercial theatre) because it allows you to interact with so many members of the production team.

Hairdresser. Performers often hire their own personal hairdresser to design a fitting style for the character they are creating. Depending on a show's budget, the hairdresser either does the performer's hair before each performance or merely designs and instructs. In film, a *key* and *assistant hairdresser* are generally on-staff to dress and style the actor's hair in such a way as to enhance the photographic realization of the character. Besides shampooing, barbering, styling, and setting the hair at the start of each production day, the hairdressers touch up, comb, dry, and spray actors' hair between takes, and select and style all wigs, toupees, falls, etc. Entertainment hairdressers work within the industry; they rarely take on private customers or full-time salon jobs.

Lighting Designer. This job is found in theatre; in film (where the lights are used to enhance the photography), the DP is responsible for the design and the gaffer for the implementation. Theatre lights enhance the set, the actors, and the mood, and reproduce all the effects of natural light. On the live stage, lighting plays a crucial part in establishing a scene, and the creator of the lights is an important member of the production team. He conceptualizes the director's interpretations, hires and supervises a production electrician, selects the lighting equipment, determines which instruments are to be used at any particular time and their placement, focusing, and framing, and works with the costume and set designers in the creation of a cohesive look. Big budget productions will employ an *assistant lighting designer* to prepare and keep up-to-date lighting documents (hanging plot, board hook-up plot, focus chart), inform the stage manager of changes and new light cues, act as liaison between the designer and the *shop* and production electrician, and generally assist the designer. See *Electrician* for related and entry-level jobs.

Make-up Artist. In theatre, performers apply their own make-up, although a consultant might be called in for character and/or special effects make-up. In film, specialists who understand the effect of lights on various skin colors and have techniques to improve or alter an actor's look are employed at production time. A key make-up artist, an assistant make-up artist, a powderman, and a body make-up artist are all a part of the make-up crew.

Key make-up artist. He styles the make-up for the director and colors it for the DP. He prepares the make-up schedules (lists of the type of make-up styling called for, the make-up items needed, a plot of the application of make-up by scene number). He supervises the make-up crew and assigns specific artists to certain actors. He is responsible for between-take touch-ups and supplies his own make-up kit. Often he applies special effects make-up and supervises his staff in the application of street make-up.

Assistant make-up artist. He assists his superior in applications and touch-ups, but rarely styles and designs.

Powderman. He is specifically assigned to the task of between-take touch-ups and alterations, and is called on to apply powder (or other make-up) to cover an actor's perspiration caused by the heat of the lights.

Body make-up artist. He is responsible for applying and removing make-up to the body to assure a good photographic effect.

Model Builder. A model builder is employed on films using models or miniatures. He is responsible for their creative and functional design and for their construction, painting, and finishing. He may also be called on to operate, set up, dress, and disassemble the models. For related jobs, see *Special Effects Person* and *Property Maker*.

Painter. A painter assists the scenic artist in theatre and film. He mixes and applies the paint to the floors, walls, props, set, and the environment. He also takes direction from the scenic artist regarding the color, texture, and effect of the paint to be used. This is a traditional first job for would-be production and stage designers. Inexperienced painters on crew are often referred to as paint boys or girls.

Paperhangers. A paperhanger works under the supervision of the scenic artist and is required on sets where paperhanging assistance is needed. He is responsible for applying paper, tile, and other coverings to the surface of the sets, floors, walls, ceilings, and props.

Production Designer. In film, the production designer visualizes, designs, and supervises the execution of the sets for the director. The job is similar to that of the theatre's stage designer, but the production designer has many more visual scenes to design and the photographic effect to consider. The production designer is the first of the staff to be concerned with the film's visual image; all others (art director, set decorator, prop master, key carpenter, location manager and scout, costume designer, *et al.*) involved with the film's look are guided by his interpretations. He determines from the final script the number and types of sets required, then oversees their actual construction. He supervises location and studio scouting, propping, and set decorating. He often designs the picture titles and credits (choosing typeface, logo, color, size, etc.). For additional information, see the profile of Mel Bourne on page 137. For related jobs, see *Stage Designer*, *Set Decorator*, and *Art Director*.

Projectionist. The job of projectionist is found in both theatre and film. In theatre, a projectionist is employed to operate any slide or film equipment used to project a special effect on stage at performance time. In film, a projectionist screens the "dailies" at the time of production, the rough cut for editing and mixing purposes, and the completed film for VIP screening. A *theatre operator* screens the released film in cinemas to paying audiences.

Property Master. The job of property master is found in theatre and film. In commercial theatre, he is a member of the house staff who is responsible for all scenic and costume props and for supervising the property personnel. He maintains the furniture and properties, and is in charge of the provision and handling of articles during a performance. In addition, the related job titles of production property person, property handler, and property maker are found in theatre, and property maker, film property master, set dresser, outside property person, greensman, and metalworker in film. Each title is described below. The number and kinds of property crew members employed on a production will depend on the amount and kinds of props required.

Production property person. He is hired for a particular show and assists the set designer in finding and/or manufacturing props. For as long as a show is housed in the property master's theatre, the two (property master and production property person) share responsibilities. Once the show moves on, the property master becomes responsible to the house and the production property person to the show. Noncommercial theatres generally employ just one property master.

Property handler. Assists the property master to "set" (put in the proper place) and hand the props to the actors. He also helps "strike" (remove from the set) the props and store them until the next performance.

Property maker. In both film and theatre, he makes all properties that cannot be purchased because of special requirements (e.g., a light barbell) or budgets. He plans, designs, executes, and sets up all special props; he may also be asked to operate and disassemble the props he has created.

Film property master. He is responsible for securing and maintaining the film's props (for a set decorator, if one is on-staff) and for supervising the other property crew members. He prepares the property list and maintains a close watch on the properties throughout production. He makes certain that prop continuity (i.e., the same prop and placement) is maintained from one take to the next, and will often ask the still photographer for a "record still" to record prop placement in each scene.

Set dresser. Assists the film's property master by securing each day's prop items, dressing and cleaning the set and props daily, marking the position of prop items, and striking them from the set.

Outside property person (Buyer). Responsible for locating properties and arranging for their purchase, rental, and transportation to and from the set.

Greensman. Responsible for maintaining all exterior props or greens (e.g., plants, foliage, trees). He selects, rents, or buys the plantlife necessary for the film; cuts, trims, and places it in a greenery if need be; places it on the set; and colors or alters it as the set decorator requires.

Metalworker. He is skilled in shaping metal to any shape or size. He works with the special effects department in constructing metal armatures or frames for artificial trees, spiral staircases, spaceship frames, water tanks for underground shooting, and so on.

Scenic Artist (a.k.a. Head Stage Set Painter and, in film, Chargeman). A scenic artist is responsible for the decorating, painting, papering, and draping of a set. He creates special designs, scenic art, and finishing touches needed to complete the set construction. In theatre, the scenic artist might paint anything from a lavish design to simple lettering. In some cases a whole crew of stage painters will work under his supervision, and in others he will be the only one painting. In film, the scenic artist is responsible for supervising the painters, drapers, and paperhangers. He orders set-decorating materials and special equipment needed to prepare the sets, does all special painting (airbrush, line work, etc.), treats all props for age and design, treats the costumes for special effects, and treats the natural components of the set (tinting the water, painting the grass).

Script Supervisor. A job specific to film, the script supervisor is responsible for maintaining the shooting script. This entails a great deal: keeping a detailed, accurate, up-to-date script for the director and editor by recording all such details as changes in dialogue and action, camera placement and movement, actor and prop positions, actor distance from the camera, prop and set dressing locations, costume conditions and placement. The script supervisor is also responsible for maintaining continuity between takes; he keeps a detailed record of everything that happens during a take so that juxtaposed scenes may be matched. Other responsibilities include prompting actors, assisting the director during rehearsals, providing scene numbers for slating, recording satisfactory takes, timing all takes, and organizing all script notes, scene changes, and modifications to be delivered to the director and film editor at the end of production. In this way, the script supervisor acts as a liaison between the director and editor. The accurate final script that the script supervisor prepares during production is crucial to the successful editing of a film.

Set Decorator. The job of set decorator is found in film. It's the set decorator's job successfully to implement the production design-

er's set designs. More specifically, he studies the floor plans, drawings, sketches, and lists prepared by the art department and, using
them as a guide, selects and has built suitable furniture, dressings,
and props. His choices are made with the production designer's and
camera's demands in mind: he must know how things "read" on
camera, as well as how they will look to the production designer's
naked eye. The set decorator oversees the work of the scenic artist,
carpenter, painter, draper, and property crew as they build the sets.

The jobs of set decorator and property master are sometimes held
by the same person, particularly on low budget films.

Sound Designer.   This theatre job is a new one. Until the late
1960s, sound was handled by either a tech director or master sound
technician. As sound equipment got more sophisticated, experts
from the music field and design companies were called in to solve
acoustical problems. It's the sound designer's job to acoustically interpret a play for the director, select sound equipment and effects,
choose the placement of the sound equipment, and supervise the
sound technicians.

Soundman.   Film and theatre include several sound jobs, but because of the nature of the medium, there are more in film. Theatre
offers the jobs of master sound technician and sound operator. In
film, there are the jobs of production mixer, boom operator, cableman, playback operator, chief re-recording mixer, re-recording mixer, music/sound effects mixer, recordist, dummy loader, and
maintenance engineer. Each title is described below.

Master sound technician.   In theatre, he supervises the work
of the *sound operator* when both are on-staff. Together, they
maintain the quality of sound during performances. They install speakers, microphones, and the stage manager's sound
communication system. They position the sound equipment on
stage and, when necessary, have microphones "flown" from
above. They operate the console, adjust the microphones during a performance, and communicate with the stage manager
at all times via a headset. When sound effects and/or incidental music are required, the master technician is responsible for
recording them and the operator for playing them on cue during performance times.

In film, there are two types of sound jobs, production sound and
studio sound. Production sound people are responsible for the mixing and recording of sound during shooting; studio sound people for
recording, re-recording, and transferring sound performed in the recording studio.

The production sound jobs are as follows:

Production mixer. He is the head of the sound crew, responsible for the quality of the sound he records on location and on the set. Some of his duties are to select the sound equipment and raw stock; to supervise the transportation, setting up, and breaking down of the equipment; to operate the mixing console and recorder; to select (along with the DP and camera operator) a "safe" position for the recording equipment (out of the camera's view); to keep sound reports; and to supervise all sound personnel in their work.

Boom operator. He operates the microphone boom in order to pick up the actors' voices, the sound effects and/or the music during shooting. He makes certain no microphone or boom shadows appear within the camera frame.

Cableman. He is responsible for supplying, connecting, dressing, disconnecting, and storing all power and microphone cables used in conjunction with the sound equipment. He also assists the mixer, recordist, boom operator, and playback operator in their work.

Playback operator. He sets up, maintains, and operates the playback equipment during rehearsals and shooting times. He is needed where pre-recorded music and dialogue are used to cue the actors in synchronizing their lip movements to the film.

The studio sound jobs are as follows:

Chief re-recording mixer. Supervises all personnel connected with the mix. He is responsible for the successful combining of all tracks and/or units.

Re-recording mixer. Assists the chief in the combining of the tracks and/or units and in all his other duties. He is specifically responsible for maintaining the proper sound levels during the mix.

Music/Sound effects mixer. Performs two functions: he records original sound effects and live scoring, then assists the chief re-recording mixer to combine all the music and sound effects tracks.

Recordist. Operates and maintains the recording equipment, organizes and keeps reports and logs pertaining to re-recording, and assists the production mixer.

Dummy loader. Assures proper interlock and track feed of the "dummies" for which he is responsible during each run.

Maintenance engineer. Responsible for maintaining the

electronic and mechanical equipment found in the recording studio. He repairs the electronic equipment, projectors, microphone cables, and other wiring.

Special Effects Person.   The job of creating special effects is found in both theatre and film. The special effects person is responsible for planning and rigging all special effects such as firearms, explosives, incendiaries, man-made rain, floods, wind, snow storms, smoke, and so on. He takes precautions to ensure the safety of the cast and crew and anyone else coming within proximity of the set-ups. Often an *assistant* is employed to rig a set-up or prepare material. All special effects people working with explosives must be licensed by the state to do so. In film, there is also the job of creating photographic effects that when photographed appear to exist (e.g., a "painted" mountain inserted behind two actors in a studio photograph as though the actors were actually outdoors). For additional information on the job of creating photographic effects, see *Animator*.

Stage Designer (a.k.a. Set Designer and, in film, Production Designer).   In theatre, the stage designer is responsible for designing and supervising the execution of the sets. He visually interprets a play for the director within the given limitations of budget, space, sightlines, and equipment, and works closely with the costume and lighting designers to coordinate all design elements. He is concerned with creating a style, mood, and geographic location on stage. He prepares sketches, floor plans, and models of each set. Once these are approved, he prepares detailed drawings for the carpenters, so that they are able to build and install the scenery. He designs methods of moving the scenery between scenes and supervises all aspects of the building, painting, and working of the scenery from start to finish; he also selects or designs all stage properties and small pieces of scenery. For related jobs, see *Production Designer* and *Scenic Artist*.

Stage Manager.   The job of stage manager is found in the theatre. Every production employs at least one stage manager and large shows employ a staff of managers, including a production stage manager (PSM), a stage manager, two or three assistant stage managers (ASM), and, for touring companies, an advance manager. Each title is described below.

Production stage manager.   He is responsible for the overall supervision of all other stage managers and stage-managing business. He functions in a managerial position during rehearsals, but stays in touch with all elements of the production. Once a play opens, the PSM sits out front three or four times a week to make certain the director's artistic intent is being carried out. The PSM is sometimes called on to restage a production for a TV show or advertising spot or a road company, and to recast and rehearse replacement actors. (The PSM of the original *West Side Story* was twenty years later asked to direct the play.) In institutional theatre, the PSM hires and supervises all other stage managers and coordinates the production elements of the shows.

Stage manager. He schedules, organizes, plans, and attends all rehearsals, keeps the acting company informed of performance schedules, assembles and maintains the production book (i.e., the script, stage floor plans, and rehearsal records), maintains discipline and goodwill within the acting company, and "sits on book" (calls cues to the electricians, sound people, curtain person, stage crew, and house manager).

Assistant stage managers. They do everything the stage manager is too busy to do, which might include sweeping the stage, supervising the deck crew, running props, and maintaining quiet backstage.

Advance manager. Hired for shows on tour (road companies, packaged tours), he arrives in town a week or so ahead of his show, provides the house stage manager with a prompt script, makes certain the props are in order and that the theatre is generally ready for the production to be packaged in. Advance managers remain with a company through technical rehearsals, then travel on to the next town in the tour route. For additional information, see the profile of Zoya Wyeth on page 142.

Still Photographer. The job of still photographer is found in theatre and film. In film, it's the still photographer's job to take the still photos for the director and DP (to test composition and lighting), for the script supervisor, make-up, prop, and wardrobe people (so that continuity is maintained between takes), for the costume and production designers (to get a "reading") and, most important, for the publicist (for use in press releases, print advertising campaigns, posters, reviews, and anthologies). For the last, he must be able to get relevant and dramatic shots on a catch-as-catch-can basis, since the rehearsing and shooting don't stop for the still photographer. The film still photographer stays with a company throughout production, including long- and short-term location trips, determines the types of camera(s) and equipment, keeps reports and captions in order, and relinquishes the undeveloped film to the unit publicist (who in turn passes it on to a *picture editor*, who will process and select stills).

In theatre, it's the still photographer's job to shoot the pictures that will appear in newspaper and magazine articles, print advertising, reviews, *Playbills*, theatre lobbys, published plays, and anthologies. He holds "photo calls" (stage reproductions of the various scenes) and takes candid shots at dress rehearsal and performance times. He processes his film and chooses prints for the producer.

Technical Director (TD).   The "tech" director is responsible for supervising the execution of the technical elements of a play. The job is most often an on-staff resident theatre company position; still, some project work is available. The TD first establishes from the set designer's plans and models how well a proposed set will work in the intended theatre, then determines what materials are needed to build the set, lights, sound system, and special effects. He prepares a budget, orders supplies and materials, and supervises the entire tech crew in the execution of technical elements. It is the TD who is ultimately responsible for the proper functioning of stage equipment, scene changes, and technical elements. The position calls for a highly skilled, versatile person who has vast tech experience and is thoroughly familiar with stage equipment.

Wardrobe Supervisor (Wardrobe Mistress and Master).   The job of wardrobe supervisor is found in theatre and film. It's the wardrobe supervisor's job to maintain the costumes and supervise the dressers. In theatre, he is hired on a project basis (when one is employed permanently by a theatre he is also known as a *housekeeper*) and works for the run of the show. He makes certain the costumes are washed, dry cleaned, pressed, repaired, and look and "perform" perfectly for every performance. He supervises the activities of the dressers, and makes certain the performers are satisfied with the dresser assigned to them and the condition of their costumes.

In film, the wardrobe supervisor does much the same; he prepares wardrobe plots, supervises costume alterations, makes minor repairs, assigns dressing rooms, assembles changes of costumes and accessories for the actors, maintains the costumes, and supervises the dressers and costumer. For related jobs, see *Costumer* and *Dresser*.

9   Production Artisan Profiles

Susan (Sandy) E. Morse,
Editor of *Manhattan*

The editor's job is to help the director to make his film as clear, as entertaining, and as dramatic as possible. He analyzes the material at hand, interprets what the director has to say, and brings out the strong points. From the 300,000 or more feet of film shot and delivered to the cutting room, the editor selects, cuts, trims, and moves scenes around until the director sees the film that he intended emerge.

Sandy Morse is a picture editor. The director she most frequently edits for is Woody Allen.

"It's a mistake to think of the editing process as something that is carried on by a single person. It's a collaboration between editor and director. The director is the one trying to get a point across to the audience and the editor is there as his objective eye. Because the editor generally comes to the film late in the game—when the shooting begins, or even in some cases when the shooting has been completed—he has the advantage of distance. That coupled with his experience in manipulating film footage leads to suggestions about dropping lines, shortening scenes, rejuxtaposing material for greater impact, and even losing scenes; but the major decisions are almost always joint ones."

Sandy Morse is a young woman, still in her twenties, whose credits include assistant editor on *Annie Hall* and *Interiors* and editor on *Manhattan, Stardust Memories*, Steve Gordon's *Arthur*, Walter Hill's *Warriors*, a PBS production of Thurber's *The Greatest Man in the World*, various documentaries, and other independently produced feature films.

In high school in her native New Jersey, Sandy attended a showing of an incongruous double feature, Leni Riefenstahl's *Triumph of the Will* and Alain Resnais's *Night and Fog*. The viewpoints of the two films were polar opposites, yet they were equally affecting. It was seeing those films together that led Sandy to write her senior thesis on "Film as a Medium for Propaganda" and to consider a

Barry Sonnenfeld

SANDY MORSE

career in film. She thought she might want to direct but had no idea how to pursue it. She put the thought in the back of her mind.

Sandy's career began to take shape some years later in London, where she went after graduating from Yale with a major in history.

"I didn't know I was going in any direction when I went to England. I just wanted to get away. In London I gravitated toward people working in communications. I took some film courses at the Central London Polytechnic, observed BBC production crews on location, wrote my own scripts, and finally came to the decision that I not only loved film but wanted to pursue it as a career. I've always felt that most people got a job for eight hours of the day so that they could have the remaining four hours to do what they wanted. I could never understand that. I wanted to do something I enjoyed twelve hours of every day. I didn't realize, of course, that that meant I'd be working twelve hours of every day."

Sandy felt the best way to approach her goal was through education. She applied to and was accepted by the NYU graduate film school. She took out loans and opted to live with a relative in Brooklyn to save on dorm expenses. In October of her first semester a notice was posted on the bulletin board. It was for a job in the cutting room on a PBS film directed by one of her professors. Sandy didn't hesitate to apply for the job. She got it.

"I was nominally the apprentice on the picture but, by the end, I was doing a bit of everything. It was a low-budget film and I worked essentially for carfare and for the thrill of working. When I started, I had never seen mag track [sound track]. At NYU, you begin by making silent pictures. The editor I was working for had to show me what a synchronizer *was*, but I caught on quickly. I had to. There was no one else to do the work.

"I remember we had two weeks to do the sound editing, which I now know is a ludicrous amount of time for a feature-length film. A second sound editor was brought in but, even so, both of them were working around the clock. Not that sound editors ever get enough time to do their job, but two weeks was ridiculous! So, in addition to building tracks and preparing cue sheets, I was in charge of selecting all sound effects and occasionally even laying them in. I was also, of course, the gofer; I got coffee, I put away trims.

"I think my biggest thrill was in the 'foleys' session, where one records sound effects that must appear in sync with the picture but for some reason were not recorded on the set. The most common variety is footsteps, and since the main character in this particular film was a fourteen-year-old boy and I was by far the lightest member of the cutting room staff and therefore had the lightest tread, I was elected to do all his 'foleys'!

"I never stopped working—I was so grateful for the opportunity to be in a cutting room working with professionals. I never imagined I'd ever get another job. I'd ask the editor, who got a kick out of my wide-eyed enthusiasm and tireless pace, how I should get started. It never occurred to me, probably because I wasn't getting paid, that I *had* gotten started."

Once the mix was completed—in January—Sandy went back to film school. In March, all first-year students at NYU film school shoot their third and final film of the year. Like her classmates, Sandy worked in every capacity from director to cameraman to crew member. It was an exhausting but productive time.

By the end of the month she was so depressed and drained that when she was wakened from sleep on April 1 by a call from someone in Ralph Rosenblum's office asking her to work for him as an apprentice editor, she thought it was an April Fool's Day joke and hung up. They called her back and she found it was no joke. The editor she had worked for on the PBS project had recommended her to Ralph Rosenblum, one of the country's most respected and brilliant editors.

"The interview with Ralph was a great experience. I was perfectly honest and told him I had worked on one 16mm feature and had never touched film before I entered film school. I had no experience with 35mm at all. I didn't want to misrepresent myself. I told him I picked things up quickly but didn't want to suggest I had a lot of experience."

Sandy was hired. The film was *The Great Georgia Bank Hoax.* Not a great film, but a chance to work and learn from one of the best.

"I sat in on dailies screenings, where the director and Ralph would discuss which take to use, whether enough coverage had been shot. An experienced director will take more chances and shoot in a way that guides the editor. A less-experienced director generally shoots more standard coverage because he just wants to make sure he's got everything that he could possibly need. In the latter case, of course, the editor has more choices to make and less of a clue as to the director's point of view on a given scene."

In addition to sitting in on the dailies, Sandy's apprenticeship consisted of organizing the cutting room: rolling up trims, making sure the trims and out-takes were filed where they could be easily found, and taking the burden of menial tasks off Ralph and the first assistant. The better the apprentice (and assistant, which Sandy became on that job), the more initiative he takes.

Sandy knew Ralph was going on to edit Woody Allen's next film and she was hoping he'd ask her to join him. He hadn't asked by the time *The Great Georgia Bank Hoax* was completed. After agonizing over it, she decided she had to give it a shot and tell him she was available if he wanted her.

"It was a terrifying call for me to make. I am very shy. I was somewhat in awe of Ralph and I was working in the big time. I thought it was just a fluke that I had gotten the job on *Bank Hoax* and I had no way of judging whether I was any good. I didn't have anything to compare myself to."

Sandy made the call. She was hired as an assistant. The picture was *Annie Hall*—an opportunity to work with Woody Allen.

"With Woody, editing begins when shooting ends, because he wants to be present in the cutting room for the entire editing experience. Many films are edited as you go along. You edit a scene the day after you see the dailies, so you keep up with the shooting. That way, the director sees as soon as possible whether a scene works as he intended. If he's not satisfied, he can go back and get additional footage the next day. Woody does not work that way. Instead, he budgets for additional shooting after the rough cut has been assembled. That way, he doesn't spend time getting additional coverage for scenes that may never make it into the final cut."

Working on *Annie Hall* and meeting Woody Allen was a great experience for Sandy. From the beginning, she felt that something magical was taking place. It was a film that was going to work. Each new scene that turned up seemed better than the last—it was exciting to watch it all come together. It was a wonderful way to learn about editing because this was a film that was restructured in the editing room.

"Editing can be simply a matter of making individual scenes work, dropping out a couple of scenes here and there because they're not contributing to the point of the film or because they're slowing the pace, and then putting the remaining scenes in script order. Or, editing can entail problems of structure. *Annie Hall* lent itself to restructuring because it was pastiche; it was written as stream of consciousness with each scene essentially complete unto itself so that you could almost put them together in any order. For example, when you needed an extra beat for an emotional pause, you could move a scene from elsewhere in the film and put it in there and it would work. It was fascinating to participate in the process—you really saw the way a film was dramatically structured.

"The ending for the film came after several attempts. It evolved out of three episodes of additional shooting. Once the picture was assembled, it still seemed we needed a voice-over to wrap it up. Ralph suggested ending in the same way that the picture had begun, with an old joke that summed up Alvy's [the character Woody Allen played] feelings. Woody agreed. He went into the recording booth and came out with a joke that was absolutely perfect. It was recorded live to play back at a premix. We didn't even have it on a separate track to adjust it. It was the perfect ending for the film."

Sandy joined the union while she was working on *Annie Hall* (that old "Catch 22"). She continued to cut friends' films, work on her own weekends and nights, and learn about editing wherever she could while she was working professionally.

"I loved it because I wanted to get as much experience as quickly as I could. So, I did a lot of cutting on my own. The first professional film I edited was a film entitled *The Orphan*. It was a film that had been in the works for ten years. Ralph had been hired to re-cut it and to come up with ideas for additional scenes. I was hired as his assistant but because Ralph couldn't stay with the picture, I was asked to take over as editor. At that point we thought we were very close to finishing it, but as it turned out we ended up totally restructuring the film in an attempt to make the central character more sympathetic. I was thrilled when we screened it for Ralph and he told me he thought I had a 'real film sense.' "

From *The Orphan*, Sandy went on to edit two documentaries (one of which was directed by her mentor, Ralph Rosenblum) and a PBS production, and then was back working with Woody and Ralph on *Interiors*.

"Ralph was the editor of *Interiors* and I was hired as his assistant, but Ralph had enough confidence in me as an editor and enough perception of Woody's growing desire to be more intimately involved in the editing process to suggest that Woody and I work together on one scene while Ralph put together another."

Interiors was cut. Ralph Rosenblum had a film to direct (editing is said to be a good way to learn directing); Woody Allen wanted to participate more in the editing of his pictures; Sandy Morse had worked hard and well for both these men. It was a natural sequence of events that Sandy be asked to edit *Manhattan*. She was and she did, ultimately earning a British Academy Award nomination for her efforts. From *Manhattan* Sandy went on to work on Marshall Brickman's *Simon*, Woody Allen's *Stardust Memories* and Steve Gordon's *Arthur*.

Sandy suggests that the reason she has managed to keep working and has been continually recommended for jobs is commitment. "When I work on something, I live the project twenty-four hours a day. I give it everything I have. I don't think I realized that until I had been working in film for a couple of years. I then learned that people took lunch hours, and even left the machine. These things never occurred to me because I wanted so much to learn. I thrived so on an actual professional experience that I never let myself stop. I think that's what makes the difference. People who want to get involved in editing should take whatever job is available and work as hard as they can on it; the opportunities and recommendations will follow. Film school can be great, but you get out of it only what you put in. Commercials and industrials are good ways to learn the techniques involved in cutting and to get a quick overview. Documentaries are often 'made' in the cutting room. They teach you structure and force you to impose clarity and order onto what frequently seems to be a random accumulation of footage. Fictional and narrative films are more structured because they begin with a script, and thus rely on the editor primarily for rhythm and pace.

"I think working hard and showing enthusiasm on your projects, whatever they are, is the answer to getting the opportunities, and given the opportunities, the rest will follow."

Mel Bourne, Production Designer of *Annie Hall*

The production designer creates and coordinates the "look" of a film. The director describes what he has in mind, and the production designer explores the visual possibilities. He is involved with all the visual elements: style, color, details.

"A good production designer," says Mel Bourne, "gets involved with everything from concept through location scouting, propping, carpentry, painting and areas outside of the backgrounds such as costumes, make-up, and hair. And he always remembers that he's working for the director. Only after he tells you what he wants can you begin to make a contribution."

Mel Bourne has been making his contribution as a production de-

© *Kerry Hayes*

MEL BOURNE

signer for over twenty-five years. He designed for Bernardo Bertolucci and Woody Allen, directors known for their high visual
standards. Mel's film credits include *Annie Hall, Nunzio, Interiors*
(for which he received an Academy Award nomination), *Luna,
Manhattan, Corky, Stardust Memories, Thief,* and *Stab.* He has
designed countless TV commercials, TV films, and plays.

When Mel was a child growing up in Illinois, he thought about
working in films (as a director, because that's all he knew about) but
considered the idea a fantasy. Instead, he went to school and graduated as a chemical engineer. His career was stopped short, before it
ever really began, by war.

"After the war I decided I wanted to do something with my life
that I would enjoy. I had always loved to paint. And I always loved
the theatre. I wanted to do something that would combine both of
these. I went over to the Paper Mill Playhouse and managed to get a
job, more like an apprenticeship really, as a scenic artist and prop-
man. I painted and ran errands by day and handled the props at
night. Most important, I learned that the job of scenic artist existed.
Now I had a career goal: I would be a scenic designer. Realizing I
had a lot to learn, I enrolled in Yale's graduate drama school and
studied design. At that time I hadn't considered working in any other medium but theatre."

Having made the decision to work in theatre, Mel journeyed to
New York, at that time pretty much the place to go if you wanted to
work steadily. Armed with painting skills, some experience in stock,
and a tenacious attitude, he managed to find work as a scenic artist
Off Broadway and in community theatre (there was no Off Off
Broadway to speak of). He took one summer off to study and prepare for the union exam (United Scenic Artists) and passed on the
first go around. He was then able to find work as a union assistant to
some of the most brilliant theatrical set designers of the time (Robert
Edmond Jones, Donald Oenslager, Lemuel Ayers). He worked on
Broadway on *Call Me Madam, The Male Animal, The Millionair-
ess* with Katharine Hepburn, and Off Broadway for the newly
formed Actors Studio with Paddy Chayefsky, Sidney Lumet, and
Delbert Mann, to name a few.

"I began to get involved with television through the people at the
Studio. They'd accept a project and ask me to design it. At that time
live television was thought of as a challenge, a new medium; it was
all very exciting. From there I began designing TV commercials.
That was in 1952, and except for several plays and some work as an

assistant designer on a few films I continued to do so for twenty years. [Mel is responsible for the look of the Sam Breakstone spots and the "I Can't Believe I Ate the Whole Thing" Alka-Seltzer commercials.] The money was good and the training turned out to be by far the best I could get. I learned to work quickly, to solve technical problems, and to get to know how the camera interprets the elements of design. My work in commercials, specifically a spot I did for White Owl Cigars, led to my career in films. Woody Allen was looking for a new look, a 'New York look,' for his film. Woody's executive producer and I had worked together on the White Owl spots. He was an assistant director at the time and I was an art director. He moved on to become a production manager of a made-for-TV film that I designed. He became Woody's production manager, then his executive producer, and suggested me as the designer who could give the new film the look he wanted it to have. I met with Woody and I was hired. Woody was the kind of director willing to hire an unknown, which despite all those years I spent in theatre and TV, I was considered."

The film was *Annie Hall*. It launched Mel on a new career. He has worked exclusively in film since that time.

"In film, the production designer works essentially with the director. He is the first person after the production manager to be hired and the very first to approach the visual elements of the film. Sometimes you meet with the screenwriter, but only if there's something unique about the script he wants to get across. Basically, my dealings are with the director. In the beginning, you sit and discuss with the director what he's trying to get out of the script—whether the film is to have a realistic look or whatever. Very basic concepts are discussed. When I worked for Bertolucci, he pretty much told me what he wanted the picture to look like. He was very definite. Others aren't always definite and you have to show them with the sketches. The first ones are very rough but indicate to the director what the scene will physically look like. Once the basic sketches and plans are completed (there are endless revisions), you confer with the director again. Some can't work from sketches or even photographs. The only time they can make a decision is right on the set." [Woody Allen rejected Mel's original decor for the interior of the Southampton house in *Interiors* after it had been executed. Mel had to do it all over; new draperies, carpets, and furnishings were brought in.]

Once the director approves the designs, they are passed on to an art director and staff of artists, who then develop them into working drawings.

"On some films I'll do the working drawings myself. I did everything on *Manhattan* because it was fairly simple visually. There are some designers, mostly those who have set-decorating backgrounds, who don't draw at all. They verbally convey their ideas to the artists. The working drawings are then passed on to the carpenters, grips, etc., who turn them into actual sets. Which brings me to all the other things a production designer is responsible for.

"In addition to the art directors, scenic artists [chargemen], and draftsmen, a crew is needed to carry everything out. Prop people, carpenters, grips, outside buyers, set decorators, and location scouts are all responsible to the production designer. Putting the crew together is administrative but ends up a creative endeavor because if you have a bad carpenter, he's not going to come up with the little details that you don't necessarily put on your drawings but that will affect how the completed set will look. Bad chargemen don't get painters who really know how to paint, etc., etc. And you want to put together a crew that's compatible with your way of thinking. It's so important to the final outcome."

Another of the production designer's responsibilities is to find adequate stage space. He shares this task to some extent with the production manager. He also gets involved in finding locations and propping.

"I like to get involved in the propping; some designers don't. In Hollywood [Mel works and lives in New York] the set decorators and prop buyers think I'm crazy to go with them, but I think every detail is important. One prop can say so much. The production designer is also responsible for coordinating the hairstyle, make-up, and costumes of the actors."

Mel has been designing and planning the way sets will look for twenty-five years. His career has spanned all the media. His advice to those wanting to follow in his footsteps is this:

"It would seem to me that a career is formed from many parts of your life the way a river is formed from many mountain streams. In this case, the mountain streams that contribute are a basic interest in things visual, a talent in the way you use your hands, and education, not only in the visual arts but in literature as well.

"Learn what a word can do to set the mood, because that's essentially what a designer does—he transforms words into pictures. Develop ways to use your knowledge. Work in theatre, in TV, in commercials. Commercials are a fantastic 'summer stock' way of learning about film. Be a gofer in the art department of film companies. Just working near good designers will teach you about design. In the beginning don't worry about being paid, worry about paying your dues. And study. U.S.A. is still one of those unions you can get into if you're qualified. Then look for work as assistant to designers you want to be influenced by. These qualities and experiences will be your mountain streams that will eventually flow into and form your career."

Zoya Wyeth, Equity Stage Manager

Stage managers are responsible for bringing together all the elements of a production and keeping them that way throughout the run of a show. It's a challenging and multifaceted job. The amazing thing about stage managers is how they function without electronic computers for brains and the limbs of an octopus.

Zoya Wyeth, a young successful Equity stage manager working in New York City, describes the job this way:

"Stage managing has three phases to it. There's the servant phase, the mothering phase, and the executive phase. That keeps the job exciting, but you must be careful not to allow your ego to get in the way of your work.

"The first, or 'servant' phase, begins before rehearsals. The stage manager is usually hired two weeks before a play goes into rehearsal to perform pre-production work. This can mean almost anything: making telephone lists of cast and crew, having the manuscript retyped with the author's changes, and running auditions for those few parts still not cast. Once rehearsals begin, the stage manager must do whatever is necessary to keep order and get on with it: mark and sweep the stage, check the actors' attendance, know and execute the Equity contract rules if it's an Equity production, call a cab for the star, and sharpen a pencil or two if need be. At this point, the stage manager is an invisible necessity scurrying about doing everything for cast, crew, director, and management alike. All the while, he is preparing and revising the prompt script [an accurate record of the play's production elements] so that an eventual smooth performance pattern will take place.

"The second, or 'mothering' phase, begins during the final weeks of rehearsals. It's the time for the stage manager to start cleaning up the prompt script, revise and elaborate the plots, and start 'mother-

Paul Myrvold

ZOYA WYETH

ing' the cast, crew, designers, directors, and management. The stage manager is elected to this surrogate mother role for two reasons. First of all, really good stage managers have the ability to remain cool, calm, and collected under the worst conditions, and they are the only ones capable of stroking and soothing at this time. Secondly, it's the business of a stage manager to be as involved as possible in everyone else's responsibilities. So, he's the natural person to turn to when help is needed.

"The technical, design, and acting elements must be brought together. It's the stage manager's responsibility to see that this happens harmoniously. If he's been organized, communicated with everyone concerned, maintained an accurate prompt book (including all stage business, cue sheets, plots, daily records), the first technical rehearsal will be a quiet fusing of the elements; if not, it will resemble a head-on collision."

Regardless of how well rehearsals go, the point at which the first run-through occurs is always a tense and frenetic time. Designers, working around the clock, will need an actor for an extra fitting—it's the stage manager they ask. The star will be overworked and fatigued—it's the stage manager who must inform the director. Everyone seems to need the stage manager. The mothering phase of stage managing is perhaps the most trying; certainly, it's the most exhausting.

"The third and final phase, the 'executive' phase, begins once the play opens and the director is gone. It continues through the run of the play. Now the stage manager assumes full control of the production: managing the performance is his primary responsibility. It is the stage manager who sees to it that the performance given on the first night will be the performance given on the last. Well-trained and informed assistant stage managers will be a great help in this phase. If there is a production stage manager, he will often sit out in the house and take notes, leaving the stage manager free to call the show. Depending on how complicated the performance notes are, the stage manager will either rehearse the scene with the actors or communicate the problem verbally. Even if the director has been in the house, watching and taking notes, it's the stage manager who transmits them to the appropriate parties. From here on in, the stage manager functions as the boss, representing both the director and the management."

This progression—from pencil sharpener to authority figure—requires a great deal of skill and knowledge. Some schools offer majors in stage managing. However, like so many jobs in the performing arts, experience seems to be the best teacher. Gaining that experience can be difficult at first. The trade papers aren't very helpful because at the point where the producers are ready to announce a show is going up, they have already hired the stage manager and the assistant stage managers.

Zoya suggests showcase theatres as good places to start.

"Volunteer to be a second, third, or even fourth assistant stage manager on a showcase production. Be willing to sweep stages, paint scenery, and bring the director coffee. The more work you do, the more people you'll meet. Exposure and experience is the name of the game at this point in your career. Competition at this level will be stiff; stage managing has long been considered a step in the right direction for would-be directors as well as a means to an end (paying the rent) for actors. Let it be known verbally, and in your attitude and work, that stage managing is a career choice for you, and you'll be ahead of the game. If you must take a 'nine to five' during this time, try to get one in the arts where you can make contact with other theatre professionals. Some likely jobs are stage carpenter, stage electrician, production secretary and/or typist. Better yet, plan while still in school to work and to save every penny you can so that when you do come to New York or Los Angeles (or wherever you choose to live and support yourself) you will be able to afford to take low-paying theatre jobs that in the long run will pay off."

Zoya Wyeth has stage-managed dinner, repertory, resident, children's, multimedia, ballet, and Broadway theatre. She's been a production stage manager, a production manager, a stage manager, and an assistant stage manager. She's worked with Joe Papp, Bob Moss, and other distinguished producers and directors. Zoya is only thirty years old. Her story is typical of working professionals—she made up her mind and worked until her goal was realized. Zoya got her first taste of stage managing at Syracuse University.

"As a directing major I could get out of crew by stage-managing a class production, so I did it. I liked it, and in my senior year I farmed myself out to the stage manager at the Syracuse Repertory Company to be her assistant stage manager. Looking back on it, it was the smartest thing to do. Many of my jobs have come from that one contact. I didn't know that then, though. At the repertory I learned to work with Equity regulations and how to work with a professional theatre company. I went there every afternoon after my classes were over and came back for the performance every night. I thought then, and still do, as a matter of fact, that this must be what is meant by paying your dues. I didn't seem to mind sweeping floors or taking guff from different actors, or working until I was exhausted as long as I was there—in on rehearsals in a theatre.

"The summer I graduated, the production stage manager I worked under at the Syracuse Repertory Company got a stock job as a stage manager. She liked my work and my attitude and hired me as her first assistant. Then the general manager at the stock company quit, the production stage manager moved to that job, and I was hired as the stage manager. It was ideal for me. I got my Equity card (the only way to join is to be offered a contract from an Equity company) and I had my mentor overseeing my work and teaching me what I needed to know."

Zoya spent ten weeks stage-managing ten shows (a week for rehearsal and a week for performance) and loved every exhausting minute of it. She "picked the brains" of the entire company, and when she came to New York that fall, she had some idea as to where to look for work and she had the confidence gained from a successful experience. Despite this, she couldn't find work. Instead, she volunteered on showcase productions and took a job with a record company in the publicity department. It was there that she realized just how committed she was to a career in the theatre; she simply wasn't prepared to sweep floors to build a career in the record industry. As luck would have it (or luck combined with sending out hundreds of résumés to producers and general managers), a lighting designer she met on a showcase production told her of a stage-managing job in a dinner theatre in Ohio. She took the job and went to Ohio. There she worked with Ann Miller, June Allyson, and other star performers and directors. Because a stage manager in dinner theatre is expected to do more than in repertory or stock, she learned new skills (mostly technical) and grew more confident.

Back in New York, Zoya took a seasonal job with the not-for-profit Chelsea Theatre. The second show of the season was *Strider*, a musical. The theatre ran out of funds, but because the company believed in the show, they offered to work for free. Equity allowed them to do so for three weeks but no more. As it happened, a commercial producer "picked up" the play and brought it to the Helen Hayes Theatre, where it played the 1979–80 season. Zoya achieved her goal of stage-managing a Broadway show before her thirtieth birthday.

She notes that of her entire graduating class there are only a few actually working within the performing arts. She attributes her success to realistic goals, hard work, humility, and tenacity. She said she would never dream of saying to a director, "I don't do that," when asked to sweep a floor or prepare a rehearsal space. She says part of the thrill of being in theatre is to work your way up. "Never feel that you shouldn't give your all and be one hundred percent committed; never stop questioning; learn from all your experiences . . . catastrophes included. Don't stop growing, and remember that if you want it bad enough, and you're willing to pay your dues, you have a good chance of realizing a career as a professional stage manager."

Fred Schuler, Camera Operator of *The Deer Hunter* and Director of Photography of *Gloria*

It is the director of photography's job to translate the director's conceptions into visual terms. He is in charge of the visual quality of a film. He is responsible for the movements and setting of the camera and for the lighting of the scenes. During production, he—along with the production manager—runs the entire crew and makes certain their efforts are visually well chosen. The DP's job is among the most important on a film.

Fred Schuler, a man of forty, just recently stopped working as a camera operator and began working as a cameraman (a synonym for DP). While still an operator he handled the camera for some of the world's most respected cinematographers, including Gordon Willis, Sven Nykvist, and Vilmos Zsigmond.

"The cameraman is in charge of the photography. It is his job to create something that is visually impressive. You want to show something—that's why you are doing photography in the first place. The DP's contribution is the look of the film. And he has to make sure the look does not overpower the story. The audience should not be aware of the photography. On the other hand, the DP needn't follow the clichés (that a comedy must be light, a tragedy dark, a street picture not beautiful); if he does, he will stop being a creator and start being a mechanic. There is no such thing as 'It has to be.' The cameraman must remain open. A movie is make-believe; you can do practically anything with it as long as it adds to the story."

Fred's is a classic story of someone who started out knowing no

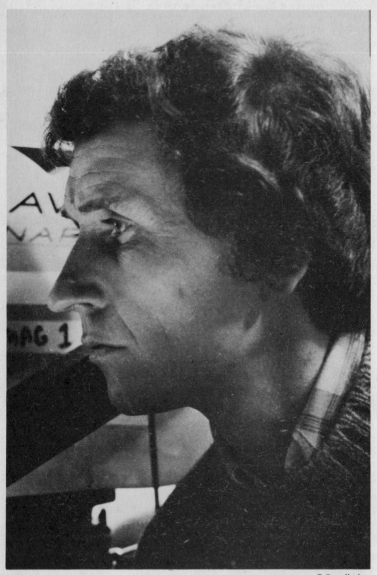

FRED SCHULER

one in the business yet managed to build himself a successful career and fine reputation as one of *the* up-and-coming cinematographers of our time.

Born in Munich he came to this country on a vacation from a job with a West German firm specializing in motion picture equipment design. He was doing well, having progressed from technician to research and development engineer, but after touring the States for six months he decided to stay in New York. He had no real ties in Germany, and was young enough to do as he wished. Also, in the back of his mind was this gnawing ambition to leave equipment design and "get into" production. He had studied film in Munich and was a pretty good photographer even then. In New York, he took a job with an American equipment rental firm because that's where he could get one. He stayed there for a number of years, progressing to designer but, more important, building a reputation with New York cameramen and operators as someone who knew cameras inside out. Whenever he could, he let it be known that he wanted to work with the cameras he was designing and enter the union (I.A. Local 644) as an assistant.

"I didn't want to go out there on my own on a nonunion basis because I was insecure about finding a job. Working as a designer through the years gave me the opportunity to meet many cameramen. Those who knew me and respected my work told me I had a chance of getting into the union as an assistant. I made an application and was accepted. I knew it would be psychologically difficult to be an assistant after having already been in a supervisory position but, on the other hand, it was very difficult to get into the union. This seemed to be my chance and I took it. It turned out to be a good thing, to come in as an assistant. I got to know the cameras and equipment and the people and gradually worked my way up. I would have been buried had I come in as an operator; I was not capable of it at that time.

"My first job offer was as a loader but with my past experience and age [he was 27] I just couldn't handle it, so I asked to leave the picture after three weeks. My first assistant job was on a TV commercial for a camerawoman who had herself just recently gotten into the union. A friend recommended me to her and she took a chance and hired me. My first movie job was also through a recommendation; it came five months and a number of commercials later. It was with Haskell Wexler on *The Thomas Crown Affair*. He became my idol because I was so impressed with the way he did things. He was very unconventional and avoided clichés. I was lucky in that for all the years I worked as an assistant, I worked for people I could learn from."

After five years as an assistant, Fred had had it. By that time he was more than capable of handling a camera on his own—more capable, in fact, than many of the people he was assisting.

"I'll never forget that day. It was on a Friday, April 13. I was to work as an assistant on *Serpico* but got a call from the production manager telling me a new director would be coming on the film and he might not want the same camera crew so the job was off. Two hours later I got a call from a DP I had worked for as an assistant asking me if I'd like to change my classification and work for him as an operator on *Man on the Swing*. At first I hesitated and asked to call him back. Everyone I spoke to told me to go ahead and do it. I was always fortunate in that whenever I was ready and able to upgrade myself, someone gave me the chance to do so. Of course, I called him back and accepted the job offer. From there I kept on going."

For the next five years Fred did keep on going, operating the camera on *Dog Day Afternoon*, *The Deer Hunter*, *Network*, *Annie Hall*, *Manhattan*, *Hide in Plain Sight*, *Willie and Phil*, and *Jaws*, where he operated second camera for the water scenes. In the middle of the filming of Paul Mazursky's *Willie and Phil* he was offered his first DP job and had to leave the film to take it. It's every cinematographer's dream to become a director of photography, Fred included, but he liked working as an operator.

"It's the best job on the crew. If the photography is good you can take the credit; if it's bad you can say you were only the operator! Actually, the camera operator is a very underrated job. Both the DP and the director depend on him. He is the only person who can see the image as it is being recorded. The rest of us have to wait till the next day, at the dailies. He may be told upfront [by the DP or director] to try to keep this or that in the shot, but what ultimately gets into the frame is in his control. For instance, maybe an actor is looking down at a newspaper but the paper isn't in the frame. The shot has been set with the newspaper in and everyone knows it should be in but only the operator knows if it really is. Sometimes a little thing the actor does to enhance the scene can only be caught by the operator. It's not his job to decide if the piece of business should be in or out, but it is his responsibility to bring it to the attention of the DP and the director. He should also be aware of the lighting; often the DP needs the operator to tell him if something is wrong. Many times, operators don't do all they could do, they don't know what to 'play with.' I know, because so many movies are so very average and not well composed. Too many operators just operate and don't realize they should be creative, that the DP and director look to them for help."

Despite his fervor for operating, Fred moved on and up. First came a chance to do completion photography on *Manhattan*. Fred operated the camera for the gifted cinematographer Gordon Willis. When it came time to do additional shooting, Willis was too busy. Believing Fred to be capable of the job (DP'ing the additional shots), Willis suggested it to Woody Allen, who agreed with him. It was a producer on *Manhattan*, Bob Greenhut, who suggested Fred to John Cassavetes as the DP on his film *Gloria*. After *Gloria*, Fred DP'd *Stir Crazy*, directed by Sidney Poitier and starring Gene Wilder and Richard Pryor, then went on to *Arthur* with Dudley Moore and Liza Minnelli, and other films.

Though Fred began his cinematography career pretty late, at twenty-seven, he quickly worked his way up the ladder, and today, at forty, is considered to be one of New York's best. (He's also one of L.A.'s best, as he is one of the few DP's who work on both coasts).° His was a case of taking it nice and easy and smart. Fred is just as passionate about his work as a DP as he was about operating.

"Working with each director is different. The inexperienced ones rely heavily on you for angles, positions, flow of cuts, and so on. The experienced ones work with you on more of a cooperative level. The DP has several weeks of pre-production time, depending on how large and elaborate the picture is. It is the most important period for the movie. It's the time you make your feeling for the script known to the director and others and see how they respond. And it's the time you learn from them what they have in mind. It's as though you are gradually building up a friendship with them. It cannot be done overnight. I generally read the script three times. The first time I fly through it just to learn what it's about. The second time I get more involved in the story, and the third time I begin to digest it emotionally and technically. Then, I think about what I would like

°When he was still an operator and working on *The Deer Hunter*, Fred joined the L.A. local (I.A. 659). He was already a member of the New York local (I.A. 644). Now that he is a DP and a member of both locals, the unions have no choice but to allow him to work both coasts. This is something that is generally considered impossible to accomplish.

to do with the movie, do I want to make it light, do I want to add colors, do I add some filters, what type of filters, and so on. It all depends on the mood. You have to make the photography work with the story, so it is a combination of what the director has in mind and what you have in mind. You meld those together and work it out.

"A great responsibility the DP has is to pick the equipment and the right people to work with. You are only as good as your crew. The entire camera, lighting, and grip crew is my responsibility. I select the operator, gaffer, and key grip and they select the people they want under them. [The production manager does the actual hiring, negotiating fees, etc.] You want to make sure you get the best equipment. You can't choose which firm to rent from [again, it is the production manager's job to "bid out"], but you can say what equipment you want. You have some influence regarding locations. The production designer is way ahead of you picking locations and creating on his end, so you get together with him and talk about colors and styles, also with the costume designer and set decorator. It's my job, as DP, to express my opinion on what will work visually, that is, what would be better photographically. Everyone listens to each other because no one wants to work against what the others are doing. It's a great collaboration of people working for the good of the movie; you pull from every corner to get it all together. During production I am in charge of the photography and all things that have anything to do with it, including, of course, lighting, setting the camera moves, conferring with the director, the make-up people, the crew, the set decorator.

"The next thing is the lab. I choose it and I make sure it is one that responds to my needs, because I could be the best photographer in the world but if the lab does a lousy job the film will look lousy. It often happens that a lab will ruin a film. My final responsibility is the timing of the movie, that is, color correction and light level of the print you select. You watch it at the lab and correct the prints. That happens a month or so before the picture is totally finished."

For would-be cinematographers, Fred suggests the following:

"Start as soon as possible. And start at the bottom so you can *learn* your way up. Progressing slowly not only helps you learn your craft, it helps you get to know the people you will be working with later on in your career. It allows them to develop confidence in you and it allows you to develop confidence in you. There is no such thing as starting at the top; you'll fall down as fast as you rose up. It's much better and more secure to experience each level.

"If someone wants to work on major movies, I suggest they try to get into the union as quickly as possible, because it's tough as a nonunion person. It's easier to try to get into the union on the lower classifications. If someone wants to be an assistant, the best thing is to get to know equipment by working for a camera rental house in the rental department, cleaning the equipment, setting it up, doing low-level maintenance, and most important, meeting cameramen. One of them might be the one to give you a shot at a job. That's exactly what happened to me. But you must be good at your job, as well as ambitious and nice, to get the shots. Photography skills are the most important thing in this line, but just as in everything else, personality counts too.

"Try to work on good films. It helps in this business to be associated with good films because people relate you to the movies you worked on. If the movie's good they think your work was good, regardless of whether that's true or not. For a type of person like me, who can't get out there and knock on doors and push, it's particularly important to develop a good reputation. I would have starved to death if I had had to do that, so instead, I just worked hard."

A. Christina (Stia) Giannini, Costume Designer to Agnes de Mille and Alvin Ailey

The costume designer's job is to create and supervise the execution of the costumes based on the director's/choreographer's concept.

A. Christina Giannini, "Stia," is a working costume designer who can be involved with a ballet, a Broadway show, and a showcase production all at the same time. Her philosophy is to work and meet the challenge. She's met the challenge at such places as the Joffrey, the American Ballet Theatre, Alvin Ailey Dance Theatre, the Spoleto festivals in Italy and the United States, and at the North Carolina School of the Arts as their resident designer. She's designed for such choreographers and directors as Agnes de Mille, Robert Wilson (*Einstein on the Beach*), and Alvin Ailey. Because being a designer allows for varying degrees of involvement with the job at hand, designers will often take on one or more projects at the same time. In addition to enormous talent, imagination, skills, and knowledge, this requires the energy and tenacity of an athlete.

Stia designed the costumes for *A Midsummer Night's Dream* based on certain "ideas" thrown at her from the director. "I want the whole thing to look like a disco with the Athenians having one

Merri Anne Milwee

STIA GIANNINI

look and the fairy people looking Turkish." It was Stia's challenge to do, as she puts it, a "Turkish-cum-disco version of *A Midsummer Night's Dream.*"

From the director's/choreographer's concept, the designer prepares the first renderings or "roughs." "There is no set rule as to how much direction one will get from a director/choreographer; it's a real mixed bag. Once the roughs are prepared, they are submitted to the director and reviewed along with other designs [set and lighting]. Concessions are made by everyone, but from this pre-production meeting the designers—costume designer included—will have a good solid idea of what the finished designs will look like. The final renderings are prepared in detail and swatched with fabric whenever possible. Before the execution of the costumes begins, the renderings must be approved, usually by management, the director/choreographer, and sometimes by the star. Dorothy Loudon, for example, has a clause in her contracts stating that nothing goes on her back without her approval. Other performers with difficult-to-dress bodies have similar clauses in their contracts."

Once the renderings are approved, the designer switches gears and sets out to have the costumes executed. In noncommercial situations this means working with the company costume supervisor and staff; in commercial situations it means sending the renderings out to costume shops to be bid on. Stia points out that before either of those things are done, she tries to get what she can for free. Often, vendors will loan a production expensive lush furs or original hats for a mention in the program.

The designer works closely with the costume shop and oversees all work. If the designer or the designer's assistant is to "shop" the fabric, now is the time. If the costume house has a good buyer, the designer will approve the fabric selection before any work begins.

"The finished costume now has its first true test: it is fitted on the performer. If it passes, I will watch it in action to see if it works— looks perfect on the performer, enhances the performance, moves well, says what it's supposed to say about the character being portrayed, and blends well with the other designed elements. It must also create the effect the director/choreographer envisioned."

Stia watches all the rehearsals she can and constantly changes the costume to make it perfect. As she puts it: "The designer must make the costumes move for the choreographer and director. You are constantly improving the sculpture during the final few days." Changes and adjustments are made up to opening night.

The last thing a designer does is submit a final list of expenditures, and then it's time to look around for the next project. Stia tries to come around to a performance now and then to make sure that her designs haven't slowly changed. Actors have a tendency to wear what's comfortable rather than what's been designed for them, if they can get away with it.

For the most part, designers need enormous and varied skills: drawing and sewing, and the ability to balance a budget. Yet, when asked to give advice to young designers, Stia said: "Artistic talent is important but you must develop a certain kind of attitude to survive as a designer. You cannot melt every time you are criticized and you must realize a play is a collaboration. If you can only do your own thing, then perhaps you should work as an artist alone in a studio, and if you don't have the personality to stand up to directors and communicate with them, well then become a craftsman. God knows the shops need more good ones.

"Having talent, skills, and knowledge are simply prerequisites; being tenacious and making contacts will keep you working."

In aspiring toward a career as a designer, there are very definite actions you can take to improve your skills and make contacts.

"Do about three things at once! First of all, take as many drawing classes as possible. Second, try to find work in the field, not necessarily as a designer, but as an assistant to a designer or in a costume shop. Third, volunteer to work on showcases and Off Off Broadway productions. The contacts made from working for little or nothing will pay off in the long run!

"The transition from apprentice to designer is difficult to make and can take years. One short cut is to take a class at Lester Polakov's Studio and Forum of Stage Design [see Appendix B]. Lester's is a good place to be for more than one reason: the teachers are professional union designers and Lester is frequently asked to recommend young designers for Off Off Broadway and showcase productions. The ideal way, and the way I did it, is to work as an assistant to a designer. The day will eventually come (after long hours and proven trust) when your designer has one too many jobs to handle and will give you one to design on your own. That's how I got my first design job. Also, write to every designer you admire and try to work for them in any capacity they need; develop a reputation as a dependable and knowledgeable person who can be trusted. Often designers will hire a nonunion assistant (they credit them in the

Playbill as secretary or administrative assistant), but union assistants work more than nonunion assistants do.

"Entrance to United Scenic Artists, the designers' union, is difficult and requires taking an entrance examination which consists of an interview, a home project, and a practical exam. Few applicants pass the exam the first time, but taking it is an excellent way of finding out where your weak spots are. All applicants are interviewed and given a portfolio evaluation. The entrance committee will give you the opportunity to ask questions and will provide you with some good sound professional answers. Make the exam a learning experience each time you take it and your chances for admittance will improve.

"A word on money. Although union designers get paid handsomely for their work on Broadway, Broadway work is scarce. Some designers work in the dance and opera to supplement that income, others in TV and films, but it is almost impossible to support oneself solely by designing for theatre. An alternative is working in regional or university theatres. There you needn't worry about joining a union (although the union has created contracts and minimum scales and conditions for regional theatres to adhere to) and the work is steady and the pay regular. Many designers enjoy working as a resident designer for a regional theatre even if only for a short period of time, and they say it's the perfect training ground. You work with different guest designers, learn how to stay within a modest budget, and learn valuable designing skills when forced to execute your own designs."

Stia's work as a costume designer has taken her all over the world from North Carolina to Italy and back. Her first design job was with the McCarter Theatre but before she got it she took any odd job that would allow her to be near a theatre. She volunteered and worked as a scenery painter, costume technician, dresser, shopper, teacher, and assistant designer. Her advice to others who want to be designers:

"Let nothing interfere with getting the thing done, whether it's finding work, coming up with a workable design, or executing a particularly complicated one. Designing can be exhausting, emotionally as well as physically, and a strong will is needed if you intend to survive. So many people think that talent alone will get them through. It won't, and the sooner you come to terms with this fact, the more likely you are to succeed."

PART V

SUPPORTING

SERVICES

The Supporting Services People

Supporting services people help the managers, creators, and artisans get the job done. Some supporting services jobs are on the fringe of the entertainment industry, while others are very much at its core.

Supporting services people are the facilitators behind the scenes of theatre and film.

10 Supporting Services Job Descriptions*

Advertising.   In addition to work in the advertising department of a film studio (described in Part II under *Studio Executive*), work is available with advertising agencies that specialize in theatre and film advertising. Some of the large ad agencies have entertainment divisions (e.g., J. Walter Thompson's Entertainment Group) and some small agencies specialize in the field (e.g., Ash-Ledonne, Serino, Coyne, Nappi). There are also companies that specialize in making two-to-three-minute trailers for use in advertising campaigns. They employ a variety of behind-the-scenes personnel. Jobs in the advertising field include *account executive* (liaison between client and agency), *copywriter* (creator of ads and TV commercials), *art director* (graphic designer of ads and commercials), *producer* (supervisor of TV commercial production), *media director* (researches best publications and stations to place advertising), and *office workers* (secretaries, receptionists, etc.).

Agent.   In theatre and film, agents represent actors, writers, directors, producers, designers, composers, choreographers. They keep up with all contacts in order to obtain work for their clients, get to know the tastes of the studios and producers, and offer only those clients who might be "right" for a job. Once they get work for their clients, agents negotiate contracts, including wages, working conditions, deadlines, special benefits, concessions, and prestige. Agents are expert in the marketing and packaging of talents. The contemporary agent is an essential element in putting together or "packaging" a motion picture and/or theatrical production. Together with personal managers, agents have taken over the role of "talent guardian" once held by the major studios and powerful theatrical producers. Agents must be officially sanctioned by Actors' Equity and the other trade unions and guilds, and receive 10 percent of their client's income. For related jobs, see *Personal Manager*, and the profile of Geoffrey Sanford on page 173.

---

*A number of supporting services jobs are in areas outside the entertainment field, making it impossible to include them all here. In some cases, spheres of work rather than specific job titles have been identified.

Animal Specialist.   In film and theatre, an animal specialist is called in when a film or play requires the use of trained animals on camera or stage. The animal specialist works with the director and is responsible for handling and directing the animals safely and effectively. He is also responsible for making sure they are treated well and that no ASPCA rule is violated. He arranges for the loading and transporting of the animals, and their food and board while on location. If an animal's owner is on hand, then no specialist is employed. On films where livestock is needed (cows, horses, mules, goats, etc.), a *wrangler* is employed to select, rent or purchase, harness, transport, lead on to the set, help the actors handle and mount the animals. The wrangler is also responsible for the proper feeding and boarding of the livestock during shooting.

Art Therapist.   Theatre, dance, and music are sometimes used as therapeutic tools. The art therapist's job is to help patients overcome their disability, be it physical or mental; in other words, psychotherapy and physical therapy are provided through the arts. *Dance therapists*, sometimes referred to as physical therapists, are trained in universities, and work in hospitals, rehabilitation clinics, and centers. The American Dance Therapy Association coordinates and offers information in this field. Certification is available. Theatre specialists work for grass roots theatre companies specializing in "theatre as therapy," and for hospitals and clinics.

Arts Council Jobs.   Each state, as well as three hundred local communities, maintains an arts council that is responsible for fostering the arts and distributing state monies to not-for-profit arts institutions in the area. Jobs range from *council members* to *executive director, deputy directors, heads of divisions* (museum programs, children's programs, ethnic programs, etc.), *staff people, panel members, assistants, secretaries, clerks,* and *receptionists.* Staff heads and members review all incoming applications for monies and pass their recommendations on to panel members. Panel members are people with expertise in specific arts areas who have been officially appointed to their positions; they review staff members' recommendations and vote on applications that come their way (dance panels vote on dance company applications, theatre panels on theatre applications, and so on). Council members are appointed by the governor of the state and make final decisions based on the panels' recommendations. Arts council directors and deputies are people with a solid education and background in the performing arts who administer the council. Entry-level assistants and secretaries are promoted from within. For related jobs, see *Arts Service Organization Jobs*.

   Arts-in-Education.   Those involved in bridging the gap between the arts and education are referred to as arts-in-education specialists. There are a number of jobs in the field, ranging from *administrator* to *artist-in-residence*. An example of an administrative arts-in-education job is that of *director of education and outreach programs* for a not-for-profit resident theatre company. His task entails administering intern programs, in-school aesthetic education programs and artists-in-residence programs; arranging for seminars and student performances; fundraising; and anything else that brings children and students in the community in touch with theatre. Artists-in-residence jobs are available in all the disciplines (theatre, dance, music, film and video, writing) and on all levels of education from elementary school up to and including the university. Arts-in-education jobs are available with resident theatre companies funded for such work, film and theatre libraries, arts service organizations, arts-in-education organizations (e.g., Jazzmobile, Young Audiences). Universities and colleges offer majors and courses of study in arts-in-education.

   Arts Service Organization Jobs.   In each city there are a number of foundations, societies, commissions, festivals, cultural and government organizations, etc., dedicated to fostering the performing arts. Each offers unique possibilities for people trained in theatre and film. Some examples are: The American Film Institute (with offices in Washington, D.C., and Beverly Hills), the Film Society of Lincoln Center, the American Theatre Wing (always asking for volunteers), New York Foundation for the Arts, Theatre Development Fund, Off Off Broadway Theatre Alliance, and the National Endowment for the Arts. The list is endless and each provides a possible place of employment. For related jobs, see *Arts Council Jobs* and *Film Commission Jobs*.

   Camera Supply House Employee.   Most camera equipment used on feature and other films is rented from camera supply houses. Working for such a house is the traditional entry-level job for those interested in learning about the technical side of filmmaking, particularly would-be cinematographers. *Camera supply house repairmen* get on-the-job training by breaking down and repairing every kind of camera available. *Camera supply house salespeople* are in constant contact with working cinematographers (DP's and camera operators) and learn which camera and equipment are used for specific situations. In addition to the practical aspects of the work, the contacts and talk of who's doing what next can be invaluable for someone looking for film production work. Names of specific camera supply houses can be found in the technical journals and magazines (e.g., *Millimeter*) where they advertise.

Concessionaire.   This theatre job is found in both commercial and noncommercial houses. The people who sell foodstuff and gifts work for the theatre owners, and are responsible for setting up and selling the foodstuff, drinks, programs, and souvenirs to patrons before a play begins and during intermissions. Because of the hours and opportunity to see plays free, this is a popular entry-level job with students.

Corporate Contributor.   A number of the Fortune 500 corporations such as Mobil, Exxon, and Chemical Bank contribute monies to the performing arts and employ a staff of "arts experts" to recommend which not-for-profit companies to sponsor. Experts are given such titles as *special projects coordinator, cultural and community affairs director, corporate public relations director,* and so on. It is their responsibility to choose performing arts institutions and events of a high standard that will provide the corporation with a positive image for sponsoring them and will generate positive publicity. To this end, the arts expert views the work of many not-for-profit companies, meets with performing arts managers, makes judgments and recommendations on the work of the companies, supervises advertising and promotion (ads, posters, press kits) on projects he chooses to finance, and sometimes attends those events he has sponsored.

Critic.   Film and theatre critics review plays and movies for the general public (i.e., newspaper and magazine readers and TV and radio audiences). It's their job to communicate to their audience what the play or movie is about and what their judgment on it is, good or bad. They make suggestions as to which events are worthwhile and which should be avoided. Critics build up their audience and reputation by years of weekly or monthly reviewing, and the trustworthy ones are regarded by their audiences as an accurate "creative filter." Generally speaking, critics choose what they review and submit their work to an editor. There is also the job of *film reviewer* for trade publications, someone who reviews films for exhibitors and other professionals. For additional information, see the profile of David Denby on page 177.

Dance Notator.   Dance notators record dance scores through a language of symbols, staves, lines, dots, and crosses known as Labanotation. It's the job of the notator to communicate the dance on paper simply, accurately and quickly. Whoever reads the notation, be it teacher, dancer, or choreographer, learns from the score what the original choreographer's intent was. Dance notators are trained specialists (the Dance Notation Bureau in New York is the center for study of Labanotation in the United States, and over ninety universities throughout the country also teach it); a strong technical background in dance and an understanding of performance styles are prerequisites for training. Recently an IBM Labanotation typewriter has been put on the market for the use of dance notators. Apprenticeships to a certified notator are available through the Dance Notation Bureau in New York.

Educational Filmmaking. *Independent educational filmmakers* make films and filmstrips for schools, foundations, educational publishing companies, educational foundations, and large corporations for the purpose of teaching something to someone. The independent educational filmmaker initiates ideas (a teaching background and a knowledge of curriculum help), writes the script, fundraises, and supervises the production crew for his films. In addition to *crew members, teachers* are sometimes employed as consultants on educational film projects. A number of large corporations and publishing firms employ an *on-staff educational film expert* to run their educational divisions.

Entertainment Reporter. These journalists (not to be confused with critics or gossip columnists) report on the goings on in the entertainment industry. Jobs are available on newspapers and magazines for their entertainment pages, trade papers (e.g., *Variety*), and trade journals (e.g., *Theatre Crafts*). Entertainment reporters write on the current state of film and theatre, as well as such related topics as who is doing what role next, technical innovations, how much money a film or play grossed, and so on. They initiate ideas and are given assignments by their editors, depending on their status with their publication. They maintain and nurture all contacts within the industry to "stay on top of things."

Equipment Sales and Design. There are firms that design and manufacture technical products and systems for theatre and film. A *sales job* in such a firm can be a good experience for someone pursuing a lighting or sound job in theatre or film, or it can be a good career in itself. *Lighting and sound equipment designers* need a thorough knowledge of theatre and film equipment and an innovative approach to designing. The names of equipment sales and design firms can be found by reading the trade journals (*Millimeter, Theatre Crafts*) where they advertise.

Film Archivist.   Film archivists work for libraries, archives, foundations—anywhere there are funds for and an interest in preserving old films. They search out, collect, preserve, and catalogue films that would otherwise deteriorate.

Film Commission Jobs.   Forty-four states and seventeen cities have film offices (as do several U.S. and Canadian territories) to lure filmmakers to their area. They provide practical services—location scouting and survey work; coordination of in-state transportation for visiting production personnel prior to shooting; liaison between production companies and local businesses, government agencies, and labor unions; and coordination and assistance with press coverage and communications—to producers, production managers, and others whose business is filmmaking. Jobs range from *director* to *locators* to *permit "fetchers"* to *office staff workers*, and vary from office to office depending on allocated funds and the size of the office.

Film Technician.   Film technicians are employed in laboratories where film is transformed into prints. All employees except the administrative staff (i.e., corporate executives and salespeople) are unionized (IATSE Local 702 in New York and 683 in Los Angeles). Film technicians are required to understand and operate sophisticated machines. Some jobs are: *developers, raw stock clerks, splicers, color timers* (evaluate each scene for color and density), *printers, finishers* (mount the reel to the client's specification), *projectionists, can carriers, cleaners, mechanics,* and *shippers.* Since all film technicians are unionized and highly specialized, it is rare that one moves to another part of filmmaking; however, *salespeople* (i.e., those who deal with film production people) do have such opportunities.

Food Caterer.   Films on distant and local location use firms specializing in motion picture catering to feed their cast and crew. It's the *motion picture food caterer's* job to work with a production manager, location manager, or food coordinator in setting up a food service for the company that will satisfy cast and crew and still keep within the "cost per head" allotted in the budget. It's the job of the *person in charge of location service* at the caterers to arrange for equipment (trucks, steam tables, duckboards, etc.), serving arrangements, and food to be sent to the location and served as quickly as possible. For a related job, see *Food Coordinator.*

Food Coordinator.   A food coordinator is employed on films with plans to shoot on distant and local location. He is part of the production crew, and is responsible for planning, preparing and/or catering breakfast, lunch, dinner, and snacks for cast and crew. He plans out the meals, based on the food budget, the cast and crew diet requirements (vegetarian, low calorie, etc.), available facilities, and catering services. On low budget films, he sets up meals (arriving on the location set before the crew, sometimes as early as 5:00 A.M.), purchases beverages and snacks, coordinates local catering services, prepares some meals, and in general makes sure everyone is well fed. This above-entry-level job is a good way to get onto a set.

Food Stylist (a.k.a. Home Economist). Food stylists work in film, TV, and advertising, being responsible for making the food used on camera look the way the script calls for it to look. They research, plan, and prepare food so that it is authentic and will photograph effectively. They may be asked to produce anything from a beautiful Thanksgiving turkey to a medieval feast to a Vietnamese mess kit. Food stylists work independently, and are called on to solve all "food problems" such as keeping butter from dissolving under the hot lights, pleasing the star's palate (for on camera meals only), or cooking in portable ovens and makeshift location kitchens. Most universities offer a course of study in home economics.

Industrial Filmmaking (Business Filmmaking). Industrial filmmakers create business films. A number of industrial filmmakers function as one-man production companies in that they go after new business, write proposals, prepare budgets, write business film scripts, produce, and sometimes direct the films for their clients. The large industrial filmmaking companies employ *salesmen, producers, writers, directors, et al.* with expertise in elements of industrial filmmaking. Production crews are smaller than but similar in make-up to crews on theatrical films. There are also *industrial film distributors,* responsible for identifying and reaching target audiences.

Marketing Research. As the entertainment industry becomes more and more of a business, additional business practices are being used to assure large profits. Marketing research is such a practice and there are now marketing research firms that specialize in servicing the entertainment industry. Clients include studio marketing personnel, production company executives, entertainment advertising specialists, and anyone else interested in the public's reaction to their product. Entertainment marketing research consists of random phone interviews, ad testing, focus groups, audience testing, and other standard research techniques. Results influence production activities (Francis Ford Coppola tested audience reactions to various endings of *Apocalypse Now*), script selection (a film company commissions a survey to find out which genres are most interesting to the corps of the movie-going public), advertising decisions (an agency surveys whether critics' quotes enhance an ad campaign), and general knowledge (a major studio wants to find out the average age of the movie-going public). Marketing research jobs include *analysts, statisticians, field operators, supervisors, interviewers,* and *studio research personnel.* Generally, phone interviewing jobs are part time and easily available. Marketing research techniques can be learned in most university business departments. For a related job, see Part II, *Studio Executive—Marketing.*

Merchandising Executive.   Merchandising executives work for film companies (Columbia, Fox, Universal, Paramount, United Artists, and Disney all have merchandising departments) and for independent licensing consultant firms. It's their job to lease the names and likenesses of characters, personalities, logos, and themes identified with their company's (or client's) movies, plays, and TV shows to manufacturers. Studio merchandising executives determine which of the company's properties (films, TV shows, plays) to merchandise and what about the property is licensable. Once the characters, themes, or logos are identified, a marketing plan is created, brochures produced, and ads taken out in licensing newsletters and trade papers. The merchandising team then sells the concept to various manufacturers (e.g., the Superman doll to a toy company, Hulk toilet paper!). One way to learn entertainment merchandising is to work for a toy manufacturer as their *director of licensing,* whose job it is to negotiate fees and contracts with merchandising executives.

Optical Designer.   Optical designers design and execute the creation of movie titles, credits, and optical effects. There are firms that specialize in this field (such as R. Greenberg & Associates, creator of the *Superman, Hair,* and *Alien* logos). For related jobs, see *Animator* in Part IV.

Personal Manager.   Personal managers manage performers' careers and act as a buffer between their clients and the world. Managers are less concerned with finding specific jobs for their clients than with helping them to advance their careers, although managers do contact agents in behalf of their clients for that purpose. Managers involve themselves in all aspects of their clients' lives—money, career strategy, image building, finding suitable properties; some even take phone messages, keep financial accounts, and accompany clients on interviews, auditions, and shopping trips. Because they spend so much time on each client, they have far fewer of them than agents do and charge more for their services (15 percent of the client's income as compared to the agent's 10 percent). It's the personal manager's job to give his or her client good, sound advice in all areas, ranging from whether to take a role in a film or play to what color they should dye their hair. Personal managers need not be sanctioned by unions.

Publicity Jobs. Public relations is the art of communicating a message from a client to the public through the communications media. Films, plays, stars, studios, production companies, and theatres all employ a public relations person (either free-lance or on-staff) to represent them. In film, PR jobs can be found on-staff with movie studios and free-lance on films in production (known as the film's *publicist*). In institutional theatre, a *director of publicity* and his staff handle the PR on a daily basis, and in commercial theatre an independent *press agent* is hired, for a fee, to handle the production. Successful press agents maintain offices where they are capable of servicing a great many clients simultaneously. Whatever the title, public relations people are responsible for favorably publicizing their client's name, product, and staff in all media, for disseminating information to outside sources, and for initiating and executing special promotional ideas. They write and distribute biographies, press releases, feature stories, and blurbs, make arrangements for interviews and press conferences, maintain news clippings and files. Along with a *picture editor* (not to be confused with a film editor), they arrange for photo calls and photography of special events, supervise the still photographer, make sure the still photographer's film is properly developed, and determine which are the best stills from a promotional standpoint. They also maintain photographic files, order prints as needed, and disburse photos (to producers, ad agency, media, etc.) for special promotions. The theatrical union, ATPAM (see Appendix B), offers an apprenticeship. For related jobs, see *Studio Executive—Advertising, publicity, and exploitation,* in Part II.

Shop Jobs. Most theatre and film sets and costumes are built in shops (Eaves-Brooks Costume Co., Atlas Scenic Studios), where costume technicians, model builders, carpenters, and so on are employed. Additional shop jobs are those of *project manager,* the liaison between the designer and the shop; *costumer (a.k.a. "rag-*

picker"), the rental coordinator; *dry cleaner,* the person responsible for the in-service cleaning service; and *hairdresser,* the person who prepares wigs. Both costume and carpentry shops maintain an *administrative staff* to run the office.

Stunt Coordinator. On films requiring a large number of stunts, a stunt coordinator is employed to hire stunt men and women, coordinate their activities (days they are required on the set, stunts they are required to perform, costume and wig fittings, make-up, etc.), and supervise the logistics of the stunts.

Teachers. Teachers teach theatre and film in elementary schools, junior and senior high schools, colleges, graduate, and trade schools (acting, film, and theatre schools not affiliated with a university). They teach acting, directing, playwrighting, film production, crafts, criticism, theatre games, and a number of other subjects. In most cases, theatre and film teachers are required to have a master's degree or its equivalent and/or a good deal of experience in their discipline. There is also the job of teacher to child actors. These teachers (more common and unionized in Los Angeles—IATSE Local 884) teach required subjects to child actors, on the set, during production time.

Theatre Architect and Consultant. There are architects and consultants who specialize in performing arts facilities design as well as those who do such work as an adjunct to their existing architectural practice. The *theatre architect's* responsibility is to execute the intent of his client, the theatre owner, and to supervise engineers, consultants, and contractors for that purpose. *Consultants* (sometimes college teachers and lighting and sound designers "moonlight" as consultants) design room acoustics, electro-acoustics (i.e., speech reinforcement, sound effects, recording facilities), space planning, seating, and sightlines. They specify lighting equipment, stage machinery, shop equipment, orchestra shells, and so on. They prepare drawings and specifications for construction, supervise construction, and evaluate bids. Architects must be licensed, but consultants don't have to be.

Theatre Manager. In theatre and film, the person responsible for the house (theatre building) is the theatre manager. He hires, fires, and supervises the house staff (house manager, ushers, box-office personnel, concessionaires, porters), he sees that the lighting, heating, air conditioning, and alarms are working properly, and communicates with the theatre owners on all house matters. He meets and greets VIPs and shows the house to prospective customers (i.e., producers interested in renting it). But his main concern is the comfort, safety, and well-being of the people who enter his theatre.

Theatre Owner. Theatre owners own and operate theatres. There are independently owned theatres and those owned and operated by large chains (e.g., the Shubert Organization). In addition to the house personnel, the large theatre owners employ an administrative staff (general manager, treasurer, etc.) and a *director of operations* to handle the daily maintenance and operations of their theatres. Any producing done by the theatre owners (theatre owners will co-finance and/or co-produce a play they want to bring to their theatre) is generally handled by the owners themselves and/or the top executives of the company.

Film theatre owners (a.k.a. exhibitors) also employ house staffs for each of their theatres and a staff of *administrators, buyers*, and *theatre operations managers*. Of the 30,000 cinemas around the country, most of the first-run houses are owned and operated by chains, while the neighborhood theatres are still independently owned and operated. The *film buyer* is responsible for choosing the films for his theatre; this is accomplished by viewing every film offered by distributors.° The buyer is also responsible for making the financial arrangements for leasing the film (initial fee, percentage of box-office take, who pays for advertising, etc.). There are firms that specialize in booking films into theatres on a fee basis, and theatre owners on occasion will hire these outside *bookers*. The *theatre operations manager* supervises the individual theatre managers, deals with the various unions (e.g., projectionists, ushers), and oversees the maintenance of the movies (repairs, construction, etc.).

Theatrical Attorney. Theatrical attorneys are lawyers whose clients are in the entertainment industry. They perform the same services for their entertainment clients as other lawyers perform for their "civilian" clients (prepare wills, form corporations, sell real estate, etc.). In addition, they handle and are expert in all contracts and negotiations pertaining to their clients' services as actors, directors, producers, writers, and so on. Theatrical attorneys may be asked to obtain the rights to a literary property for a producer, draft a contract for an actor, or negotiate a screenwriter's deal with a studio's business affairs person. Some theatrical attorneys function more or less as their client's personal manager, offering advice on

°Except in those states where blind bidding—the practice whereby a distributor offers a film and financial deal to the exhibitor without screening the film for him— is allowed by law.

career moves; there are legal firms specializing in this kind of repre-
sentation. Lawyers interested in working with not-for-profit arts
groups may do so by volunteering their services through Volunteer
Lawyers for the Arts in New York City.

Translator.   This film job is to translate foreign-language dialogue into English so that subtitles can be prepared. The work is
generally done on a free-lance basis for distributors of foreign films
and requires absolute proficiency in both languages.

Transportation.   Often, a film production crew will include a
driver to transport cast, crew, sets, and equipment, and generally
help expedite the production. He maintains the vehicle in constant
readiness and operates it when called on to do so by the production
manager, producer, or other category head. He may be called on to
load and unload equipment, props, etc., take cast members to and
from location, operate loading lifts or winches attached to his vehicle. The job of driver is a good entry-level position on low budget
films, and is not to be confused with the *teamsters*, who are employed on union film crews for transportation purposes.

Union Employee.   The theatre and film trade unions and guilds
(IATSE, NABET, SAG, etc.) employ people to carry on union business and maintain internal operations. Many of the union employees
come from within the ranks of the union; still, there are employees
who have been educated in union relations and find jobs with the
entertainment unions. Generally, unions employ *business agents* to
negotiate contracts with management and handle member complaints; a *membership education person* to educate members as to
their rights and benefits; and an *office staff*. The rich unions, with
membership improvement and benefit programs and internships,
employ people to run those programs.

Usher.   Theatre ushers in commercial theatre are union members who are responsible for showing patrons to their seats, providing them with a *Playbill*, and calling the house manager's attention
to any problem. They are required to wear an usher's collar (they
receive $1 a week to maintain it) and carry a flashlight. The *head
usher* supervises the others, provides *Playbills* for each aisle, and
communicates with the house manager. Noncommercial theatres often ask for volunteers to usher and in lieu of a salary allow them to
view performances.

Starting something new.   If you have a particular talent, skill,
or service that hasn't yet been thought of, offer it. There are shops
that specialize in selling theatre and film books, T-shirts, memorabil-

ia, posters, and actors' used clothing. There is a theatre party agency that selects plays for organizations to take their theatre parties to. There are artists who do theatre portraits. Believe it or not, there is even an insurance company that specializes in writing insurance coverage for the entertainment industry. Someone had to think of the idea and be the first to start it. So if your talent or service doesn't fit any of the jobs described in this book and you think the entertainment industry can use it, offer what you've got.

11 Supporting Services Profiles

Geoffrey Sanford, Hollywood Literary Agent

Literary agents represent writers and directors. Their job is to sell talent and stories and get their clients work.

"There are different kinds of literary agents. Some just take a script and sell it; others talk over potential deals, talk over concepts, and try to offer some help, both creative and practical."

Geoffrey Sanford is the latter kind. He represents writers such as Deric Washburn (*The Deer Hunter*), Chris DeVore and Eric Bergren (*The Elephant Man*), and Robert Moore (*The Cheap Detective*). His four partners represent actors, including Jack Nicholson, Hal Holbrook, Judd Hirsch, and Diahann Carroll. Together, the five partners form The Artists Agency, located in Beverly Hills.

Although Geoffrey grew up "in the business," it was a long time before he knew what it meant to be an agent. "Nobody seems to know what an agent does. My father was an agent, yet I had no idea what he did until I was twenty-five years old. I was in L.A. on my first day as an agent and I said to myself, 'Ah ha, so that's what my father's been doing all these years.' I have two partners who also grew up in the business but living in California they had a slightly different experience. I grew up in a suburb of New York and my father's friends weren't in the business. In a sense I had an advantage in not knowing that much about it in my early years."

Geoffrey wasn't interested in show business as a child, nor was he particularly interested in it as a career when he grew up.

"I was at Columbia University preparing for a career as a philosophy teacher and having a bad time of it because it was the heyday of something called 'logical positivism,' which was reducing philosophy to a branch of symbolic logic. I had come to study Jean-Paul

Madeline Porter

GEOFFREY SANFORD

Sartre and Camus. Somehow I got to be a senior, but the prospects in philosophy looked bleak. Then my wife got pregnant and I needed a job. I went to my father for advice. He told me there was a job where people would pay you to stay at home and read books and do a synopsis on them. I thought that was fabulous. I got a job at Columbia Pictures as a free-lance reader. I sat home and read for two years. Otto Preminger's office was down the hall from Columbia's story department and one day when I was around I heard he was looking for a story editor. I told them I was available and I got the job. I was to solicit books as well as read them, which meant talking to agents and publishers and trying to find out what new books would make a good film property. I started doing that when I was twenty-three, which is awfully young. I was fortunate to get that job."

As is so often the case with talented and conscientious story editors working for production and/or film companies, Geoffrey was given the chance to get involved with actual production activities.

"We were producing a film called *Hurry Sundown*, which was shot on location in Baton Rouge. I went along with the company and Preminger. Working on location is the most wonderful, magical experience because you become a family, and you're actually doing something constructive, which is not as frustrating as so many other aspects of the film business are. I fell in love with it. It didn't matter to me if it was a good picture or a bad picture as long as we were having fun. When we came back, I was thoroughly hooked on the film business. I wanted to be a film producer. In those days—and it is still true today—the way to become a producer was to go to Hollywood and be an agent."

Geoffrey set out to find a way to get himself to Hollywood and a job as an agent. He knew that Zeigler and Ross was considered to be the best literary agency, and that Zeigler often came to New York to meet with Harold Matson, one of his co-agents. Geoffrey made it his business to meet Zeigler, and when he did, offered his services as a free-lance reader. Zeigler accepted and Geoffrey had an "in." As it happened, Zeigler was looking for an agent for his West Coast office.

"This is a business of interrelationships and contacts. Zeigler offered the job to a woman I had worked with when I was at Columbia. She wasn't interested so she recommended me. Zeigler knew my work and offered me the job."

In 1967 Geoffrey packed up wife and child and went west.

"The first week I was in town, Bill Goldman turned in *Butch Cassidy and the Sundance Kid*. I was sitting by the pool of the Sunset Marquis, the famous motel on Sunset Boulevard, where everyone stays the first time they come to Hollywood, reading this script and thinking, 'This is terrific, a dynamite script.' I didn't know that a script like that comes along every ten years. The deal got put together remarkably fast, in a matter of weeks. I didn't do it, Zeigler did, but it was my first exposure and a terribly valuable experience for me. I had been with Zeigler for two years when I was offered a job as the head of the literary department of CMA [now ICM]. I hired agents, was responsible for all the screenwriters, packaged screenplays with other CMA clients, and sought out properties for their big name actors like Streisand and Paul Newman. I ran the department for a year."

Geoffrey had come to Hollywood to become a producer, so he jumped at the opportunity to work for Warner Brothers studio as a production executive when the job was offered to him.

"I was hired because I had been an agent and had the contacts. My job at Warners was to find projects and bring them to the studio. I knew other agents, writers, and stars and they felt I could attract them to the studio."

Instead of continuing to find screenplays to bring to the studio, Geoffrey eventually left Warner's to write one of his own. During this period of his life he realized that of all the careers he had had or aspired to—philosophy teacher, reader, production executive, screenwriter, and agent—agenting made the most sense for him.

"One day it dawned on me that all the experiences I had had in my life added up to my being a really good agent. So I came back to it, first a job, then a partnership at The Artists Agency."

The way films are put together today in Hollywood has made the agent an indispensible element in the process. He can put together the nucleus of a project, that is, package it before it ever gets to a studio.

"We have input during the writing of a screenplay and once it's finished we have some influence as to who directs it and stars in it. The way that happens is by choosing who to show it to. For instance in the case of *Butch Cassidy*, Zeigler had a lot to say about the people to whom it got shown. If you want so and so to direct, you only show it to so and so. People are always asking agents this or that; agents are clearinghouses for information—who's available, who's looking for a certain kind of picture. We're always trading information, like maybe Al Pacino wants to do a comedy or George Roy Hill is looking for a cowboy movie. If you're a good agent you know each studio's personality; there's a certain kind of film you think is Universal or Fox or ah ha—this one's for Filmways.

"Obviously, we have a lot to say about the deal, how much ought to be asked for the script. However, if the buyers know who's to direct and star, I have little else to do with it except if they want my client to make changes. But if it's just bought and all they have is the screenplay, you still have a responsibility to the script."

On being an agent, Geoffrey remarks:

"I can be happy being an agent for the rest of my life. Had I not done other things I couldn't say that. It's endlessly fascinating to see human character up close. Just to see how people act. All agents have wonderful stories to tell because, like doctors, they see people exposed at their most vulnerable moments. It's also interesting to see the ups and downs. It's like a Victorian novel to see what made somebody successful and why. To be a good agent you should have that sort of interest in people and their lives. Besides that, you should have the ability to deal with people and to make rapid, pretty accurate judgments of their capabilities and their character. I've known I wanted to be somebody's agent by talking to them for two minutes without seeing or reading anything they've done, although I would only sign someone whose work I've read and am passionate about.

"Other than knowing somebody's uncle or brother as the best way to get a job, the quality that will help the most is perseverance. Large agencies train people to be agents. They start them in the mailroom or have them answer phones, then make them somebody's secretary. Another way to do it is to start at a small agency as an assistant. Perseverance will be needed either way. Like the world at large, the industry rewards energy, and you just have to put a lot out before you can get something in."

David Denby, Film Critic on *New York* Magazine

It's a film critic's job to introduce a movie to its audience. A film critic views movies, describes them, and shares his critical judgments. Critics try to convey the essence of a film, to point out the things that work and the things that don't.

David Denby, film critic for *New York* Magazine, thinks of him-

© Jody Caravaglia

DAVID DENBY

self as "an articulate member of the audience. It is not my job to be an insider, to know things like whether it rained on the day they were to shoot the big scene, because the only thing that matters to someone who is going to see the movie is what is on the screen. The critic is the first audience member to see the film. Presumably he has a little sharper taste and a commitment to film history. He uses his influence and writing abilities to steer people toward the good movies and away from the bad ones and to make what the movie is doing a little clearer. It is also the critic's job to draw attention to anyone or anything that is good in a movie, particularly *young* craft contributors and performers.

"An important thing a critic does is to be part of the talk about movies, to feed into the sociability, which is an important aspect of movie-going. People come back from a movie and talk it over and get into fights and lovers' quarrels, and the critic is sort of a guest in these quarrels and loving discussions between friends. That's half the fun of it.

"The ideal review is written for those who have seen the movie as well as for those who have not. [Walter Kerr defined a reviewer as someone who writes for those who have not yet seen the movie and a critic as someone who writes for those who have.] You include a certain amount of exposition: who is in it, what is it about, what does it look like, what does it feel like, and is it any good? That's all for the people who haven't seen it. You can also do a certain amount of analysis: what is the director trying to do, is it successful, what does the style say, how does it relate to older movies? That's for people who have seen the film. In other words, you can do both and meld them together, but it takes a lot of skill."

A lot of skill is something David Denby has. For over two years, *New York* Magazine's film-wise readership has come to depend on David's discriminating judgments. An English major at Columbia University in the mid-1960s, David was interested in journalism, and wrote book and concert reviews for *The Columbia Spectator*, the college paper. In his senior year he reviewed critic Pauline Kael's book *I Lost It at the Movies*.

"I was very startled by that book. It was a great event in my life and in the lives of many other young people who wanted to write criticism. It suddenly seemed that film criticism was something very exciting to do and tremendous fun. I went on to journalism school [at Columbia] and took Judith Crist's course in film criticism (which she is still teaching, by the way). We went to screenings and wrote reviews every week. I got hooked. After I got my M.S. from Columbia, I went on to film school at Stanford and made films and studied film history. I became a teaching assistant in a film criticism and a film aesthetics course and then began teaching them myself. In 1969 I took the summer off and started writing reviews for *Film Quarterly*, published in Berkeley. I started writing for the same reason that anyone starts anything. I thought I could do it better than most people who were doing it professionally. I began to think of myself as more of a writer than a filmmaker."

Once David thought of himself as a writer he set out to make himself into a working one. He knew there was no movie critic on *The Atlantic Monthly* and believed he could fill the bill. Armed with his reviews and a recommendation from Pauline Kael (he had introduced himself to her and shown her his work when she came to California to lecture), he approached an editor who was living near the Stanford campus. The editor read his work and David lucked out.

"It was sort of a fluke, landing on a national magazine for my first job. I was twenty-six and had been hanging around the university, frankly marking time [to stave off getting drafted into the Vietnam War]. All told, I wrote about twenty-five pieces for them. I found it hard writing for a monthly magazine because of the lead time of monthlies. The reviews come out later than the weeklies' and those of the news magazines. Because the editors at *Atlantic* didn't want to repeat other magazines' coverage they asked me to write trend pieces, to take three or four movies and make some essay out of them. There are really only five or six legitimate trends a year but you can take almost any three movies and put them together and deduce some trend; but it's a journalistic trick to do so. For that reason I was always uncomfortable at *Atlantic Monthly*. They fired me and I think I was relieved because the column never really worked."

For the next three years David "floated around" and free-lanced. He did some pieces for the *New York Times Magazine* and *Harper's* magazine, writing them either on spec and sending them in or first submitting a letter of inquiry, taught some at his alma mater, Stanford, traveled around the world lecturing on film for the USIS (United States Information Service, a propaganda and cultural service), and edited a number of anthologies for the National Society of Film Critics.

"It was a very bad time for me. Being a free-lance critic is a contradiction in terms because a critic has to be in regular contact with his audience or else he hardly exists. I tried to get full-time jobs but I was not successful."

In September of 1976 David received a phone call from an editor on a weekly paper, the Boston *Phoenix*, asking if he was interested in applying for the job of first-string film critic. (A first-string critic gets first choice regarding which films to cover, a second-string critic gets second choice, etc.) David went up to Boston and got the job.

"It was a great job. There was plenty of space for movie criticism and a strong tradition for it because the paper had a very 'hip' student audience who wanted to read it. So, the *Phoenix* was a place to write at considerable length and with great freedom and a place where there were high standards and low pressure and where people loved criticism and cared about movies."

David stayed at the *Phoenix* until he was offered the job at *New York* magazine with an opportunity to write for a much bigger audience and a chance to make some good money.

As a critic on a weekly magazine, his schedule is much less arduous than that of a daily critic who has to see everything that opens. He gets to choose which films he will review and writes one piece a week and the listings for the magazine. He generally sees two or three films each week and doesn't have a formula for how he chooses which ones he will review. But he is very selective.

"There are certain films that I obviously must review—the big important movie made by a major director, one that is obviously going to be a box-office hit or it has big stars in it, and so on. With the others, I go back and forth between two criteria: one, what I am interested in writing about and think the reader should know more about; and two, what I think the reader probably *wants* to know about.

"I prefer to see a movie in a theatre with a regular audience. Though, in fact, most of the time I see films in screening rooms with other critics. I take notes in a stenographer's notebook with a regular ballpoint pen. Those things with a light just annoy the hell out of everybody. I take down bits of dialogue and things that will evoke the film for me a day or two later. I don't write out whole sentences, just key words. Then I let the movie percolate for a couple of days. Sometimes when I first step out of a theatre I have a kind of mixed, unfocused feeling even though I've had a lot of emotional impressions watching the film. After a day or two things settle and I'm pretty sure of exactly what I think. Then I read my notes and try to recreate in my mind what it was on the screen that produced those feelings I was having while watching the movie. Any review that doesn't have some current of feeling in it of pleasure, arousal, anger, or boredom is going to be dry, academic and dull. If I don't have those feelings, I go back and see the movie again.

"If I have a long piece to organize, I make a new set of notes with specific headings (e.g., direction) and transfer my old set onto the new. Then I make a solid old high school outline. If I start writing in the heat of inspiration, I go well for two or three paragraphs but then the piece runs into the sands. I find it best to know where I'm going and where I'm going to end up. After the outline, I write a couple of drafts. I try to write a little essay about the movie, to organize it around what is most interesting about the film and to fit into that framework the different contributions. Otherwise it reads like a laundry list. I bring the piece in on Mondays at about noon. Then I go through edit. I have an excellent editor, Rhoda Koenig. She doesn't just cross out sentences she doesn't like, she tries to bring out what I'm attempting to say and make it more forceful. Then it's read again by a second editor. It's set in type Monday night. Tuesdays I have the luxury of doing a fair amount of fiddling with it in galleys, which really helps the piece tremendously. It goes out once more and is set again, and on the second proof I can do some fine tuning. That is usually finished by Tuesday, so I go to a movie at night or in the afternoon."

For those interested in acquiring the knowledge necessary to be a movie critic, David suggests the following:

"The single most important thing is a good liberal arts background. Movies incorporate so many other art forms. It is a synthesizing medium in that it brings together photography, painting, theatre, journalism, literature, dance, and mime in film's silent form. In structure, movies are close to fiction. So a basic education in all the arts is important. Then you have to see as many movies from the past as you can, the bad as well as the great, so you get to know the styles and genres of different periods. There are revival houses for this sort of thing and film courses at universities. All the major film programs have courses in criticism and film aesthetics. It's important for a student of criticism to be in a city where there are lots of revivals. You should read the classic writers of film aesthetics like Eisenstein and Pudovkin and read the best critics from the past as well as the present."

His advice to would-be film critics:

"The only way to write film criticism is to do it. You don't need a large institutional setting to practice your art. The way to become a film critic finally, after you've done all your studying, is to assert that you *are* one. Get something in print. When you have clippings, send them to editors and other critics who can help you. Critics will be delighted to help you if you're good, and if you're not, they'll probably tell you so.

"It's very hard to get one of the top fifteen or so good jobs around the country; they are jealously guarded and people will kill for them. Try to get a job on one of the weekly alternative papers (e.g., the Boston *Phoenix*, the L.A. *Reader*, the Chicago *Reader*); there's one in almost every major city. You won't be paid well, but you'll get space and intelligent readership and you'll be able to knock the kinks out of your writing. Daily papers don't give you the space and you have to write all the time and cover a lot of bad movies, but that's a good way to learn how to write fast and under pressure and to be entertaining. While you're looking for a job, be willing to write free-lance and do all sorts of journalism. If you want to write long analytical reviews or career pieces about actors or directors, try film magazines like *Film Comment*. You write a letter to the editor, explaining who you are and what you want to do and why the magazine needs this particular piece. If you have clippings, send them. You will get a letter or a phone call back within a couple of weeks saying yes or no. If it's a no, and you still think it's a terrific idea for a piece, write it up and send it in, because editors sometimes change their minds.

"It's not an easy life if you have high standards. When practiced faithfully and with love, film criticism is a minor literary art form. Too many people seek out a job in criticism as a way of getting themselves known; they don't have deep feelings about movies. I wouldn't advise anyone to go into it unless they really love movies and love writing and are willing to live on very little money for a while. I was writing professionally for nine years before I made decent money.

"Of course, it takes a certain arrogance to think that you know what is wrong with something and that you have the right to say so to 500,000 or 5,000 people. But behind that 'arrogance' should be a belief in what you say. You must believe that what you say matters, that whether a movie is good or bad matters, that the reasons matter, that life-and-death issues and not some frivolous show business game are at stake here. Unless you have that feeling about movies then I would say, skip it."

PART VI

FINDING A JOB

The journey of a thousand miles begins with one step.
—LAO-TSE
Chinese Philosopher

12 The First Step

It's difficult to find a job in theatre and film, but not impossible. It takes long hours, hard work, and the stamina to keep at the task until it's done. It won't be accomplished in one fell swoop, but arduously, one step at a time. Often, the first step is the most difficult to take. What follows should be of some help.

TIMING

From Norman Samnick, vice president of industrial and labor relations at Warner Communications:

"Finding a job is based on three things: timing, timing, and timing. You may be great, but if there's no job, there's no job. And sometimes they're so desperate, they'll take anyone."

There's no question; timing is paramount to a successful job hunt. It's almost always a matter of the right person being there when the job opens up. The only way to get around this is to be at as many places as possible—in person, through letters and résumés, and through contacts you've asked to keep an eye out for you. Keep up with new events (companies forming, departments expanding, plays optioned), and get your name in. Play hunches, follow your instincts.

Norman Samnick again:

"I get thousands of résumés. Unless the applicant requests a specific job that we have, the résumé goes back with a perfunctory response, a sorry and thank you. Every now and then a résumé comes through that's interesting. Once I was looking for a lawyer for this department, but wasn't exactly sure what the qualifications should be. By chance, I picked up a résumé that had just come in and noticed that the woman had been a lawyer for the Writers Guild. I liked the idea that she had worked on the other side of the bargaining table. Had she had ten times the experience in labor in another capacity I would have dumped the résumé. I called her in for an interview and eventually hired her. It just happened that her résumé popped up at the time that I needed her. It was good timing."

From nothing comes nothing. From doing comes a sporting chance. Had the woman dwelt on the fact that the odds were stacked against her, she might never have mailed her résumé, the one that arrived at the "right" time.

THE APPROACH

Ira Eaker, publisher of *Back Stage:*
"The only way to succeed in this business is to want to more than anything else. It has to be the most important thing in your life."

Looking for a job is a job in itself. You will have to spend precious time and money, do research, cultivate contacts, scrutinize your skills and talents, and deal with disappointments and dashed hopes. In other words, it's not something you can do in a hit-or-miss fashion. Finding a job requires a professional attitude.

Individuals must determine for themselves what route to take, depending on where they've been and where they want to go. Sometimes getting a job takes additional education, sometimes an internship or apprenticeship can build the bridge to the future, and sometimes detective work and legwork is what's called for. Whatever, the experts agree that the first step toward finding a job is deciding what it is you want to do, what skills and talents you possess, and what working environment is most suitable for you. This requires extensive self-examination and research. More on those . . .

SELF-EXAMINATION

Edward Lachman, cinematographer:
"You must be self-directed and know yourself well to survive in this business. Filmmaking is a lifestyle. You have to be completely dedicated to it. There isn't a day that goes by that I'm not involved in something that relates to film. I'm always asking questions. You should never fear seeking people out for advice on technical matters. There are no tricks, only knowledge."

The first question you need to ask yourself is: Do I really want to work in theatre or film, or is it only the glamour I'm attracted to? If it's the latter, you're bound for disillusionment. Eventually the glamour wears off and what you're left with is the work—you'd better like it. Ask yourself if you're willing to put up with the self-sacrifice, egomaniacal co-workers, and, in the beginning at least, the financial insecurity that goes with a career in theatre or film. Be honest with yourself early on. The job-hunting experience will weed out those of you who are serious from those of you who are not, for it will undoubtedly be a frustrating, emotionally draining, lonely, and depressing time, but why put yourself through it for a capricious dream?

If you are certain you want to make a career of it, next ask yourself what skills and talents you can offer and which you want to cultivate. Determine what levels of responsibility you are capable of handling. Set up goals for yourself, immediate and future. Decide what philosophical and geographical environment you'd be most happy and therefore most successful in. Review the jobs mentioned in this book and those you uncover on your own, and take note of the ones that interest you most. Determine which of these you are capable of doing now and which you will need additional training and experience for. It helps to write these things down and examine them. There are several books on the market that can aid you in a self-examination. Richard Nelson Bolles's *What Color Is Your Parachute?* and *Where Do I Go from Here with My Life?* (written with John Crystal) are considered to be among the best. But all that is really necessary is to focus on what it is you want to do. It's a matter of taking a formalized personal inventory. This will pay off in the long run, for no one is more likely to fail than the aimless job hunters and no one is more likely to succeed than the ones who know what they want.

RESEARCH

Joe Farrell, entertainment marketing researcher consultant:

"When I came out here [Hollywood], I literally read every issue of *Variety* from 1955 on (a twenty-year span), every daily, so that I'd have a feeling for it go through my head. It was a cultural shock to do that; it took me weeks to start talking normal English again!"

There isn't anything you can't find out if you try hard enough and delve deep enough. And that's what you'll have to do to find a job in theatre and film. The traditional way of looking doesn't work here because most jobs aren't advertised. You're going to have to locate the places where you could work and the people you could work for through research.

Use directories, almanacs, trade journals, newspapers, newsletters, pamphlets, books, out-of-state and in-state yellow pages, contacts, unions, libraries, school placement offices, employment centers, clearinghouses, bulletin boards (those in Appendix B of this book and those you'll uncover on your own). From these sources you can find out the types of organizations° that might hire you, the names, addresses, and phone numbers of specific organizations that interest you, who's producing what when, who is in a position to hire you, those who are doing what you want to do, which companies are expanding, which forming, which productions are ready to be staffed, union requirements, union apprenticeships, etc., etc., etc. Whatever you need to know to get a job can be researched. Don't assume, find out.

Make a close study of those organizations you are interested in that might hire you. Use annual reports, *Moody's* manuals, *Standard and Poor's, Playbills,* subscription brochures, directories, contacts—anything that's available. Find out specifics about the organization: when it was started and by whom, how it grew, the organizational structure that exists now, what plays and films it's been involved with, who its clients are, if the job you're interested in exists, what responsibilities it carries, what it's called (remember, job titles and responsibilities differ from organization to organization), whether they hire free lancers, and most important, the name of the person with the clout to hire you. Find a link to that person. If you can't get an introduction, make contact through a letter and/or phone call. More on that later.

During this period of your job hunt, immerse yourself in the trade papers and journals. You'd be surprised how much inside information you can get and how professional you can sound by reading the trades. (See Appendix B for a thorough listing.)

CONTACTS

Norman Samnick:
    "Finding a job depends a lot on who you know."
More than in any other business, show business people hire through the grapevine. They like to know the person they hire, or someone who does. So, mobilize your contact network. Exploit (in a

---

°The term "organization" is used here and throughout the chapter as an umbrella one to include all the various places of work in the entertainment industry: theatre companies, production companies, film studios, distribution companies, press agents agencies, and so on.

courteous way!) every relationship. If you know people in the business or remotely associated with it, reach out to them—and that includes friends, relatives, friends of relatives, relatives of friends, ex-schoolmates, teachers, employers, and spouses if need be. Seek out their advice. Ask to see them even if they don't know of a job. It's important to tell as many people as you can that you are interested and get as many people as you can in your corner. Whenever possible, meet your contacts in person (the experts believe this works better than a phone call), and follow up with a note afterwards.

"If you can't get in the front door, get in another way," says Nancy Littlefield, Director of the Mayor's Office for Motion Pictures and Television, New York City.

If you don't have any contacts, make them. Get on the mailing lists of the organizations you are interested in or that are related to what you want to do. That way you'll learn of seminars, workshops, and conferences. Go to them and mingle with the professionals and other job seekers; you're bound to learn from both groups. A number of associations run career workshops and seminars. For example, every fall the New York Chapter of the National Academy of Television Arts and Sciences runs "A Night at the Round Table" where experts discuss the newest trends and employment opportunities with novices. The American Film Institute runs various career workshops and seminars (in New York, Washington, and L.A.), as does the American Theatre Wing. You have the opportunity to learn *and* make contacts at these events.

Seek out people who are doing what you want to do and ask them for advice and the names of other people to talk to. Volunteer your services at Off Off Broadway theatres, showcase theatres, film companies, film commission offices, professional associations. The contacts you'll make will be well worth the time spent. They could very well lead to the knowledge of a paying job. Call the unions and ask them for suggestions; ask if you can come in and speak to a business agent and get some career advice. Some will be cooperative, others won't, but it's worth a try.

Needless to say, keep up the contacts you make. It's an incestuous industry and chances are your paths will cross again. Once you find a job, keep your contacts apprised of your progress. Jobs in the entertainment industry are generally short-lived; it's best to keep an eye out for the future.

LETTERS, RÉSUMÉS, AND INTERVIEWS

Norman Samnick:

"There is no formula to job hunting in the entertainment industry."

Sooner or later you're going to show your wares, so to speak. The standard way to do this, even in the entertainment industry, is through a letter, a résumé, a personal meeting.

The way to get someone to show interest in you is to show interest in them. Your letter should be hand done and addressed to a person, not a title (i.e., the person your research led you to). It should be short and to the point, and tailored for the circumstance. Wouldn't you be more apt to read a hand-done letter addressed to you than an offset copy addressed to Dear Job Seeker? Some experts believe in including a résumé with the letter, others believe it's best to highlight your relevant skills in the letter itself, adding that a résumé will be furnished upon request. Do whichever suits the situation. If after a few weeks you don't hear from the person, follow up with a phone call. Once you reach them ask if you can come in to see them even if no job is available. You can pick up invaluable privileged information at meetings such as these. Keep track of what they say. If you are asked to contact them again in a couple of months, do so; that may be the time they're going into production. Many entertainment organizations maintain a skeleton staff until they are producing something.

Your résumé, too, must be clear and tailored to meet the job specifications. If necessary, have more than one; if you are applying for, say, the job of seamstress, you don't want to have costume designer as your career objective. Always stress the link between your skills and the work that needs to be done. Potential employers are interested in what you can do for them, how you can help solve *their* problems. Consider this while preparing your résumé.

A résumé should include your name, address, and phone number(s). Printed clearly on top is your job objective—a simple statement that is tailored to meet a particular job. Present your work experience in reverse chronological order. Include the organization, the film or play title if applicable, your title, and a brief description of your responsibilities. If your work experience is limited, you might consider a functional listing. Divide your qualifications into categories that point out your skills and experience in them (e.g.,

Writer, wrote PR release for an Off Off Broadway theatre company, wrote subscriber newsletter). You need not state that these responsibilities were a part of an internship or school project. Never lie on a résumé, but do present the truth so that it shows you to advantage. If you do a functional listing, give your educational background first. If you do a work experience résumé, include it afterwards. This, too, should be presented in reverse chronological order. It's a good idea to include some personal information such as honors, hobbies, outside interests. You don't have to list references, simply state that they are available upon request. If you need help in preparing a résumé, you might consider one of the many books on the market. Richard Lathrop's *Who's Hiring Who* is considered to be a good one, and offers instruction on the interview as well.

An interview in the entertainment industry can mean anything: a formal one-on-one meeting in a corporate office, a lunch at the Russian Tea Room, a talk in the back of a dark theatre, a conversation at a Beverly Hills party. The more interviews you go on, the better you'll become at it. It's your job at an interview to demonstrate self-confidence, enthusiasm, and a clear set of goals. ("I'll do anything" translates to "I can do nothing.") One way to succeed at interviews is to prepare yourself. Before you go, research the organization thoroughly and find out what it lacks so that you can stress your applicable skills. This kind of research will accomplish two other things. It will show your enthusiasm for the organization, and it will allow you to relax and speak freely, knowing you're too well informed to put your foot in your mouth.

Bring along whatever work samples you have—reviews, sketches, writing samples, photos, a film, an ad, whatever applies and shows you off in a good light. Remember also that a positive, enthusiastic attitude is sometimes as important as your skills. Personality counts. In most cases you will develop a close relationship with those you work with (many of whom will be very difficult to get along with). Film and theatre work is collaborative by nature, so a compatible staff that remains steady under tension is a necessity.

No one likes the interview, neither the interviewee nor the interviewer, but there is no other way for people to meet each other. Beforehand, do what you need to do to relax yourself: jog, stretch, do deep breathing, whatever. Try to be yourself; be honest, but don't minimize what you've done, and stress what you can bring to the job. Follow up your interview with a note.

You may send several letters and résumés, make many phone

calls, and knock on a lot of doors before you have an interview with the person who will hire you. Don't be put off by rejection, and remember that just because you haven't succeeded yet doesn't mean you've failed. The main difference between those who are successful and those who aren't is that the former don't give up. Set a goal for yourself and fight to get there.

TO GET YOU STARTED

Nancy Littlefield:

"You've got to decide what you want to do and find out the appropriate next step to take. And then take it."

Appendix A contains a list of the jobs described in this book and examples of the types of organizations that might employ people for these jobs; also entry-level and middle-level positions related to the jobs that you might consider. The key words to keep in mind while reading these lists are "might" and "suggested." Every arts and entertainment industry organization is unique and has its own staff requirements; no list of this kind could apply to all without exception. And only you know what needs to be known in order to choose an entry-level job—your existing skills and those you will have to cultivate to attain your goal. Therefore, use this list as a reference tool to get you started and thinking, rather than as a rulebook to be followed implicitly. The directories listed in Appendix B will prove helpful in researching specific organizations.

Epilogue

Through my research I met and came to respect many people with careers behind the scenes in theatre and film. Some of them shared their goals and dreams with me and when, after a year or two, I followed up on their careers I found myself reacting as a friend would to their successes and to their failures. For instance, I was pleased to learn that *Kramer vs. Kramer*, Richard Fischoff's idea for a movie, had won the Academy Award for the best picture of the year and that Zoya Wyeth had reached her goal of stage managing a Broadway show by the time she was thirty. And it was good to learn that so many of the others were doing well. I was not pleased, nor surprised, however, to learn of the bitter disappointments others experienced. There was a failed play, a film that never made it, a brilliant executive without a job, a number of career detours to be taken. I mention these here because it is impossible to escape disappointment in show business, and those of you interested in building a career in it should face that fact early on. I believe those who succeed ultimately do so in spite of disappointment and failure. They write another play, produce another film, get a better job and learn to use the detours to their advantage.

Our final story. Two years ago my research took me to the Pittsburgh Public Theatre where I met Sally Lapiduss, a bright and funny aspiring writer of twenty-four. She was overqualified and underpaid for her job as assistant box office treasurer. As part of their repertory that year the theatre presented Katherine Houghton in a production of Chekhov's *The Seagull*. Ms. Houghton is the niece of Katharine Hepburn and as luck would have it Ms. Hepburn journeyed to Pittsburgh to see her perform. It was in that little two-by-two box office that Sally met Ms. Hepburn and offered to show her around Pittsburgh and to drive her to the airport the following day. To everyone's surprise Ms. Hepburn took Sally up on her offer. Sally

called the museums and did her best to plan an enjoyable day. She
even cleaned out her '69 Chevy for the occasion. Obviously the day
was a success, because Sally was given Katharine Hepburn's New
York telephone number and address and told to call "If ever there is
something I can do for you." Sally did keep in touch, first with a
note telling of genuine admiration and respect for Ms. Hepburn as a
performer and a "human being" and later by keeping her posted on
her career progress. Many months later Sally planned a trip to New
York to see some theatre. She wrote to Ms. Hepburn and told her of
her plan. The note she got back said "Call when you get to town."
Sally did and she learned that Katharine Hepburn was about to go
on tour with a new play entitled *West Side Waltz* and she thought
Sally would make a good production assistant. Sally had an interview with the director, made a favorable impression, and did eventually get the job. The last I saw her she was in L.A. "gofering,"
taking notes for the director, driving the company around town and
savoring the opportunity of her lifetime—the chance to watch a truly great performer at work. She said she didn't yet know what the
moral of her story was. I suggested it was that she was ready for her
opportunity when it came since she had worked so hard at menial
production jobs during the year. "Maybe," she said, but I could see
on her face she meant to say, But who would have thought it would
come from a job in the box office in a theatre in Pittsburgh.

Appendix A: Jobs in Show Business

Job	Where to Apply for Job and/or Information	Related Middle- and Entry-level Jobs
Administrative Jobs		
Arts Manager	Resident theatres;* cultural institutions; appropriate employment centers (see Appendix B)†	Almost any not-for-profit theatre job, especially administrative
Booking Director	*see* Program Director	
Box-Office Personnel	Theatre owners (e.g., the Shubert Organization); resident theatres; appropriate union and employment centers	Mailroom boy or girl; assistant treasurer
Company Manager	General managers' offices; producers' offices; resident theatres; appropriate union and employment centers	Assistant to a company manager; production secretary; production assistant; assistant to the director; bookkeeper
Comptroller	Resident theatre companies; film companies; accounting firms specializing in entertainment industry accounting	Bookkeeper
Director of Audience Development	Resident theatre companies; employment centers	Assistant to the director of audience development
Director of Funding and Development	Resident theatres; cultural institutions; appropriate employment centers	Assistant to the director of funding and development

* Throughout this list, the term "resident theatres" includes (in most cases) regional theatre companies all over the country, seasonal production companies in New York City, dance and opera companies, summer stock companies, and dinner theatres.

† A comprehensive list of employment and union centers can be found on pages 220–222.

Job	Where to Apply for Job and/or Information	Related Middle- and Entry-level Jobs
Distributor	Film studios; independent distribution companies; appropriate employment centers	Buyer; assistant to salesperson; secretary; clerk; print "checker" (checks to see prints are in good condition); receptionist
General Manager	Resident theatre companies; Broadway theatrical producers' offices; general managers' offices; appropriate employment centers	Company manager
House Manager	Resident theatres; theatre owners; appropriate union	Assistant to a house manager; ticket taker; usher
Literary Manager	see Story Editor	
Packager	Theatrical offices specializing in stock theatre	Production secretary; any work in a packager's office
Producer (Film)	Self-employed—find a property to produce! Associate producers can apply for work with independent producers and/or studios	Associate producer; line producer; production manager; unit production manager; 2nd assistant director; any other film production experience
Producer (Theatre)	Self-employed, although in some noncommercial theatres producers are employed on a seasonal basis; appropriate employment centers	General manager; arts manager; company manager; any theatre job
Production Auditor	Film production companies	Accounting experience; assistant to an office coordinator; production assistant
Production Estimator	Large film companies	Accounting and budgeting experience

Production Manager	Film companies; independent producers; appropriate union	Production assistant; 2nd assistant director; production office coordinator; unit production manager
Production Office Coordinator	Film companies; appropriate union and employment centers	Production secretary
Program Director	Cultural institutions	Booking director
Reader	see Story Analyst	
Receptionist	Everywhere (just to name a few: agents, film companies, theatrical producers, distribution companies, service organizations), appropriate employment centers	Typist; clerk
Secretary/Assistant	Again, everywhere; appropriate employment centers	Receptionist
Story Analyst (Reader)	Free-lance* and on-staff for film production companies; film studios; resident theatre companies; theatrical producers; appropriate union	A literary background such as publishing industry experience
Story Editor/Literary Manager	Film companies and studios/Resident theatre companies specializing in producing new plays	Reader; subsidiary rights publishing background
Studio Executive	Film studio	Anyone's guess: working your way up the corporate ladder is one way; bringing previously achieved skills is another. More and more, studio executives have some sort of business background

---

* The term "free-lance" refers to project-based jobs.

Job	Where to Apply for Job and/or Information	Related Middle- and Entry-level Jobs
Subscription Director	Resident theatres; appropriate employment centers	Assistant; some advertising background is helpful
Production Jobs		
Artistic Director	Resident theatre companies; generally you must start your own company!	All theatre jobs, including technical, directing, management
Auteur	Function as an independent filmmaker and win the respect (and financial backing) of colleagues	Director, writer, performer
Casting Director	On-staff with resident theatres; most work as free-lance consultants	Casting agent for TV commercials (at ad agencies); assistant/secretary to a casting consultant or talent agent
Choreographer	Theatre and film directors; dance companies; universities; appropriate union and employment centers	Dance teacher; personal assistant to a choreographer; dance arranger; dance notator; and, of course, dancer
Composer	Team up with lyricist in theatre; in film, the director hires the composer; appropriate unions offer information	Musician; arranger; orchestrator; contractor; copyist
Cuer	Film production companies	Production assistant; this is an entry-level position
Dialogue Director	Film directors hire dialogue directors	Acting or speech teacher
Director (Film)	Independent producers; film studios; TV commercial production companies; appropriate union	Editor; screenwriter; independent filmmaker; assistant director

Director (Theatre)	Resident theatres; theatrical producers; universities; appropriate union and employment centers	Stage manager; assistant director; assistant to a director; tech work; acting teacher
Fight Director	Directors hire fight directors	Dancer; assistant director
Independent Filmmaker	Self-employed	Writer; production manager; technician; fundraiser; almost any film experience will help—the more the better
Location Scout	Independent film production companies; some film studios (via production manager); scout locating companies; some film commission offices	Assistant to a scout; production assistant
Lyricist	Self-employed—team up with a composer	Work for other lyricists and composers
Musical Director	Film studios; free-lance for film and theatre producers	Musician, contractor, composer, any music-related job
Playwright	Self-employed in commercial theatre. Playwright-in-residence jobs are available at resident theatre companies specializing in producing new plays; appropriate guild	Write plays on own; learn theatre through tech jobs and any other that connects you with theatre activity
Production Assistant	Film production companies and studios; theatrical production offices; resident theatres; showcase theatres; film-editing companies; film studio facilities; TV stations (cable and network); appropriate union and employment center	This is the traditional entry-level position, but one could intern or volunteer to gain some experience
Screenwriter	Self-employed at the beginning of career; once established, producers hire screenwriters. Getting an agent is the first step	Write screenplays on spec; write TV scripts; write nightclub acts and other entertainment writing; write TV commercials

Job	Where to Apply for Job and/or Information	Related Middle- and Entry-level Jobs
Production Artisan Jobs		
Animator	Film companies specializing in animation (e.g., Disney, Hanna Barbera); film graphic and optical companies; appropriate union	Checker; opaquer; inker; in-betweener
Art Director	Film studios with art departments; production companies where work is mostly free-lance; hired by the director and/or production designer; appropriate union	Assistant art director; artist
Artist/Draftsman	Film studios with art departments; large costume and scenic shops; free-lance with busy costume designers, art directors, or set designers; appropriate union	Flunky around the art department; gofer
Camera Operator	Director of photography at production companies hires camera operator (via production manager); free-lance for TV commercial production companies; educational and industrial film companies; appropriate union	1st, 2nd assistant camera operator; salesman or technician for camera supply company
Carpenter	Scenic shops; cultural institutions (e.g., Lincoln Center); free lancers at film companies and studios are hired by production manager, production designer, or DP; appropriate union	Assistant carpenter
Cinematographer	*see* Director of Photography	

Clapper	Free-lance for film production company	This is an entry-level position sometimes handled by a 3rd assistant director or production assistant
Costume Designer	On-staff with costume shops, resident theatres; free-lance for theatre and film directors; appropriate union	Assistant to a designer; assistant designer; sketcher; costume supervisor; costume technician; costumer; dresser
Costumer	Free-lance for film production company hired by production manager and/or wardrobe supervisor; appropriate union	Costume technician; dresser
Costume Supervisor	Resident theatres; appropriate employment centers	Assistant to a costume designer; dresser; costume technician
Costume Technician	Costume shops (e.g., Eaves-Brooks Costume Co.) and resident companies with their own house shop; designers who maintain their own staff	Seamstress
Crafts Service Person	Film studios in L.A.; appropriate union	This is an entry-level position; taking the job on a nonunion basis is one way to get experience
Curtain Operator	Theatre owners; resident theatre companies	This is an entry-level position
Dance Supervisor	Director/choreographer hires the dance supervisor	Dancer; dance captain/master
Director of Photography	A film's director chooses the DP; appropriate union	Camera operator
Draper	Film production companies (via the production manager and/or scenic artist)	This is an entry-level job for scenic artists

Job	Where to Apply for Job and/or Information	Related Middle- and Entry-level Jobs
Dresser	Resident theatre companies; theatrical producers; film production companies (via the production manager and/or wardrobe supervisor); appropriate union	Costume technician; this is an entry-level position for would-be wardrobe mistresses and costume designers
Editor	On feature films, the director chooses the editor; on-staff work is available at film-editing companies that primarily edit TV commercials; appropriate union	Sound editor; music editor; assistant editor; apprentice editor; negative cutter; breakdown editor
Electrician	Resident theatre companies; theatre owners; film production companies and studios (via DP and production manager); appropriate union	Best boy; generator operator; operator
Fabricator	Free-lance for film production companies and studios (via set decorator, production designer and production manager); appropriate union	This is an entry-level job for set decorators; work in a fabric house could provide worthwhile experience
Grip	Free-lance for production film companies (via the DP and production manager); resident theatre companies; free-lance for theatre owners and producers (via the general manager); appropriate union	Production assistant
Hairdresser	Individual performers; free-lance for production companies; free-lance for TV commercial production companies; appropriate unions	Assistant hairdresser; hairdresser at a salon; costume shops that style wigs

Lighting Designer	Free-lance and on-staff for resident theatre companies; free-lance for theatrical production companies; appropriate union and employment centers	Assistant lighting designer; electrician
Make-up Artist	Free-lance for production film companies and studios; free-lance for TV commercial companies; professional make-up shops; appropriate unions	Assistant make-up artist; powderman; body make-up artist
Model Builder	Free-lance for production companies and studios; free-lance for TV commercial production companies; scenic shops; appropriate union	Propmaker
Painter	Resident theatre companies; free-lance for production companies and studios (via the production manager); scenic shops; appropriate union	Paint boy or girl; this is an entry-level position for would-be designers
Paperhanger	Free-lance for production film companies and studios; free-lance for TV commercial film companies; scenic shops; appropriate union	This is an entry-level position for scenic artists; production assistant; paperhanging for the general public
Production Designer	The director chooses the production designer; appropriate union	Stage designer; art director; set decorator; artist; painter
Projectionist	Free-lance for theatrical producers; free-lance for industrial theatre producers; free-lance and on-staff for film production companies and studios; on-staff for film-editing companies; theatre owners; appropriate union	Assistant to a projectionist

Job	Where to Apply for Job and/or Information	Related Middle- and Entry-level Jobs
Property Master	Theatre owners; free-lance for theatrical production companies; free-lance and on-staff for resident theatre companies; free-lance for film production companies and studios; scenic shops with prop departments employ property makers and metalworkers; appropriate union and employment center	Property handler; set dresser; outside property person; greensman
Scenic Artist	Free-lance for theatrical production companies; free-lance for film production companies and studios (via the production designer and production manager); appropriate union	Painter; draper; paperhanger
Script Supervisor	Free-lance for film production companies and studios; appropriate union	Assistant/apprentice to a script supervisor; production assistant
Set Decorator	Free-lance for film production companies and studios; appropriate union	Scenic artist; carpenter; painter; property crew
Sound Designer	Free-lance for theatrical producers; free-lance for musical concert producers	Sound equipment designer; soundman
Soundman	Theatre owners; free-lance for theatrical producers; resident theatre companies; sound studios; film studios; free-lance for film production companies; appropriate union	Boom operator; sound operator; cable-man; playback operator; recordist; dummy loader
Special Effects Person	Free-lance for theatrical producers; free-lance for film production companies and studios; film animation companies; appropriate union	Assistant special effects person

Stage Designer	Free-lance for theatrical producers (the director chooses); resident theatre companies; appropriate union and employment center	Production designer of films; scenic artist; painter; assistant to a stage designer
Stage Manager	Free-lance for theatrical producers; resident theatre companies; appropriate union and employment centers	Assistant stage manager
Still Photographer	Free-lance for film studio (via the publicist); free-lance for theatrical producers; appropriate union	Relevant photographic experience
Technical Director	Resident theatre companies; appropriate employment centers	All tech work, i.e, carpenter, electrician, sound operator
Wardrobe Supervisor	Theatrical producers and owners; film production companies and studios; appropriate union	Costumer; dresser

Supporting Services Jobs

Advertising	Film studios; advertising agencies specializing in entertainment advertising; trailer makers	Assistant to advertising executive of studio; junior account executive; secretary
Agent	Large or small talent agencies; personal managers are self-employed	Most large agencies have a training program that begins in the mailroom. At the small agencies it is sometimes possible to enter as someone's assistant
Animal Specialist	Animal rental companies	Help with the animals' care and feeding at such companies
Art Therapist	Hospitals; rehabilitation clinics; theatre companies specializing in arts therapy	Therapists must be trained; there are some administrative jobs available; secretary

207

Job	Where to Apply for Job and/or Information	Related Middle- and Entry-level Jobs
Arts Council Jobs	Arts Council	Staff people; assistant; secretary; clerk or receptionist
Arts-in-Education	Resident theatre companies; arts service organizations; schools; appropriate clearinghouse	Artist-in-residence
Arts Service Organization Jobs	Foundations; film societies; cultural and government organizations	Assistant/secretary; receptionist
Camera Supply House Employee	Camera rental companies (e.g., Camera Mart, N.Y.C.); rental companies; equipment design companies	This is an entry-level job for would-be cinematographers
Concessionaire	Theatre owners; resident theatre companies	This is an entry-level position for theatre people
Corporate Contributor	Large corporations that fund the arts; organizations such as Business Committee for the Arts, the Corporate Fund	Assistant/secretary to the department
Critic	Newspapers; magazines; trade journals; TV stations	Entertainment journalist; film reviewer; teacher; scholar
Dance Notator	Dance companies; choreographers; universities	Apprentice
Educational Filmmaking	Education film production companies; publishing houses with such a division	Technical work (grip, etc.); consulting; assistant/secretary
Entertainment Reporter	Newspapers; magazines; trade publications	Any writing experience
Equipment Sales and Design	Design firms	Technician (repairman)

Film Archivist	Libraries, foundations, archives; companies that specialize in this service (e.g, the Renovare Co. in Hollywood)	Researcher
Film Commission Jobs	Film commissions across the country	Office staff workers
Film Technician	Film laboratories	Salesmen
Food Caterer	Motion picture catering companies	Location service jobs
Food Coordinator	Film production companies	Production assistant
Food Stylist	Free-lance for TV commercial production companies, magazines, film production companies	Assistant to a food stylist
Industrial Filmmaking	Industrial film production companies and distribution companies	Sales
Marketing Research	Film studios; marketing research films with clients in the entertainment business	Interviewer
Merchandising Executive	Film studios; independent licensing consultants	Assistant to merchandising executive; work for toy manufacturer in licensing division
Optical Designer	Film graphic and optical houses	Sales; assistant/secretary
Personal Manager	see Agent	
Publicity Jobs	Press agent's office; resident theatre companies and film studios; public relations companies with entertainment industry clients; free-lance for production companies; appropriate union and employment centers	Assistant to a press agent; apprentice publicist

209

Job	Where to Apply for Job and/or Information	Related Middle- and Entry-level Jobs
Shop Jobs	Costume and scenic shops	"Ragpicker"; carpenter's assistant
Stunt Coordinator	Free-lance for film production companies and studios	Coordinators usually are ex-stunt people
Teachers	Public and private schools, universities, trade schools; free-lance for film studios; appropriate union	Teachers must be appropriately trained
Theatre Architect and Consultant	Self-employed; architecture firms specializing in performing arts facilities	Contractor
Theatre Manager	Theatre owners	House manager; usher; box-office personnel
Theatre Owner	Self-employed	Work for theatre owner in theatre operations; buyer
Theatrical Attorney	Self-employed; firms that specialize in entertainment law; film studios hire lawyers with entertainment law experience	Lawyer in another field
Translator	Distributors; film studios	This is more often than not a part-time job and perhaps a way for a bi-lingual person to earn some money and make contacts
Transportation	Film production companies	This is an entry-level position

| Union Employee | All unions | Most union officials come from the ranks of the union; occasionally people are hired from outside and from other unions |
| Usher | Theatre owners; appropriate union | In noncommercial (i.e., nonunion) houses this job is entry-level; in union houses ushers begin by joining the union |

Appendix B: Resources

There are a number of ways to learn about the "industry" before entering it as a professional. There are courses to take; books, newspapers, and periodicals to read; directories to refer to; trade associations to join; internships, training programs, and grants to apply for—all this and more to acquaint you with the world you wish to join. Take advantage of all the resources available. Contact organizations for literature, get on mailing lists, and let it be known you are eager to learn.

This appendix is a gathering of available resources: internships, training programs, employment agencies, schools, grants, festivals, unions, guilds, professional associations, books, periodicals, directories, newspapers, theatre and film bookstores and libraries. The resources are listed here to let you know they exist; it is up to you to decide which ones are relevant to your goals. Although the appendix is complete in itself, it is by no means comprehensive, so do some of your own research; seek out things that will help you and teach you.

Many of the programs mentioned depend on funding for their existence, therefore it may well be that they are here today and gone tomorrow. The same is true of the periodicals—a call or note will let you know of their status and any changes in prices, policy, phone numbers, and addresses.

Internships and Training Programs

An internship is a period of time spent learning while you work in a professional environment. For their work some interns earn a small stipend, others college credit, others on-the-job training, education, and contacts. At its best an internship bridges the gap between school and the professional world, at its worst it provides free labor for exploitive institutions. To avoid the latter, make certain from the start that you will be getting something (money, entrance into a union, training, college credit, seminars) in return for your work. A number of schools allow their students (graduate and undergraduate) to intern with a relevant professional organization for college credit. For a list of those see "Appendix 4: Schools with Intern/Apprentice Programs" in the American Film Institute's *Guide to College Courses in TV and Film*. Generally, the school will arrange for and supervise the internship. Those out of school can also participate. Below you will find organizations that offer internships directly and clearinghouses that suggest internships. Contact those you are interested in for additional information and application. Whenever possible, make a visit before obligating yourself. For those interested in interning at a regional theatre, see *Theatre Profiles*

3: *A Resource Book of the Nonprofit Professional Theatres in the U.S.,*
with information on their intern programs.

Alternate Media Center Apprenticeship Program, Alternate Media Center, 725 Broadway, New York City 10003. (212) 260-3990. Applicant
must be sponsored by a broadcast station. Once accepted, he/she
spends a year as a paid employee of a local cable, commercial, or
educational TV station, attends workshops, visits staff members. Requires: local sponsor endorsement letter, programming proposal, work
sample, experience résumé, sponsor information. Supported by National Endowment for the Arts and local sponsors. Apply by Dec. 13.

American Film Institute Academy Internship Program, Center for Advance Film Studies, 501 Doheny Road, Beverly Hills, CA. 90210.
(213) 278-8777. Through funding from the Academy of Motion Picture Arts and Sciences, the AFI provides a limited number of filmmakers with a weekly stipend and the opportunity to learn by
observing the work of major directors throughout the production of
a feature film. The duration of the internship varies with the length
of production. Applicants must be twenty-one and a citizen or permanent resident of the United States. Interns are chosen on the basis
of their knowledge of film and potential as directors. After an initial
screening by a review board, applicants are interviewed by participating directors who choose the interns they wish to have with
them.

Animation Training Program, Hanna-Barbera Productions, 3400 Cahuenga Blvd., Hollywood, CA. 90068. (213) 851-5000. Portfolio and
résumé are required. Applicants must have formal art training and be
good in life anatomy drawing. If accepted, applicant receives free
training in animation (i.e., layout, character design, storyboard). The
best students are selected for work assignments.

Astoria Internship Program, Astoria Motion Picture and Television Center
Foundation, 35-11 35th Avenue, Astoria, N.Y. 11106. (212) 392-5600.
A small number of "emerging professionals" are given the opportunity to earn a weekly stipend for a limited number of weeks while they
observe the making of a feature film. In addition, they are given the
opportunity for independent research and/or involvement with a
production company or service organization. The interns also meet
with their mentors, both individually and as a group, to discuss and
evaluate their experiences and to attend workshops, seminars, demon-
strations, and lectures given by film and television specialists. Interns
are selected by an independent panel representing a wide range of
the film and TV professions.

ATPAM Apprentice Program, Association for Theatre Press Agents and
Managers, 165 West 46th Street, New York City 10036. (212) 719-
3666. ATPAM trains five apprentices annually. Upon completion of
the three-year program, applicants become members of ATPAM and
are eligible to work as press agents. To gain admission into the apprenticeship program, you must be working as an assistant to a press

agent who is willing to submit your name for formal apprenticeship. All applicants are screened verbally and evaluated for potential. If accepted, the apprentice continues to work for and get paid by a senior press agent while attending seminars and field trips. Applicants must work at least twenty weeks each season, not necessarily for the same press agent. A written exam is given to those who complete the program; those who pass are admitted into the union. See also below: *Joint Managers Apprenticeship Program for House and Company Managers,* which is co-administered by ATPAM.

Black Theatre Alliance (BTA), 410 West 42nd Street, New York City 10019. (212) 564-2266. BTA has as its members seventy-five theatre and dance companies located across the country. Its purpose is to uphold a standard of excellence and to serve as a central source of information on black theatre and dance. It offers a (nonpaid) internship at the Alliance but, more important, serves as a clearinghouse for internships and employment opportunities at the seventy-five member theatres.

Boston Film/Video Foundation, 39 Brighton Avenue, Allston, MA. 02134. (617) 254-1616. A resource organization providing equipment and information to independent video and film artists. Internships and workshops on screenwriting, directing, acting, and other facets of film are available.

Camera Assistant Training Program, 8480 Beverly Blvd., Hollywood, CA. 90048. This training program is sponsored by IATSE Local 659, the photographers' local. The purpose is to train ten assistant cameramen and five special effects assistants in film production. Trainees work on-the-job for two hundred working days within one year at trainee pay scale wages and attend seminars in (for cameramen) hand tests, placemarks, running tapes, photo logs/reports, slates, reloading magazines, setting up, dismantling, moving, and use of motion picture photographic equipment; (for effects assistants) opticals, miniature photography, insert stage work, electronic equipment, animation cranes, matte painting, background projection. Upon successful completion of program, trainee's name is placed on Industry Experience Roster, making him/her eligible for hire as Group I Cameraman. Admittance into program by committee based on education, photographic knowledge, experience, results of eight-hour test, personal interview.

City of New York Department of Cultural Affairs Arts Apprenticeships, 830 Fifth Avenue, New York City 10021. (212) 360-8185. The Cultural Affairs Arts Apprenticeship Program places college students interested in careers in the arts in apprenticeships with not-for-profit arts organizations and artists throughout the city for one year. The program aims to prepare students to make informed decisions on how to use their talents in the "real" world. Student apprentices, who need not be from NYC colleges, are paid through the Urban Corps and the Federal College Work Study Program. Work Study grants are based on financial need. Students interested in Work Study should apply through their college's financial aid offices; students not eligible for Work Study should apply directly to the Arts Apprenticeship Program (above). Student apprentices can work either in arts administration positions or creative workshop situations. Workshops and conferences are held throughout the year. Ask for program brochure.

Contract Services Administration Trust Fund, 8480 Beverly Blvd., Hollywood, CA. 90048. (213) 655-4200. Training programs in various film- and TV-related fields are open to qualified applicants. Contact for details.

Design Institute of the National Arts Consortium, 30 West 57th Street, New York City 10019. (212) 246-5023. A small number of people with particular disadvantages in the labor market (e.g., a lack of educational credentials, displaced homemakers, minorities, and native Americans) receive a weekly stipend while they study lighting, set design, scenic painting, script analysis, and drafting, as well as other theatre crafts at this arts organization. Students have an eight-hour day and forty-hour week for three years, and their training consists of formal classroom work as well as field projects. They receive a stipend and tuition. Upon completion of the training, students are qualified to work in the commercial and noncommercial theatre, and the design students are ready to take the United Scenic Artists Union exam. To be eligible, you must belong to a Title 3 group designated by the U.S. Department of Labor. Admittance to the program is by portfolio and interview. As the program was funded under Title 3 of the Comprehensive Employment Act (CETA), it is not guaranteed to continue. Contact for details and future of program.

Directors Guild of America Assistant Directors Training Program, 8480 Beverly Blvd., Hollywood, CA. 90048. (213) 653-2200. Although it is called something else, this two-year training program is basically the same as the DGA, New York, program (below), with these few exceptions: Interns may work with TV series, and if they do they remain with that series the entire two years; interns must accumulate four hundred actual work days; the IQ test is an eight-hour test; no psychological profile is given; and an admission committee chooses which students who pass the written exam will go on to the interview. Fifteen to seventeen applicants are chosen each year. To apply, contact above office. There is no need to set up an interview prior to receiving application.

Directors Guild of America Producers Training Program, 1697 Broadway, Suite 407, New York City 10019. (212) CI 5-2545. This two-year training program (administered by DGA, New York) is designed for those interested in the production end of film (producing, not directing). The program emphasizes the administrative and managerial functions of assistant directors and unit production managers, and familiarizes the trainee with the paperwork and proper maintenance of records, including the preparation of call sheets, production reports, and requisitions. It acquaints them with the working conditions of the collective bargaining agreement of industry guilds and unions, and gives them a basic knowledge of the administrative procedures in motion picture production. The program provides the intern with a higher-than-average weekly stipend during periods of employment and includes both on-the-job and off-the-job training (seminars). Interns work on a number of productions during their internship and must complete three hundred actual working days during the two-year period. Upon completion of the program, the trainee is accepted into DGA as a Second Assistant Director, making him or her eligible for employment. Applicants must be graduates of a four-year accredited college or have equivalent work experience. Admission is by a four-hour IQ exam, a 600-question psychological profile, and an interview, and is highly competitive. Ten to twelve applicants are chosen each year. To apply, call Allan Burns at the above number to set up a personal interview.

Great Lakes Colleges Association Arts Program, 2182 Broadway, New York City 10024. (212) 595-3350. This program places Midwestern college students in apprenticeships in New York City arts organizations. Students receive training and college credit for their fifteen-week full-time internship. Deadline for applications is end of April for the fall semester and mid-November for the spring semester.

Institute of New Cinema Artists, 505 Eighth Avenue, New York City 10001. (212) 695-0826. The institute trains disadvantaged youths in videotape, camera, recording, and other technical fields in the entertainment industry, and provides them with a weekly stipend. The program is 9–5, five days a week for thirty weeks. The institute attempts to place participants in jobs upon completion of their training. Qualifications to become an intern are innate talent, NYC resident at least eighteen years of age, and low income status.

International Alliance of Theatrical Stage Employees and Moving Picture Machine Operators (IATSE), 1515 Broadway, New York City 10036. (212) 730-1770. A few locals of IATSE offer apprenticeship programs. As each local designs its own program, contact them directly (addresses and phone numbers are provided under *Unions*) and inquire about their apprenticeship programs.

Joint Managers Apprenticeship Program for House and Company Managers, League of New York Theatre Owners and Producers, 226 West 47th Street, New York City 10036. (212) 582-4455. This training program for company and house managers is administered jointly by the League and ATPAM. Eight people are accepted into the program annually. To qualify, you must first get a job as an assistant to a company or house manager. You then make formal application to become an apprentice and, if accepted, you work on salary for three years and attend seminars. Upon satisfactory completion of the apprenticeship, you are accepted into the union and are eligible to work for a theatrical producer, owner, or general manager.

Juilliard School Internship Program at Lincoln Center, Stage Department, The Juilliard School, Lincoln Center, New York City 10023. College students apprentice in this program in production for the performing arts for sixteen or thirty-two weeks, and receive a small weekly stipend. In addition to working with a fully professional staff, interns participate in a professional enrichment program designed to acquaint them with new materials and experimental production techniques. The program is designed for those currently enrolled in accredited theatre training programs who are looking for professional experience prior to graduate work or entrance into the profession. Interns are selected on the basis of a demonstrated capacity for professional work.

National Endowment Fellowship Program, National Endowment for the Arts, Intern Program Office, Mail Stop 557, 2401 E Street, N.W., Washington, D.C., 20506. (202) 634-6380. NEA provides a thirteen-week paid internship for arts administrators at the National Endowment for the Arts offices in Washington. The program is designed to acquaint participants with the policies and operations of the Endowment and to help give them an overview of arts activities around the country. Fellows are given the opportunity to learn about Endowment programs by observing policy development, grant-making procedures, and administration. In addition to working as members of the staff, fellows attend a series of seminars and meetings with members of the National Council on the Arts, Endowment panelists, artists, journalists, federal officials, and leading arts administrators. In order to apply, each candidate must be sponsored by a college or university, state or local arts agency, or other nonprofit arts organization. For further information write to the Intern Program Office.

National Opera Institute, John F. Kennedy Center for the Performing Arts, Washington, D.C., 20566. (202) 254-3694. The purpose of this organization is to encourage the growth and development of opera in the United States. One of their programs is an apprenticeship in opera administration and production. Apprenticeships in stage direction, stage management, lighting and technical direction, costuming, coaching, and other related professions enable outstanding young professionals to work with experts in their field. Apprentices receive a weekly stipend plus transportation to and from the location of the apprenticeship, which ranges from two to twelve months. Write for guidelines and details of eligibility.

Neighborhood Film Project, 3601 Locust Walk, Philadelphia, PA. 19104. (215) 386-1536. Internships in film projection, researching program notes, as well as filmmaking workshops, are offered.

New Dramatists, 424 West 44th Street, New York City 10036. (212) 757-6960. The purpose of this organization is to encourage and develop new playwrights. Application for membership is accepted from playwrights who live in NYC and who have written two full-length plays. Once accepted, benefits include: an apprenticeship to Broadway and Off Broadway producers and directors on one of their plays from start to finish, theatre admissions at no cost, craft discussions with established theatre professionals, workshops, free use of theatre. Membership is limited.

Northwest Film Study Center, Portland Art Museum, 1219 S.W. Park Avenue, Portland, OR. 97205. (503) 226-2811. Internships and a variety of courses on filmmaking and film criticism are offered.

Off Off Broadway Theatre Alliance (OOBA), 162 West 56th Street, New York City 10019. (212) 757-4473. OOBA serves as a resource and referral center for over two hundred Off Off Broadway theatres. One of their many services is to match up interns with theatre companies. They know which OOB theatres have programs, which need particular skills, which pay out stipends. One call to them could save you many to individual theatres. Call or write and ask about help in finding an internship.

Radio City Page Program, Radio City Music Hall Productions, 1260 Avenue of the Americas, Rockefeller Plaza, New York City 10020. (212) 246-4600. Att: Guest Relations-Page Program. This on-the-job training program provides a limited few with the opportunity to work as a Radio City page while attending seminars on various aspects of the entertainment industry and observing, first hand, production of Radio City spectaculars. Pages meet and greet patrons, take tickets, seat people, and in general act as Radio City hosts and hostesses for twenty-five to thirty-nine hours per week for eighteen months, and are paid an hourly wage. At the end of the program the most successful pages are invited to stay on as Radio City tour guides. College students who have reached their junior year and graduates interested in a career in administration and production may apply.

Shubert Internship Program, The Shubert Foundation, 234 West 44th Street, New York City 10036. (212) 944-3718. A twenty-week internship in nonperforming theatrical skills that places interns at the right hand of Broadway directors, lighting designers, general managers, press agents, and even the heads of the Shubert Organization. Besides working a minimum of thirty hours a week in their specialty, each student keeps a journal, writes critical papers, and finally a thesis.

Tune In, New York City. (212) 246-5600. This organization will "tune you into" theatre and arts organizations looking for volunteers. *Tune In* listings are not for interns or on-the-job training programs, so all you will get is experience. This is a good resource for those thinking about a career in theatre and eager for a taste but too timid to call theatres directly. Make certain to ask for *theatre* organizations because *Tune In* lists all kinds of volunteer-seeking organizations.

Walt Disney Studio, 500 South Buena Vista Street, Burbank, CA. 91521. (213) 845-3141. A talent development program offering training in all aspects of animation technique. Applicants must be able to draw.

Young Filmmakers/Video Arts, 4 Rivington Street, New York City 10002. (212) 673-9361. Young Filmmakers offers an intensive twenty-week workshop in television studio production training (in Spanish and English) to minority group members and women from the five boroughs of New York City. Priority is given to the unemployed. Participants pay a $25 fee upon being accepted. Other services are provided to the public, including a variety of film workshops. Send for flyers. This organization also runs paid workshops; be certain to ask about free workshops and/or intern program.

Employment Clearinghouses and Placement Services

Affirmative Action Register, Inc., 8356 Olive Blvd., St. Louis, MO. 63132. (314) 991-1335. This organization offers an employment listing for arts administrators and others. Ask for Affirmative Action Register *Newsletter*.

The American Dance Guild, 1619 Broadway, Suite 603, New York City 10019. (212) 245-4833. The purpose of this organization is to promote the art of dance and to serve the needs of dance artists (dancers, choreographers, dance teachers) through all phases of their careers. The guild maintains employment information for dance educators.

American Theatre Association (ATA) Placement Service, 1029 Vermont Ave., N.W., Washington, D.C. 20005. (202) 737-5608. The ATA's placement service functions as a resource and referral center and exists to aid its registrants in securing positions in theatre. Publishes the ATA *Placement Service Bulletin*, a monthly listing of current professional openings. These vacancy listings are placed in one of a number of categories: administrator, teacher, director/teacher/technical, director/designer/teacher, costumer/designer/teacher, and so on.

Artist-in-Schools (AIS), New York Foundation for the Arts, 60 East 42nd Street, New York City 10017. (212) 986-3140. AIS places artists proficient in theatre, film, dance crafts in full-time and part-time paid residencies, ranging from three months to one year. Artists interested in working in schools and community residency programs may apply by sending résumé and references to the Foundation.

Association of College, University and Community Arts Administrators, P.O. Box 2137, Madison, WI. 53701. (608) 262-0004. This organization has a placement referral service for arts administrators.

Association of Independent Video and Filmmakers (AIVF), 625 Broadway, New York City 10012. (212) 473-3400. The purpose of this organization is to foster the art of independent video and filmmaking through informational and practical services. One of those is an employment referral service. Write for membership application.

Black Theatre Alliance, 410 West 42nd Street, New York City 10019. (212) 564-2266. Serves as clearinghouse with regard to employment opportunities at member theatres. See *Internships*.

Career Planning Center, 1623 South La Cienega Blvd., Los Angeles, CA. 90035. (213) 273-6633. Offers seminars and workshops for women and students on a variety of jobs. "The Cast You Don't See on the Screen" is a seminar offered on the film industry, including ways of finding employment.

Central Opera Service (COS), c/o Metropolitan Opera, Lincoln Center for the Performing Arts, New York City 10023. (212) 957-9871. The group's purpose is to foster closer association among opera companies. One of their services is employment assistance: COS will help opera administrators and artists searching for work in opera administration, coaching, conducting, public relations, fundraising, and directing.

College Art Association, 16 East 52nd Street, New York 10022. (212) 755-3532. This organization has a placement referral service for arts administrators.

Foundation for the Community of Artists, 280 Broadway, New York City 10007. (212) 964-2180. This organization has a placement referral service for arts administrators. Ask for their newsletter, *Artists Update*.

Good People, 827 Hilldale Avenue, Los Angeles, CA. 90069. (213) 278-8221. An employment agency listing jobs in show business. Especially useful for entry-level jobs (secretary, receptionist, production secretary). Associate producer and production assistant jobs are sometimes listed.

Off Off Broadway Theatre Alliance (OOBA), 162 West 56th Street, New York City 10019. (212) 757-4473. Serves as a clearinghouse for member theatres. See *Internships*.

Off-Roster Hiring Project, Contract Services Administration Trust Fund, 8480 Beverly Blvd., Room 22, Hollywood, CA. 90048. (213) 653-7560. Commercial film and TV producers generally hire personnel listed on rosters. A skilled, experienced unlisted worker may register for the Off-Roster Project and be called for jobs if listed personnel are unavailable. By gaining enough work experience, the worker becomes eligible to be included on roster. Positions are technical in nature (make-up artist, lab operator, cameraman, etc.).

Opportunity Resources for the Arts, 1501 Broadway, New York City 10036. (212) 575-1688. Opportunity Resources serves as a placement center for arts organizations seeking professional personnel and for individuals seeking employment in the arts. OR provides candidates for administrative positions in museums, arts centers, arts councils, theatre, opera and ballet companies, symphony orchestras, and other nonprofit professional arts organizations. OR places qualified people in jobs appropriate to their skills, background, and geographical preference. Counseling in career development and advice on writing résumés for arts administration jobs are also available.

TAG Foundation Ltd., 463 West Street, New York City 10014. (212) 691-3500. TAG keeps an active list of qualified young technicians (including stage managers) from which theatre and dance companies draw. People looking for work are asked to come in for an interview.

Theatre Communications Group (TCG), 355 Lexington Avenue, New York
   City 10017. (212) 697-5230. TCG offers artistic, administrative, and
   information services to nonprofit theatres and to theatre artists, administrators, and technicians. One such service is the personnel referral. Files of directors, designers, stage managers, technicians, and
   administrators are available to theatres and colleges seeking qualified
   professionals and offering professional-level salaries. TCG will make
   referrals, supply résumés, and schedule interviews for prospective
   employers. Ask for their newsletter.

Grants and Festivals

Financial assistance—in the form of grants, scholarships, fellowships, and
contest awards—is available to independent filmmakers, playwrights, and
other behind-the-scenes people. Funding is given in support of a particular
project or talent by private and government foundations, film companies,
TV stations, private corporations. There is too little room here to identify all
these organizations or provide guidance in grant solicitation. A small sampling of grants and festivals and further research material follows.

Resources

**Gadney's Guide to 1800 International Contests, Festivals and Grants in
Film and Video, Photography, TV-Radio Broadcasting, Writing, Poetry
and Playwrighting, Journalism,** Festival Publications, P.O. Box 10180,
   Glendale, CA. 91209
Factfile #3, Film/Video Festivals and Awards
Factfile #12, Film/Television: Grants, Scholarships, Special Programs,
   AFI National Education Service, c/o John F. Kennedy Center for the
   Performing Arts, Washington, D.C., 20566
**Private Foundations Active in the Arts and Grants in Aid to Individuals
in the Arts,** Washington International Arts Letters, 115 5th Street S.E.,
   Washington, D.C. 20003. (202) 488-0800.

Services

Foundation Center, 888 Seventh Avenue, New York City, with regional
   offices in Washington, D.C., San Francisco, Cleveland. The Center
   has information on almost every foundation in the country. For those
   unable to reach a center, they have compiled the *Foundation Directory,* Columbia University Press, 136 S. Broadway, Irvington-on-the-
   Hudson, N.Y. 10533.

Grant and Festival Sampling

AFI Independent Filmmaker Program Grants, American Film Institute,
   501 Doheny Road, Beverly Hills, CA. 90210.

Purpose: To nurture new talent in filmmaking, aid established artists to explore new directions in their work.

Grant: $500–$10,000 for total/partial production or completion of film (35mm, 16mm) or videotape to be produced within ninety days after grant awarded, completed within eighteen months.

Require: Synopsis of project, complete script (for dramatic), films/videotapes, or supporting materials as work samples, biography, personal goals, budget (20% maximum living stipend).

Judging: Preliminary review by professional filmmakers, final by committee, based on potential as filmmaker, technical competence, creative ability.

Film Fund Media Grants Program, The Film Fund, 80 East 11th Street, Suite 647, New York City 10003

Purpose: To support documentary and dramatic films, videotapes, slide shows that examine structure of modern society, take a hard look at social issues, are innovative in style/content, expand perception of what is real or possible, encourage activity rather than passivity; to create supportive community among independent Third World filmmakers, encourage new funding sources.

Grant: $25,000 maximum to individuals/organizations for pre-production, research, production, editing, or distribution of noncommercial, artistic, educational, or charitable films, videotapes, slide shows on social issues.

Require: Project proposal, budget, statement of purpose, sample work, interview of finalists. Request distribution/sales income to be used to pay back grant with interest.

Judging: Initial review by staff; further by selection panels of film/videomakers, distributors, exhibitors, community activists; final by board of directors.

ABC Theatre Award, National Playwrights Conference, Eugene O'Neill Theatre Center, 1860 Broadway, Suite 1012, New York City 10023

Purpose: Development of talented writers through opportunity to work on plays with professional theatre artists. Held at Eugene O'Neill Theatre Center, Waterford, Connecticut.

Awards: ABC Theatre Award, $10,000 cash and first option to TV rights by ABC-TV. $200 room, board, transportation to pre-conference weekend (reading of plays), and conference to accepted entrants. During conference authors rewrite plays, confer with dramaturges/story editors, rehearse actors, give two staged readings of play and videotape production of scripts. Possible full production during conference.

Require: Stage, any subject: original, unproduced, not currently optioned play. Television, any subject: original, unproduced, not currently optioned script or extended outline.

Judging: By theatre and television experts.

Ann Arbor Film Festival, P.O. Box 7283, Ann Arbor, MI. 48107. One hun-

dred films shown, thirty toured to seven colleges and nineteen theatres in recent year.

Awards: $4,000 total cash, plus $750 Berman Award to Most Promising
Filmmaker. $350 minimum awarded at each tour stop. $1 per minute
for theatrical screenings.

Require: Independent 16mm film, optical/silent. Entry fee.

Judging: Preliminary by committee, final by jury, based on creativity.

American Film Festival, Educational Film Library Association, 43 West
61st Street, New York City 10023. Considered to be the most comprehensive *nontheatrical* film festival. Held in NYC and as national
traveling exhibition to libraries, schools, universities.

Purpose: To promote production, distribution, utilization of films, audio-
visual materials in education, community programs.

Awards: $500 as well as other noncash awards.

Require: Nontheatrical 16mm film in various categories (e.g., performing
arts, language arts, human concerns, travel, health education, documentary feature 50–110 minutes). Entry fee.

Judging: Preliminary by regional committees of subject/film/utilization
specialists. Final judging during festival.

Schools

At one time, not too long ago, it was difficult to find a school where you
could study (let alone major in) film or theatre crafts; the only courses available were in acting. Today, there are literally thousands of colleges, universities, and professional schools offering courses in the diverse areas of film
and theatre. Many of these offer majors and graduate programs. You can
study technical production, design, criticism and aesthetics, arts management, directing, producing, history, playwrighting and screenwriting, education, and instructional technology. There are thousands upon thousands of
courses available for those who wish to learn via the academic route. For a
comprehensive listing of graduate and undergraduate courses in the world,
see the American Film Institute's *Guide to College Courses in Film and
TV* and the American Theatre Association's *Directory of American College
Theatre.* Also, for those interested in studying arts management, the University of Wisconsin-Madison Center for Arts Administration has compiled
*A Survey of Arts Administration Training in the United States and Can-
ada* (available through the American Council for the Arts, 570 Seventh
Ave., New York City 10018).

For those interested in short-term and nonmatriculated study, there are
professional schools as well as continuing education programs at colleges
and universities (e.g., NYU offers a six-week seminar on the role of the
producer in commercial theatre). You can find entire courses of study,
short-term programs, workshops, and seminars in specific areas of film and
theatre.

Below are listed a few of the most well-known and respected colleges in the country that offer degrees in the film and theatre disciplines, as well as a sampling of professional schools that offer specialized training on a short-term basis. But for a complete picture of what's available in education, read the above-mentioned guides, the education pages of newspapers, and the advertisements in the trade journals (particularly *Theatre Crafts*).

Colleges and Universities

Theatre Programs

Boston University offers:
> B.F.A. and M.F.A. in costume design, scenic design, and technical design
> B.F.A. in production
> M.F.A. in directing and theatre education
>
> For program information contact:
> Director
> School of Theatre Arts
> 855 Commonwealth Ave.
> Boston, MA. 02215

Columbia University offers:
> M.A., M.E.D., M.F.A., Ph.D. in directing, management, playwriting, history, and criticism of theatre
>
> For program information contact:
> The Center for Theatre Studies
> Columbia University
> 605 Dodge Hall
> New York, N.Y. 10027
> (212) 280-3408

North Carolina School of the Arts offers:
> B.F.A. in costume, scenic design, lighting design, technical production, and stage management
>
> For program information contact:
> Director of Admissions
> NCSA Box 12189
> Winston-Salem, N.C. 27101
> (919) 784-7170

Film Programs

New York University Film School offers:
> B.F.A., M.A., and Ph.D. in cinema studies

For information on graduate and undergraduate film criticism and aesthetics, history, and appreciation, contact:

Department of Cinema Studies—New York University
School of the Arts
51 West 4th Street
New York City 10003
(212) 598-7777

For information on undergraduate film production, writing, and TV study:

Undergraduate Institute of Film and TV—New York University
(212) 598-3701

or:

Graduate Institute of Film and TV
40 East 7th Street
New York City 10003
(212) 598-2416

University of Southern California offers:
B.A., M.A., M.F.A., M.S. in cinema
Ph.D. in communications-cinema
M.F.A. in professional writing
M.S. in film education

Peter Stark Motion Picture Producing Program at USC. (The first academic curriculum designed to turn out film and TV production executives and independent producers)

Contact:
University of Southern California
Division of Cinema
School of Performing Arts
University Park
Los Angeles, CA. 90007
(213) 741-2235

University of California, Los Angeles, offers:
B.A., M.F.A. in production and writing
B.A., M.A., Ph.D. in critical studies

Contact:
University of California, Los Angeles
Theatre Arts Department
405 Helgard Avenue
Los Angeles, CA. 90024
(213) 825-7891

Short-Term and Specialized Programs

For programs in dance lab analysis:
  The Dance Notation Bureau
  505 Eighth Avenue
  New York City 10018
  (212) 736-4350

For programs in the artist as therapist:
  School of Visual Arts
  209 East 23rd Street
  New York City 10010
  (212) 679-7350

For programs in design for the theatre (including costume, lighting, set, model making, research, drawing, etc.):
  Lester Polakov Studio and Forum of Stage Design, Inc.
  727 Washington Street (Bank Street)
  New York City 10014
  (212) WA 4-5035

For programs, workshops, and seminars in the art of filmmaking, write for brochures to:
  The American Film Institute
  Center for Advanced Film Studies
  501 Doheny Road
  Beverly Hills, CA. 90210

  Sherwood Oaks Experimental College
  6353 Hollywood Blvd.
  Hollywood, CA. 90028
  (213) 462-0669

  Women's Interart Center
  549 West 52nd Street
  New York City 10019
  (212) 246-1050

  New School for Social Research
  66 West 12th Street
  New York City 10011
  (212) 741-5625

  Division of Liberal Studies, School of Continuing Education
  New York University
  2 University Place, Room 21
  New York City 10003
  (212) 598-2371

  Master Lecture Series
  Astoria Motion Picture and Television Center
  34-31 35th Street
  Astoria, N.Y. 11106

Unions, Guilds, and Professional Associations

Whether and at what point to join a union, guild, or professional association is a question you will have to face sooner or later in your career. In some cases you will have to decide which union to join. The following should provide some food for thought.

Unions and guilds were originally created to protect workers and negotiate contracts. Generally speaking, unions represented so-called craftsmen, and guilds represented so-called artists. Professional associations in one way or another look after the interests of a particular group, be it management or otherwise. All of these unions, guilds, and professional associations do a great deal for their members (e.g., establish wage scales and working conditions, negotiate contracts, settle disputes and establish ground rules, work toward the passage of government bills beneficial to members, and provide fringe benefits such as health insurance). Each admits into its organization only those it deems worthy.

Unions, guilds, and associations do not find work for their members, but your chances of finding employment improve as a union member. Future employers feel more confident about your potential, your professional status is improved, you meet more people in a position to hire and/or recommend you for a job, and you'll have concentrated opportunities (at meetings and functions) to make friends and contacts within the industry.

Getting into professional associations is generally not difficult. Several associations allow nonprofessionals to enter as a subscribing or associate member. You pay less dues than active members and receive many of the same benefits (newsletters, seminars, workshops, libraries, career guidance, etc.). Contact the professional associations listed below that interest you and ask for their literature. If you can't find a listing here that is relevant to your interest, look through *The International Motion Picture Almanac.* Chances are you'll find one does exist.

Unions, on the other hand, are generally very difficult to get into. Admission requirements vary from one local to the other. Some require that you pass a lengthy exam, others that you are offered a job on a union project, and others again that you go through an apprenticeship program. In most cases, executive board and general membership approval is ultimately needed in order for you to be accepted. Admission information is best gotten directly from each local, but in some cases even this won't be an easy task. It is best to write down the questions you wish to ask and make certain you are 100 percent clear about the reply. If you are told an exam is given every three years, find out when the next one will be and where they will advertise the date. If there is any way for you to meet and ingratiate yourself with union members, do so and let it be known you wish to join their local. Ask their advice, show them you care and how good you are at your job.

Joining a union actually means joining a local of that union. A local is a (generally autonomous) chapter or branch of a larger international union with jurisdiction over a specific place and job, e.g., I.A. Local 1 represents New York stage carpenters, property men, and electricians. Entrance into one local does not necessarily mean entry into a sister local is assured. A person may belong to more than one union, although in some cases (e.g., NABET and the I.A.) membership is mutually exclusive. The same job might be unionized in one city and not unionized in another. It is best to contact the international office of the union to find out the specifics. All unions require an initiation fee, which varies greatly.

Many unions, guilds, and associations provide literature for aspirants. Some even provide career information booklets (e.g., American Cinema Editors, 422 Western Ave., Los Angeles, CA. 90020 publishes *Career Information on Film Editing*). Contact these organizations and ask them to send you any literature they might have that could be helpful to you: membership requirements, testing procedures, the organization itself; much can be learned from this kind of material.

Below is a listing of the major entertainment unions, guilds, and professional associations representing behind-the-scenes personnel. Once again, a thorough listing can be found in *The International Motion Picture Almanac* or the *Pacific Coast Studio Directory*.

Actors' Equity Association. In addition to representing all professional performers in the legitimate theatre, Equity represents stage managers. The union's jurisdiction extends to Broadway, Off Broadway, touring companies, stock, repertory theatre, industrial shows, dinner theatre, and theatre for young audiences. There are two ways of becoming an Equity stage manager: to be offered a job with an Equity company, or to participate in the Equity Membership Candidate Program, whereby you must work as an assistant to a stage manager (not as an ASM) in an Equity-approved stock theatre for fifty weeks, not necessarily consecutive. For further information and literature, contact:

(National Office), 165 West 46th Street, New York City 10036. (212) 719-9447.
(Chicago), 360 N. Michigan Ave., Chicago, Ill. 60601. (312) 641-0393.
(Hollywood) 6430 Sunset Blvd., Los Angeles, CA. 90028. (213) 462-2334.
(San Francisco), 465 California St., Suite 210, San Francisco, CA. 94104. (415) 781-8660.

American Dance Guild, Inc. This guild represents dance teachers across the country and operates a job express registry for members. Contact: American Dance Guild, Inc., 1133 Broadway, Room 1427, New York City 10010. (212) 694-7773.

American Federation of Musicians. This union represents (in addition to 320,000 musicians) arrangers, orchestrators, copyists, editors, librarians, and proofreaders in musical productions (theatrical and industrial), revues, dance units, symphonic orchestras, ballet troupes, opera companies, etc. There are 604 locals throughout the United States, Canada, Puerto Rico, and Guam. Contact: (National Office) 1500 Broadway, New York City 10036. (212) 869-1330. (California) Local 47, 817 North Vine Street, Hollywood, CA. 90038. (213) 468-2161.

American Guild of Authors and Composers (AGAC). A protective association run by and for songwriters. AGAC maintains Composers and Lyricists Educational Foundation (CLEF) to provide music scholarships to low-income and minority group students and to conduct seminars for instruction in the music business. Conducts ASKAPRO, a weekly session with record producers, publishers, lyricists, composers, etc., and aspiring music authors and composers. Also conducts workshops. Associate membership available. Contact: AGAC, 40 West 57th Street, New York City 10019. (212) 757-8833.

American Society of Composers, Authors and Publishers (ASCAP). Represents over 23,000 authors, composers, and publishers of music. For literature and information, contact: ASCAP, Lincoln Plaza, New York City 10023.

Artists Managers Guild. This guild is the official organization of artists' managers, representatives, and agents in Hollywood. Contact: Artists Managers Guild, 9255 Sunset Blvd., Suite 930, Los Angeles, CA. 90069. (213) 247-0628.

Association of Independent Video and Filmmakers (AIVF). The AIVF is a trade association open to independent film and videomakers and others interested in the production and promotion of independent video and film. Membership benefits are plentiful and include a monthly newsletter, *The Independent.* For further information, contact: AIVF, 625 Broadway, New York City 10012. (212) 473-3400.

Association of Motion Picture and TV Producers. A trade organization representing producers, production companies, and studios in labor negotiations. Contact: Association of Motion Picture and TV Producers, 8480 Beverly Blvd., Los Angeles, CA. 90048. (213) 651-0081.

Association for Theatre Press Agents and Managers (ATPAM). This union represents house managers, company managers, and press agents working in the legitimate theatre throughout the United States and Canada. Membership through an apprenticeship program. ATPAM administers the press agent apprenticeship program, and the League of New York Theatres and Producers, together with ATPAM, administers the house and company managers apprenticeship program. For further information, see Internships, and contact: ATPAM, 268 West 47th Street, New York City 10036. (212) 582-3750.

Broadcast Music Inc. (BMI). BMI represents songwriters and publishers. Contact: BMI, 320 West 57th Street, New York City 10019. (212) 586-2000.

Composers and Lyricists Guild of America. Union for composers working in film and television. Contact: 6565 Sunset Blvd., Hollywood, CA. 90028. (213) 462-6068

Directors Guild of America (DGA). The DGA negotiates minimum salaries and working conditions for directors, assistant directors, and unit production managers working in film (theatrical and nontheatrical), TV, and radio, as well as associate directors, stage managers, and production assistants in TV and tape. The DGA bargains with the producers' associations (representing the major motion picture companies), independents, networks, local stations, makers of commercials, producers of industrials and educational films. Its jurisdiction extends to all regions of the United States as well as American-financed productions overseas. Main office is in California; other offices in New York and Chicago. The DGA maintains an internship program. For further information, see *Internships,* and contact: DGA, National Office, 7950 Sunset Blvd., Hollywood, CA. 90046. (213) 656-1220. DGA, 110 West 57th Street, New York City 10019. (212) 581-0370. DGA, 40 E. Oak Street, Chicago, Ill. 60111. (312) 944-6040.

Dramatists Guild. The Dramatists Guild represents playwrights, composers, and lyricists throughout the United States. Three categories of membership are available: active members, associate members, and subscribing members. The last must be engaged in a drama-related field or simply a student or patron of the arts. Subscribing membership fee is approximately $15. In addition to protecting the rights of its members, the guild offers advice, symposia, workshops, a library, and the *Dramatists Guild Quarterly,* a magazine, plus the guild's monthly *Newsletter.* For further information, contact: The Dramatists Guild, 234 West 44th Street, New York City 10036. (212) 398-9366.

Foundation for the Extension and Development of the American Professional Theatre (FEDAPT). A consulting service for management personnel in nonprofit theatre. Contact: FEDAPT, 165 West 46th Street, New York City 10036. (212) 869-9690.

International Brotherhood of Electrical Workers (IBEW). IBEW is a huge organization with some 1,500 locals, only 85 of which represent technicians working in the broadcast, recording, and cable television industries. IBEW represents the technicians at CBS network and some 300–400 independent television stations and cable systems throughout the country. Their members are not filmmakers and only occasionally get involved with production activities. For further information on entrance requirements, apprenticeships, etc., contact: IBEW, attention Broadcast and Recording Dept., or attention Cable TV Dept., 1125 15th Street, N.W., Washington, D.C. 20005. (202) 833-7000.

International Alliance of Theatrical Stage Employees and Moving Picture Machine Operators of the United States and Canada (IATSE, pronounced Yatsee, a.k.a. the I.A.). The I.A. is the largest entertainment union, comprised of over nine hundred locals representing film and theatre artists, cameramen, cartoonists, costumers, editors, electricians, grips, laboratory technicians, make-up artists and hairstylists, moving picture machine operators, motion picture assistant directors and script clerks, production designers, production office coordinators and accountants, projectionists, property men and makers, publicists, scenic and title artists, script supervisors, set designers and model makers, set painters, sound technicians, special effects, story analysts, stage carpenters, studio mechanics, studio teachers, television film costume designers, treasurers and ticket sellers, theatrical wardrobe attendants, ushers, and others. Specific admission information must be sought from the locals, but generally speaking, they do give tests (general knowledge) every three years, and those who pass are placed on an apprentice list and must work enough to gross a set amount each year for three years to gain experience. Apprentices who meet these requirements are placed on an admissions list. The names on the list go into a hat and each month five new members are taken in from a draw. It can take years before your name "comes up," and certain locals have been accused of pushing the names of their relatives up front. For further information, contact the national office, IATSE, 1515 Broadway, New York City 10036. (212) 730-1770. Ask for a copy of the *Official Bulletin* containing names and addresses of the business agents of each local, or contact one of the locals located in New York and Los Angeles below:

New York—area code (212)

Local 1—Represents stage carpenters, property men, and electricians, 1775 Broadway, N.Y.C. 10019. 489-7710.

Local 52—Represents studio mechanics, 221 West 57th Street, N.Y.C. 10019. 765-0741.

Local 161—Represents script supervisors and production office coordinators, 251 East 50th Street, N.Y.C. 10022. 686-7724.

Local 304—Represents film projectionists and audio-visual workers, 745 Seventh Ave., N.Y.C. 10019. 586-4018.

Local 644—Represents cameramen, 250 West 57th Street, Suite 1723, N.Y.C. 10019. 247-3860.

Local 702—Represents lab technicians, 165 West 46th Street, N.Y.C. 10036. 757-5540.

Local 751—Represents treasurers and ticket sellers, 227 West 45th Street, Room 213, N.Y.C. 10036. 245-7186.

Local 764—Represents theatrical wardrobe attendants, 1501 Broadway, Room 1604, N.Y.C. 10036. 221-1717.

Local 771—Represents film editors, 630 Ninth Ave., N.Y.C. 10036. 581-0771.

Local 798—Represents make-up artists and hairstylists, 1790 Broadway, N.Y.C. 10019. 757-9120.

Local 818—see L.A. locals; 125 East 23rd Street, N.Y.C. 10010. 477-0719.

Local 841—Represents screen cartoonists, 25 West 43rd Street, N.Y.C. 10036. 354-6410.

Los Angeles—area code (213)

Local 33—Represents stage carpenters, property men, and electricians, 4605 Lankershim Blvd., Suite 833, N. Hollywood, CA. 91602. 985-0633.

Local 44—Represents motion picture studio property men, swing gang men, nurserymen, set dressers, propmakers, upholsterers, prop miniature men, drapers, and special effects men, 7429 Sunset Blvd., Hollywood, CA. 90046. 876-2328.

Local 80—Represents studio grips, 6926 Melrose Ave., Hollywood, CA. 90038. 931-1419.

Local 165—Represents motion picture studio projectionists, moving picture machine operators, 6640 Sunset Blvd., Hollywood, CA. 90028. 461-2985.

Local 659—Represents cameramen, 7715 Sunset Blvd., Hollywood, CA. 90046. 876-0160.

Local 683—Represents laboratory technicians, 6721 Melrose Ave., Hollywood, CA. 90038. 935-1123.

Local 695—Represents sound technicians, 15840 Ventura Blvd., Suite 303, Encino, CA. 91436. 842-0452.

Local 705—Represents motion picture costumers, 14 North La Brea Ave., Hollywood, CA. 90028. 851-0220.

Local 706—Represents make-up artists and hairstylists, 11519 Chandler Blvd., Hollywood, CA. 91601. 877-2776.

Local 717—Production Office Coordinators and Accountants Guild, 7715 Sunset Blvd., Hollywood, CA. 90046. 843-6000.

Local 727—Represents motion picture crafts services, 12754 Ventura Blvd., N. Hollywood, CA. 91604. 877-0541.

Local 728—Represents motion picture studio chief set electricians, floormen, lamp operators, and all persons employed on electrical apparatus used in the making and taking of motion and still pictures, 3400 Barham Blvd., Hollywood, CA. 90068. 851-3300.

Local 729—Represents motion picture set painters, 11650 Riverside Drive, N. Hollywood, CA. 91602. 984-3000.

Local 767—Represents first aid employees, 8736 Swinton Ave., Sepulveda, CA. 91343.

Local 768—Represents theatrical wardrobe attendants, 5909 Melrose Ave., Hollywood, CA. 90038. 467-3862.

Local 776—Represents film editors, 7715 Sunset Blvd., Hollywood, CA. 90046. 876-4770.

Local 790—Represents motion picture studio art craftsmen, 7715 Sunset Blvd., Hollywood, CA. 90046. 876-2010.

Local 816—Represents scenic artists, 7429 Sunset Blvd., Hollywood, CA. 90046. 876-1440.

Local 818—Represents unit publicists and publicists who work in PR agencies throughout the United States, 1427 N. La Brea Ave., Hollywood, CA. 90028. 851-1600.

Local 839—Represents screen cartoonists, 12441 Ventura Blvd., Studio City, CA. 91604. 766-7151.

Local 847—Represents set designers and model makers, 7715 Sunset Blvd., Suite 210, Hollywood, CA. 90046. 876-2010.

Local 854—Represents story analysts, 7715 Sunset Blvd., Hollywood, CA. 90046. 876-1600.

Local 857—Represents treasurers and ticket sellers, 6513 Hollywood Blvd., Room 204, Hollywood, CA. 90028. 464-2846.

Local 871—Represents script supervisors, 7715 Sunset Blvd., Hollywood, CA. 90046. 876-4433.

Local 876—Represents art directors, 7715 Sunset Blvd., Hollywood, CA. 90046. 876-4330.

Local 884—Represents motion picture studio teachers and welfare workers. 334 N. Cordova, Burbank, CA. 91505. 553-2786.

Local 892—Costume designers guild, 1420 S. Mansfield, Los Angeles, CA. 90019. 397-3162.

League of New York Theatres and Producers. Represents Broadway producers and owners. The league implements the collective bargaining agreements, widens theatre audiences, conducts marketing studies, and in general acts as a support group for Broadway theatre producers and owners. It also co-administers an apprenticeship program for company and house managers (see *Internships*). For information, contact: League of N.Y. Theatres and Producers, 226 West 47th Street, New York City 10036. (212) 582-4455.

Motion Picture Association of America, Inc. (MPAA). A trade association of the larger motion picture production and distribution companies whose aim it is to look after the interests of the motion picture industry. They maintain an office in Washington for this purpose. Contact: MPAA, 522 Fifth Avenue, New York City 10036. (212) 840-6161.

National Academy of Television Arts and Sciences (NATAS). College students with an interest may become student affiliate members of the NATAS and attend special events twice a month and meet television professionals. Contact: NATAS, 110 West 57th Street, New York City 10019. (212) 765-2450.

National Association of Broadcast Employees and Technicians (NABET). NABET consists of forty-five local unions across the country representing film and tape personnel, broadcast technicians, newswriters. Of the forty-five locals, five represent film and tape personnel and are in direct competition with the I.A. for members. The five film and tape locals are a.k.a. the Association of Film Craftsmen, and represent the same job categories as do the I.A. (i.e., camera, sound, electric, grip, hair, make-up, wardrobe, carpentry, script clerks, etc.). However, NABET's structure is different from that of the I.A. Also, the size is different; the I.A. is approximately four times the size of NABET. All tape- and film-related jobs are represented by the same local in the area. For instance, Local 15 represents all film and tape personnel in New York.

NABET prides itself on being an "open" union, and in fact was originally started in the 1950s in response to the closed-door policy of the I.A. Even today, it is much easier to gain entry into NABET (perhaps because the I.A. tradition of nepotism has not yet taken hold). To join in New York you must pass an exam and be sponsored by a member. Although the NABET locals do enter into contracts with feature film producers, the union's primary strength lies in commercial and other nontheatrical film and tape production and the networks. For further information, contact: NABET Local 15, 1776 Broadway, Suite 1900, New York City 10019. (212) 265-3500; NA-

BET Local 531, 1800 Argyle, Los Angeles, CA. 90028. (213) 462-7485; or the international headquarters, NABET, 80 East Jackson Blvd., Chicago, Ill. 60604. (312) 922-2462.

National Association of Performing Arts Managers (NAPAMA). An association of managers of classical musicians. They are planning a project for would-be managers. Contact: NAPAMA, 1860 Broadway, Suite 1610, New York City 10023. (212) 582-5792.

Screen Publicists Guild. Represents publicists who work directly for the New York home offices of the film studios (e.g., Columbia, Paramount). They do on occasion get requests from the studios for trainee publicists. Contact: Screen Publicists Guild, 13 Astor Place, New York City 10003.

Society of Motion Picture and Television Engineers (SMPTE). SMPTE is a professional organization dedicated to advancing the engineering and technical aspects of the motion picture, television, and allied arts and sciences. College students may become members if recommended by an SMPTE member or faculty member of the applicant's school. Student members may attend monthly local chapter meetings and national conferences, and receive the SMPTE *Journal* and *News & Notes.* Contact: SMPTE, 862 Scarsdale Avenue, Scarsdale, N.Y. 10583. (914) 472-6606.

Society of Stage Directors and Choreographers (SSDC). SSDC is an independent national labor union, which represents directors and choreographers in every major sector of the legitimate theatre. SSDC's jurisdiction extends to Broadway, national tours, Off Broadway, resident theatres, stock and dinner theatre. SSDC protects the integrity of the directors' and choreographers' work, their royalties, and their artistic rights in all areas of professional theatre. The union sets minimum wage and benefit scales for directors and choreographers working in Broadway, Off Broadway, Off Off Broadway, LORT, COST, and stock theatres.

United Scenic Artists, Local 829. USA Local 829 is an autonomous local of the Brotherhood of Painters and Allied Trades. The only other local affiliated with the brotherhood is Local 350, in Chicago. USA Local 829 has labor jurisdiction over scenic designers, art directors, scenic artists, costume designers, and lighting designers in theatre, opera, ballet, motion pictures, television, and industrial shows. Entrance to the local is achieved through an extensive exam given annually, for which a fee is charged; generally, the exam is given in late May or June. Prerequisites for membership include extensive knowledge and an ability to organize and to execute projects, as well as the practical experience of mounting a production for stage or camera. The exam consists of an interview, home project, and a practical. All applicants are interviewed, and their portfolios and professional experience graded. The practical exam tests the applicant's skills (design ability, drafting, sketching, color and use of light, knowledge of fabric, form and line perception, layout and painting) under pressure of severe time limitation; many designers take it over and over before they pass. Since the interview is conducted by a panel of prominent craftsmen, the smart applicant can learn from the portfolio evaluation. The full membership category is being phased out, so that applicants now take an exam only in the category of their major interest and are authorized to work within that particular area only. The person may take other exams to qualify to work in additional areas. Initiation fees vary. For further information, contact: USA Local 829, 1540 Broadway, New York City 10036. (212) 575-5120; USA Local 350, 343 South Dearborn Street, Chicago, Ill. 60604. (312) 431-0790. In Los Angeles, the parallel locals are I.A. Local 816 and 876.

Writers Guild of America (WGA). The Writers Guild is a labor union formed to represent writers in motion pictures, television, and radio. To join, you must have a contract or letter of agreement from a producer. Due to differing corporation laws in New York and California, the guild is organized as the Writers Guild of America, East, and the Writers Guild of America, West. The Mississippi River serves as a dividing line. Twice a year a national council meeting is held to coordinate policy and action and to keep a common purpose in spite of the different labor markets and the distance between headquarters. The total membership of WGA, East, is approximately 2.500; of WGA, West, approximately 4,500. The guild is in effect a single organization, and membership is on a national basis, carrying with it the benefits and privileges of a national organization. Since 1954, the WGA has negotiated with major film producers and broadcasting networks and stations, covering theatrical and television films, live and tape TV, documentary film and radio. WGA East and West offer a registration service for members and non-members. For a nominal fee you may register scripts, outlines, formats or ideas with the guild. This registration is in case of future dispute over who had the idea first. The newsletter of WGA, West, reports on current job information. For further information, see *Theatre- and Film-Related Publications,* and contact: WGA, East, 22 West 48th Street, New York City 10036. (212) 575-5060; WGA, West, 8955 Beverly Blvd., Los Angeles, CA. 90048. (213) 550-1000.

Theatre- and Film-Related Publications

There are books, directories, magazines, newspapers, newsletters, and pamphlets published that are advantageous for you to read—some because they teach skills, others because they keep you informed and aware of trends, and others again because they provide practical advice and career-related information. A "how-to" book has been written for just about every job in show business. A few of these are listed below, but for a comprehensive look at what is available, consult the subject index at your library, the film and theatre sections of general bookstores, and the bookstores and libraries specializing in film and theatre literature. The specialized bookstores publish catalogues of available books. If you are unable to reach one of them in person, write and ask for their suggestions. In most cases they will do business via the mail.

It is a good idea to read the newspapers and periodicals read by those you wish to work with. You will find a list of most of those below. It is also a good idea to read the *New York* and *Los Angeles Times*, choosing the most pertinent articles. In addition to articles and interviews, newspapers and periodicals provide you with film and theatre book reviews, festival and grant notices, production schedules, news of new equipment and school programs, and, most important, in their classified sections and elsewhere, job opportunities.

The directories are meant to be used as a reference tool. If you are just starting out, use them to learn the names and addresses of potential employees. If you are already working, consult them for your various jobs; it is important that you know they exist. The more you know, the more employable you are. The more you read, the more you'll know. Following is a list of books, directories, and periodicals that cover the industry, and the bookstores and libraries where they can be found. Become familiar with these and other materials you are introduced to and you will learn much about show business.

Books

Herman Buchman. *Film and Television Make-up*; also *Stage Make-up*. New York: Watson Guptill Publications. Guides for the make-up artist.

Bert Gruver. Revised by Frank Hamilton. *The Stage Managers Handbook*. New York: Drama Book Specialists. A how-to book for would-be stage managers.

Stephen Langley. *Producers on Producing*. New York: Drama Book Specialists. A collection of commentaries by two dozen theatrical leaders in the areas of grass roots theatre, educational theatre, regional theatre, Off and Off Off Broadway theatre, Broadway, cultural centers, and government agencies.

Terence St. John Marner. *Film Design*. London: Screen Textbooks. A guide for art directors, set designers, and others interested in this area.

James Monaco. *American Film Now, The People, The Power, The Money, The Movies*. New York: Oxford University Press. A good book about contemporary American filmmaking.

Motley. *Designing and Making Stage Costumes*. New York: Watson Guptill Publications. A guide for costume designers.

Danny Newman. *Subscribe Now*. New York: Theatre Communications Group. A how-to for audience developers in not-for-profit theatre.

Karel Reisz and Gavin Millar. *The Technique of Film Editing*. London: Focal Press. Considered to be the classic textbook on film editing.

Ralph Rosenblum and Robert Karen. *When the Shooting Stops . . . the Cutting Begins*. New York: The Viking Press. An inside look at what goes

on in the cutting room. More conceptual than technical, with entertaining "show biz" stories.

Directories

Available at most libraries and specialized bookstores:

Audiovisual Market Place: A Multimedia Guide, New York: R. R. Bowker
    Co. Annual. A directory for the audio-visual industry (education and
    industrial). Covers producers, distributors, production companies, and
    related associations.

Back Stage TV Film Tape and Syndication Directory, California: Back
    Stage Productions. Annual. Arranged by geographical regions.

Broadcasting Cable Sourcebook, Washington, D.C.: Broadcasting Publica-
    tions. Annual. A comprehensive resource for the cable television
    industry.

Film Daily Year Book, New York: Film Daily. Directory of motion picture
    companies, services, and personnel.

Guide to Film and Video Resources, ed. Abigail Nelson, Cambridge, MA:
    University Film Study Center. Includes listings of film and video pro-
    duction companies and their policies on hiring free lancers.

International Motion Picture Almanac, New York: Quigley Publishing Co.
    Annual. A major reference book for the film industry. Includes 4,500
    biographies, the corporate structure of companies, lists of producers
    and distributors, services, agents, organizations, unions, the world
    market, the press. Comprehensive and accurate. The almanac is cor-
    rected and updated each year, running some 700 pages, and found in
    most libraries. An important reference book for those looking for a
    job.

Pacific Coast Studio Directory, Hollywood, CA. Quarterly. Lists production
    companies, representatives and/or agents, unions, guilds, organiza-
    tions, and associations connected with theatrical and nontheatrical
    film and video industries. Covers seven Western states and British
    Columbia. See *Periodicals* below.

Theatre Profiles, New York: Theatre Communications Group. A resource
    book of not-for-profit professional theatres in the United States.

Theatrical Index, A major reference tool. See *Periodicals*.

Newspapers and Periodicals

If not at your local newsstand, contact publishers for availability and cost:

Action. Published bi-monthly by the Directors Guild of America, 1516
    Westwood Boulevard, Suite 102, Los Angeles, CA. 90024. Covers film
    and television news relevant to guild members and entertainment
    business professionals (i.e., agents, production managers).

AFI Factfile. Published by the National Education Services Publications,

American Film Institute, John F. Kennedy Center for the Performing Arts, Washington, D.C. 20566. A series of periodically updated documents on various topics (film music, animation, Third World cinema). Write for list of subjects.

The Alpha Viewfinder. Published quarterly by Alpha Cine Laboratory, 1001 Lenora Street, Seattle, WA. 98121. Free. Includes classified for jobs available and jobs wanted in the motion picture and audio-visual industries.

American Cinematographer. Published monthly by the American Society of Cinematographers, 1782 N. Orange Drive, Hollywood, CA. 90028. Written for those in professional motion picture and TV industry responsible for producing 16mm and 35mm films and for purchasing equipment. Articles relevant for people working in television, film, industrial film, motion picture laboratories, sound studios, etc. A current film, feature, documentary, or industrial is highlighted in each issue. Interviews with technical personnel; reviews of equipment and books.

American Cinemeditor. Published quarterly by the American Cinema Editors, 422 South Western Avenue, Los Angeles, CA. 90020. Free. Articles on film editing and related film news.

American Film, Magazine of the Film and Television Arts. Published monthly by the American Film Institute, John F. Kennedy Center for the Performing Arts, Washington, D.C. 20566. News, features, periodical reviews, interviews with the pros. Regular feature is "Dialogue on Film" seminar between the Fellows of the AFI Center for Advanced Film Studies and prominent film and television personalities.

Back Stage. Published weekly by Back Stage Publications, 165 West 46th Street, New York City 10023. (212) 581-1080. *Back Stage* newspaper is edited for the entire communications entertainment industry. Includes relevant news and career information for behind-the-scenes personnel. "Staff and Tech" column lists openings for technical directors, costumers, set designers, etc. A must.

Daily Variety. Published daily except Sat., Sun., and holidays by Daily Variety Ltd., 1400 N. Cahuenga Blvd., Hollywood, CA. 90028. (213) 469-1141. *Daily Variety* endeavors to provide complete objective news as well as news analysis of the entertainment business—motion pictures, TV, radio, theatre, nightclubs, music, and related enterprises. Coverage is local, national, and international. Lists job availabilities in motion pictures. Referred to as the bible—a must.

Dance Magazine. Published monthly by Danard Publishing Co., Inc., 10 Columbus Circle, New York City 10019. Articles and news of all areas of dance, edited for professional dance people and dance buffs. Often includes info on alternative careers for dancers.

Film Comment. Published bi-monthly by the Film Society of Lincoln Center, Film Comment, 140 West 65th Street, New York City 10023. A good magazine for film buffs.

Filmmakers Monthly. Published monthly from P.O. Box 115, Ward Hill,

MA. 08130. A magazine for those involved in feature film and video independent production, business, educational, and instructional media. Articles on production, interviews with directors and cameramen, festivals, etc. "Bulletin Board" section announces jobs wanted and jobs available.

Film Quarterly. Published by the University of California Press, Berkeley, CA. 94720. Articles, interviews, and in-depth reviews of films for film buffs.

The Hollywood Reporter. Published daily except Sat., Sun., and holidays by the Hollywood Reporter, 6715 Sunset Blvd., Hollywood, CA. 90028. (213) 464-7411. *The Hollywood Reporter* provides national and international coverage of the entertainment industry. Includes a help wanted column. A must.

The Independent. Published by the Foundation for Video and Film, 625 Broadway, New York City 10012. This newsletter reports on everything of interest to the independent filmmaker. Includes "Opportunities/Gigs/Apprenticeships," where positions available for independent film- and videomakers are listed.

Millimeter. Published monthly by Millimeter Magazine, Inc., 12 East 46th Street, New York City 10017. *Millimeter* covers theatrical motion pictures, broadcast TV, and TV commercials. Issues contain feature stories on current projects of directors, producers, cinematographers, editors, and other production technicians in the film and video fields. Columns spotlight current events in New York, Chicago, and California.

On Location. Published bi-monthly from 6311 Romaine, Hollywood, CA. 90038. Reports the experience of film and tape production while on location. Interviews with filmmakers.

Pacific Coast Studio Directory. Published quarterly from 6331 Hollywood Blvd., Hollywood, CA. 90028. A major reference tool—see *Directories*.

Ross Reports Television. Published monthly by Television Index, 150 Fifth Avenue, New York City 10011. Detailed information on script and casting requirements of continuing television programs, including how and when to submit work.

ScriptWriter Magazine for Entertainment Writers. Published monthly by ScriptWriter News, Inc., 250 West 57th Street, Suite 1432, New York City 10019. News and feature articles on the entertainment industry edited for entertainment writers. Includes in-depth interviews with the pros, hints on selling your work, what's been sold to whom, etc.

Show Business. Published weekly by Leo Shull Publications, 134 West 44th Street, New York City 10036. (212) 586-6900. *Show Business* newspaper is edited for show business people in various crafts: performers, producers, technicians, costumers, designers, directors, investors. Publishes lists of agents, names of shows and pictures in production with name of production manager and/or stage manager. Must read.

SMPTE Journal. Published monthly by the Society of Motion Picture and

Television Engineers, 862 Scarsdale Avenue, Scarsdale, N.Y. 10583. (914) 472-6606. *SMPTE Journal* is edited for executives and professional engineers and others in motion pictures, TV, and related fields. Articles cover the motion picture and television aspects of broadcasting, cameras, cinematography, color, data processing, film and tape editing, lighting, optics, photographic theory, production, news of products, developments, and activities. Jobs listed.

Super-8 Filmmaker. Published eight times a year from P.O. Box 10052, Palo Alto, CA. 94303. Technical information for those beginning to make their own films with super-8 equipment—includes buying guides, how-to columns.

Take One. Published monthly from Box 1778, Station B, Montreal, Quebec, Canada, H3B 3L3. Interviews with filmmakers, reviews, and surveys.

Theatre Communications (formerly the *TCG Newsletter*). Published monthly by Theatre Communications Group, Inc., 355 Lexington Ave., New York City 10017. A digest of not-for-profit theatre activities throughout the country. Includes monthly production schedules, articles relating to theatre and the arts in general. The "Callboard" section provides classified listings of positions available, positions sought, new publications, and training opportunities.

Theatre Crafts. Published seven times a year by Rodale Press, 250 West 57th Street, New York City 10036. (212) 582-4110. *Theatre Crafts* magazine reports on current developments in lighting, sound, set design, costuming, make-up, and administration for various types of theatrical productions. Often includes news for the behind-the-scenes up and comer—grants, internships, career guidance, union information, training, etc.

Theatrical Index. Published weekly by Price Berkley, 888 Eighth Ave., New York City 10019. (212) 586-6343. The *Index* is a comprehensive and accurate weekly publication, which is used on a regular basis by most of the people and firms in the entertainment industry who wish to be fed advance theatre information (i.e., film and individual entertainers) and kept abreast of the New York theatre scene. It includes listings of current Broadway, Off Broadway, and some regional shows, those in preview, those trying out, those in rehearsal, those set to open in the future. The listings supply the producer's and general manager's name, address, and telephone, staff, cast when known, press and advertising agency, and other up-to-date info. The *Index* is invaluable to anyone looking for a job in theatre. Single copies and subscriptions available through the publisher.

(Weekly) Variety. Published by Variety Inc., 154 West 46th Street, New York City 10036. (212) 582-2700. *(Weekly) Variety* is edited for those in the entertainment, broadcast, and advertising professions. It reports on and critically reviews films, stage, café, opera, ballet, and arena performances. Special issues include anniversary, international film, radio-TV reviews and previews, Canadian, auditorium-arena, international TV. A must.

View. Published monthly by Macro Communications Corp., 150 East 58th Street, New York City 10022. (212) 826-4360. A magazine edited for those working in the cable TV industry.

WGA, West, Newsletter. Published by Writers Guild, West, 8955 Beverly Blvd., Los Angeles, CA. 90048. (213) 550-1000. *WGA Newsletter* reports on jobs and current information regarding jobs, residuals, awards, and other news of interest to writers. Each issue includes the TV Market—a list of TV series that are open to submissions, written in-house only, or accept material through agents only. Professional typing and duplicating services for writers in the L.A. area are listed.

Bookstores That Specialize in Books on Theatre and Film

New York

The Drama Book Shop, 150 West 52nd Street, New York City 10019. (212) 582-1037. *The* source for plays, scripts, books, periodicals, vocal scores connected with the performing arts in New York or anywhere. If they don't stock the book or script you need, they'll find it for you. Books on all performing arts topics, including theatre, film, circus, opera, ballet, crafts, books imported from Europe, biographies, research material. They even keep chairs around for those wishing to browse through a book or script on the premises. Cooperative staff.

Cinemabilia, 10 West 13th Street, New York City 10011. (212) 989-8519. The largest film bookstore on the East Coast, stocks film and theatre books. Maintains a catalogue covering all phases of film—i.e., history, criticism, film personalities, technique, and crafts. Also souvenir programs, posters, etc.

California

Larry Edmunds Book Store, 6658 Hollywood Blvd., Hollywood, CA. 90028. (213) 463-3273. The largest film and theatre bookstore on the West Coast. Books and periodicals on all phases of show business. They publish a catalogue.

Birns & Sawyer, 1026 North Highland Ave., Hollywood, CA. 90038. (213) 466-8211. A film equipment supplier that operates a book division it calls "The Book Nook." Stocks a huge amount of film books.

Libraries and Study Centers That Specialize in Theatre and Film Material

Academy of Motion Picture Arts and Sciences, The Margaret Herrick Library, 8949 Wilshire Blvd., Beverly Hills, CA. 90211. (213) 278-4313. Books and periodicals on film and television (production, biography, general subjects). Stills collection. Scripts and historical manuscript collection. The *National Film Information Service* of the library offers mail access to its research holdings. Nominal fee for research assistance, preparation of research guides, and copies of stills.

American Film Institute, Charles K. Feldman Library, Center for Advanced Film Studies, 501 Doheny Road, Beverly Hills, CA. 90210. (213) 278-8777. The Feldman Library offers books and periodicals on film, clipping files on films and personalities, a film festival file, archival collections of scripts and stills, transcripts of AFI seminars. Mail and telephone reference service.

American Film Institute, National Education Service and the Kennedy Center Reference Collection, Kennedy Center, Washington, D.C., 20566. (202) 933-8300. Books and periodicals on the performing arts. Stills collection. Mail and telephone reference. Nominal fee for copying stills and print material.

Anthology Film Archives, 80 Wooster Street, New York City 10012. (212) 226-0010. Books and periodicals. Specializes in avant-garde films and film history.

Center for Arts Information. This organization serves as a clearinghouse of information for and about the arts in New York State. It is equipped with a library of over 4,000 reference books, pamphlets, and directories. The Center offers special information and referral services for independent film- and videomakers. In addition, it publishes directories and other management aids.

International Museum of Photography at George Eastman House, Film Department Archives, 900 East Ave., Rochester, N.Y. 14607. (716) 271-3361. Books and periodicals on cinematography. Stills collection.

Library of Congress, Motion Picture Section, Thomas Jefferson Building, Room 1046, Washington, D.C., 20540. (202) 426-5840. Reading room open to public. Books and early periodicals. Film collection of over 50,000 titles, including films produced before 1915.

Museum of Modern Art Film Study Center, Museum Library, 11 West 53rd Street, 10019. (212) 956-7236. Books and periodicals on various film topics, with emphasis on early motion picture history.

New York Public Library—Lincoln Center, 111 Amsterdam Avenue, New York City 10023. (212) 930-0800. Books and periodicals on film and theatre, television, and other arts. Clipping files, archival collections of scrapbooks, personal papers. Scripts. Stills collection. Telephone and mail reference service.

Northwest Film Study Center, Portland Art Museum, Southwest Park and Madison, Portland, OR. 97205. (503) 226-2811. Books and periodicals. Interviews with filmmakers on tape and in transcript form. Telephone and mail reference service.

University Film Study Center, Massachusetts Institute of Technology, 18 Vassar Street, Room 120, Cambridge, MA. 02139. (617) 253-7612. Books and periodicals, clippings file, festival information, scripts of U.S. films. Telephone and mail reference service.

University of California—Los Angeles, Theatre Arts Library, University

Research Library, 405 Hilgard Avenue, Los Angeles, CA. 90024. (213) 825-4880. Books and periodicals, clipping files, festival information, stills collection, television and film scripts, oral histories.

University of Southern California, Department of Special Collections, Doheny Library, University Park, Los Angeles, CA. 90007. (213) 741-6058. Books and periodicals, private papers collection, production files, clippings, scripts and stills, taped interviews, and oral histories.

Wisconsin Center for Film and Theatre Research, The State Historical Society of Wisconsin, 816 State Street, Madison, WI. 53706. (608) 262-0585. Books, periodicals, original manuscripts, archival materials, scripts, stills, film collection.

Index

accountants:
  general, 33
  production, 33
account executives, 161
Ackerman, Robert Allan, 89–97
  advice given by, 97
  background of, 91–92
  on casting, 96
  as theatre director, 89–90, 92–97
Atherton, William, 95
acquisitions departments, in studios,
    33
Actors' Equity, 16, 161
Actor's Fund Drive, 28
Adler, Stella, 7
administration departments in studios,
    33–34
administrators, 23–61, 197–200
  function of, 23
  job descriptions of, 25–35
  profiles of, 35–61
advance managers, 129–130
advertising agencies, 161
advertising departments, in studios,
    33–34, 161
agents, 80, 81, 89, 161
  profiles of, 173–177
Albee, Edward, 55
Alexander, Jane, 4
Allen, Woody, 65, 131, 135, 136, 137,
    139, 140, 151
American Dance Therapy Association,
    162
American Zoetrope, 6
"angels," 7

animal specialists, 162
animation cameramen, 109
animation designer, 109
animation editors, 109
animators, 109–110
Annie Hall, 131, 135–136, 139, 140,
    150
Apocalypse Now, 168
apprentice editors, 116, 117, 118–119
  profiles of, 133–135
apprentice treasurers, 25
Arena Stage (Washington, D.C.), 14
Aronovitch, Ricardo, 104
arrangers, 66
art directors (film), 70, 110
  assistant, 110
art directors (graphics), 161
Arthur, 131, 137, 151
artistic directors, 65
  profiles of, 72–77
artists, 110
Artists Agency, The, 173, 176
artists-in-residence, 163
arts centers, 15
arts council jobs, 162–163
arts experts, 164
arts-in-education, 163
arts managers, 25, 28
arts service organization jobs, 163
art therapists, 162
assistant art directors, 110
assistant camera operators:
  first (follow-focus), 111
  second (loaders), 111
assistant carpenters, 111, 112

assistant costume designers, 113–114
assistant directors (ADs):
    first, 67–68
    second and third, 68
assistant directors of audience devel-
    opment, 26
assistant directors of funding and de-
    velopment, 26
assistant editors, 116, 117, 118
    profiles of, 135–137
assistant lighting designers, 122
assistant make-up artists, 122
assistant special effects persons, 128
assistant stage managers (ASMs), 66,
    128, 129
assistant treasurers, 25
assistant unit production managers,
    30, 31
associate directors, 67
associate producers, profiles of, 82–89
Atlantic Monthly, The, 180
Atlantic Records, 48
auditions, 96
auteurs, 65
Avon Books, 80
Azure Productions, 102

Babe, Thomas, 95
background artists, 109
ballet masters, 115
Barr, Richard, 55
Bent, 95
Benton, Robert, 4, 87
Bergman, Ingmar, 65
Berkshire Theatre Festival, 95
Bertolucci, Bernardo, 139, 140
Best Boy, 20
best boys, 118, 120
*Best Little Whorehouse in Texas,
    The*, 7
Bloomgarden, Kermit, 93–94
body make-up artists, 122
Bolles, Richard Nelson, 189
bookers, 171
booking directors, 31
bookkeepers, 26
books, film- and theatre-related, 237–
    238

bookstores specializing in theatre and
    films, 242
boom operators, 126, 127
Bourne, Mel, 137–142
    advice given by, 141–142
    background of, 139
    as production designer, 137–142
box-office personnel, 25
breakdowns, 117, 119
Brickman, Marshall, 137
Broadway, 95
Broadway theatre, 11, 12, 14
Burstyn, Ellen, 59–60
business affairs departments, in stu-
    dios, 34
business affairs experts, 34
    profiles of, 45–51
business agents, 172
business film, *see* industrial film
Butch Cassidy and the Sundance Kid,
    176
buyers, 114, 124

cablemen, 126, 127
cable television, 89
cameramen, 111, 115–116
    animation, 109
camera operators, 110–111
    first assistant (follow-focus), 111
    profiles of, 147, 149–151
    second assistant (loaders), 111
camera supply house employees, 163–
    164
    repairmen, 163
    salespeople, 163–164
Carlino, Lewis John, 60
carpenters, 111–112
    assistant, 111, 112
    key, 111, 112
    master, 111
    production, 111–112
Carroll, Vinnette, 72–77
    as actress, 74, 75–76
    advice given by, 76–77
    as artistic director, 72, 75–77
    background of, 72–74
    ghetto program headed by, 74–75
Cassavetes, John, 151

cassettes, 6
casting assistants, 65
casting consultants, 65
casting directors, 65, 96
chargemen, 125
checkers, 109
chief executive officers (CEOs), 32
chief re-recording mixers, 126, 127
children's theatre, 17–18
choreographers, 65–66
cinematographers, 113, 115–116
clappers, 111, 113
Clurman, Harold, 7
Cobb, Lee J., 7
cobblers, 115
Cohen, Alexander, 12
Columbia Pictures, 4, 19, 87, 88
commercial producers, 7–8, 9, 28, 29
commercials, television, 21
commercial theatre, 7–8, 9, 11–12
    types of, 12, 14
community theatre, 14, 15–16
company managers, 25–26
composers, 66, 70
comptrollers, 26
    profiles of, 47
concessionaires, 164
construction managers, 111, 112
consulting editors, 117
contacts, 190–191
contractors, 66
Coppola, Francis Ford, 6, 168
co-producers, 29
copyists, 66
copywriters, 161
corporate contributors, 164
COST (Council of Stock Theatres), 16
COST producers, 28
costume designers, 113
    assistant, 113–114
    profiles of, 153–157
costume drapers, 116
costumers, 114, 169–170
costume supervisors, 114
costume technicians, 114–115
crafts service persons, 115
Crawford, Cheryl, 7
Crist, Judith, 179

critics, 164
    profiles of, 177–183
cuers, 66
cultural institutions, 15
curtain operators, 115

dance captains, 115
dance companies, 17
dance masters, 115
Dance Notation Bureau, 165
dance notators, 164–165
dance supervisors, 115
dance therapists, 162
Davidson, Gordon, 54
Deer Hunter, The, 150, 151n
Denby, David, 177–183
    advice given by, 182–183
    background of, 179–180
    as film critic, 177–183
dialogue directors, 66
dinner theatre, 17
directories, film- and theatre-related,
    238
directors, 66–69
    animation, 109
    assistant (AD), 66, 67–68, 69
    associate, 67
    in film, 5, 67, 68, 69
    producing, 51–57
    in theatre, 68–69, 89–97
director's assistants, 69
    profiles of, 41–42
directors of audience development,
    26, 35
    assistant, 26
directors of education and outreach
    programs, 163
directors of funding and development,
    26
    assistant, 26
directors of licensing, 168
directors of operations, 171
directors of photography (DPs), 111,
    115–116
    profiles of, 147–153
directors of publicity, 169
distribution departments, in studios,
    34

distribution executives, 34
distributors, 27
  independent, 5
  industrial film, 167
division heads, in studios, 32–33
documentary film, 20
documentary film editors, 118
draftsmen, 110
drapers, 116
dressers, 116
drivers, 172
dry cleaners, 170
dummy loaders, 126, 127
dyers, 114

Eaker, Ira, 188
Eastman House and Archives, 85
editors, film, 116–119
  animation, 109
  apprentice, 116, 117, 118–119, 133–
    135
  assistant, 116, 117, 118, 135–137
  consulting, 117
  documentary film, 118
  music, 117, 118
  picture, 116–118, 131, 137
  profiles of, 131–137
  sound, 117, 118
  supervising, 117
educational film, 21, 165
educational theatre, 17–18
electrical operators, 119, 120–121
electricians, 119–121
  master (house), 119
  production, 119–120
employment clearinghouses, 220–222
entertainment reporters, 165
equipment sales and design, 165
Equity waiver theatre, 16
executive producers, 29
exhibitors, 171

fabricators, 121
fabric cutters, 114–115
Farrell, Joe, 3, 189
feature film, 18–19
festivals, 5, 222–224

fight directors, 69
film archivists, 166
film buyers, 171
film commission jobs, 166
film directors, 5, 67, 68, 69
film producers, 6, 28, 29–30
  "creative-" vs. "financier-type," 29
  independent, 3, 4–5, 29
film production:
  financing and distribution in, 3–5
  in future, 6–7
  geography and, 5–6
  types of, 18–21
  unions in, 9–10, 33
  see also specific jobs
film reviewers, 164
film technicians, 166
film theatre owners, 171
finishers, 15
Fischoff, Richard, 82–89, 195
  advice given by, 88–89
  as associate producer, 82–84, 87–89
  publishing background of, 84–87
fitters, 115, 116
flyers, 111, 112
follow-focus, 111
food caterers, 166
food coordinators, 166–167
food stylists, 167
Ford Foundation, 14
Fosse, Bob, 65–66
Fox, Maxine, 35–45
  advice given by, 44–45
  background of, 38–39
  as director's assistant, 41–42
  as receptionist in theatrical offices,
    39–41
  as theatre producer, 35–38, 42–45

gaffers, 119, 120
Garfield, John, 7
Gazzara, Ben, 72
general accountants, 33
general managers, 27, 36, 40
generator operators, 119, 120
Giannini, A. Christina (Stia), 153–157
  advice given by, 156–157

Giannini, A. Christina *(cont'd)*
  as costume designer, 153–157
Gloria, 151
Goldman, Bill, 176
Gordon, Steve, 131, 137
grants, 8, 20, 21
  list of, 222–224
grass roots theatre, 14, 15–16
Grease, 36, 43–44
Greatest Man in the World, The, 131
Great Georgia Bank Hoax, The, 134–135
Greenberg, R., & Associates, 168
Greenhut, Bob, 151
greensmen, 124, 125
grips, 121
  key, 121
Group Theatre, The, 7
Grubman, Patti, 1

hairdressers, 121, 170
head stage set painters, 125
head treasurers, 25, 35
head ushers, 172
Hepburn, Katharine, 195–196
Herzog, Werner, 80
Hoffman, Dustin, 4, 87
Hollywood film, 19
Holt, Stella, 54
Home Box Office, 6, 20
home economists, 167
home video films, 19–20
Horovitz, Israel, 95
Hospital, 20
Houghton, Katharine, 195
house electricians, 119
housekeepers, 130
house managers, 27–28
Hurry Sundown, 175

I Lost It at the Movies (Kael), 179
in-betweeners, 109
independent distributors, 5
independent educational filmmakers, 165
independent filmmakers, 69
  profiles of, 97–105

independent films (indies), 19
independent producers and production companies, 29
  in deals with studios, 3, 4–5
  untraditional financing of, 5
industrial film, 20, 167
  distributors, 167
industrial shows, 18
inkers, 109–110
Interiors, 131, 136, 139, 140
internships, 213–220
interviews, in job hunting, 193
Ionesco, Eugene, 93
Ionescopade, 93–94

Jackson, Kate, 87
Jackson, Lewis, 97–105
  advice offered by, 104–105
  as independent filmmaker, 97–99, 102–105
  production jobs held by, 99–102
Jaffe, Stanley, 4, 84, 87, 88
Jaffe, Stanley, Productions, 4, 84, 87
jobs in show business:
  administrative, 23–61, 197–200
  contacts and, 190–191
  looking for, 187–195, 197–211
  middle- and entry-level, 197–211
  production, 63–105, 200–201
  production artisan, 107–157, 202–207
  researching of, 189–190
  self-examination and, 188–189
  supporting services, 159–183, 207–211
  timing and, 187–188
Kael, Pauline, 101, 179, 180
Kanin, Garson, 39–40
Kennedy Center (Washington, D.C.), 15
Kerr, Walter, 17, 179
key carpenters, 111, 112
key grips, 121
key make-up artists, 122
Kiwitt, Sidney, 33, 45–51
  advice given by, 50–51

Kiwitt, Sidney *(cont'd)*
  as business affairs expert, 45–47,
    48–51
  as comptroller, 47
Kleiner, Burt, 103
Koenig, Rhoda, 182
Kramer vs. Kramer, 4, 84, 87–88, 195

Labanotation, 164–165
labor relations experts, 33
Lachman, Edward, 188
La Mama Etc., 14
Lansbury, Angela, 41, 42
Lansing, Sherry, 4
Lao-tse, 185
Lapiduss, Sally, 195
Lathrop, Richard, 193
lawyers, 33, 36, 171–172
League of New York Theatres, 26
League of Resident Theatres (LORT),
    14
letters, in job hunting, 192
libraries specializing in theatre and
    film, 242–244
lighting designers, 120, 121–122
  assistant, 122
lighting equipment designers, 165
Lincoln Center (New York), 15
line producers, 30
literary managers, 32
Littlefield, Nancy, 11, 191, 194
loaders, 111
location designers, 70
location managers, 70
location scouts, 69–70
Loews Corporation, 6
LORT (League of Resident Theatres),
    14
Loudon, Dorothy, 155
lyricists, 70

McCarter Theatre, 157
MacShane, Anita, 76
made-for-pay-television films, 19–20
made-for-TV films, 19
mailroom "girls" and "boys," 25
maintenance engineers, 126, 127–128

make-up artists, 122
  assistant, 122
  body, 122
  key, 122
Mame, 41–42
Mamet, David, 95
Manhattan, 131, 137, 139, 141, 150,
    151
Man on the Swing, 150
marketing departments, in studios, 34
marketing research, 167–168
master carpenters, 111
master electricians, 119
master sound technicians, 126
matte artists, 110
Maysles Brothers, 20
MCA Universal, 86–87
Meat, 20
media directors, 161
membership education persons, 172
merchandising executives, 168
Merrick, David, 12
metalworkers, 125
Midsummer Night's Dream, A, 153–
    155
milliners, 115
Missel, Renee, 59, 80, 81
mixers:
  chief re-recording, 126, 127
  music/sound effects, 126, 127
  production, 126, 127
  re-recording, 126, 127
model builders, 123
Monette, Paul, 77–82
  advice given by, 81–82
  background of, 77–79
  as screenwriters, 77, 79–82
Morse, Sandy, 131–137
  advice given by, 137
  as apprentice editor, 133–135
  as assistant editor, 135–137
  background of, 131–133
  as picture editor, 131, 137
Morton, Jack, Production, 18
Moss, Bob, 51–57, 145
  advice given by, 57
  background of, 53

Moss, Bob *(cont'd)*
  in 42nd Street redevelopment, 51–
    53
  as producing director, 51, 54–57
  as stage manager, 54
Mount, Thom, 80–81
musical directors, 70
music editors, 117, 118
music/sound effects mixers, 126, 127

NABET, 71
National Endowment for the Arts, 8,
  13, 56
Nederlander Organization, 12
negative cutters, 117, 119
newspapers, film- and theatre-related,
  238–242
New York magazine, 177, 179, 181
New York Shakespeare Festival, 91
New York State Council on the Arts,
  8, 56, 74
New York Street Caravan, 15
Night and Fog, 131
No Contest, 80–81
noncommercial producers, 9, 28
noncommercial (not-for-profit)
    theatre, 7, 8, 9, 13
  types of, 12–18
non-fiction film, 20
Nosferatu, 80
not-for-profit theatre, *see* noncommer-
    cial theatre
Nova, 21
NRC (New Repertory Company), 92–
  93

Off Broadway theatre, 11, 12–13
Off Off Broadway theatre, 9, 12, 13–
  14, 16
Off Off Broadway Theatre Alliance,
  14
opaquers, 110
opera companies, 17
optical designers, 168
orchestrators, 66
Orphan, The, 136
outside property persons, 124

packagers, 28
painters, 123
paperhangers, 123
Papp, Joe, 13–14, 95, 145
pay-television, 6
periodicals, film- and theatre-related,
  238–242
personal managers, 161, 168–169
"photo calls," 130
photocopying machine operators, 110
picture editors (film), 116–118
  profiles of, 131, 137
picture editors (still photography),
  130, 169
placement services, 220–222
playback operators, 126, 127
Players Guide, 96
playwrights, 68, 70
  in residence, 70
Playwrights Horizon, 51, 56, 57
Playwrights Unit, 55
Polakov's, Lester, Studio and Forum
    of Stage Design, 156
powdermen, 122
Prayer for My Daughter, A, 95
Preminger, Otto, 175
press agents, 169
Pressman, Edward, 103
Prince, Hal, 12
print people, 27, 34
producers, 28–30, 161
  associate, 82–89
  co-, 29
  COST, 28
  executive, 29
  line, 30
  seasonal, 28
  see also film producers; theatre
    producers
producing directors, profiles of, 51–57
"producing-in-law," 9, 35
production accountants, 33
production artisans, 107–157, 202–207
  function of, 107
  job descriptions of, 109–130
  profiles of, 131–157
production assistants (PAs), 70–71

production auditors, 30
production carpenters, 111–112
production departments, in studios,
    34–35
production designers, 69–70, 123, 128
    profiles of, 137–142
production electricians, 119–120
production estimators, 30
production executives, 35
    profiles of, 57–61
production heads, 35
production managers, 30–31, 152
    unit, 30, 31
production mixers, 126, 127
production office coordinators, 31
production people, 63–105, 200–201
    function of, 63
    job descriptions of, 63–71
    profiles of, 72–105
production property persons, 124
production secretaries, 32
production stage managers (PSMs),
    128–129, 144
program directors, 31
projectionists, 123
project managers, 169
property handlers, 124
property makers, 124
property masters, 123–125
    film, 124, 126
    theatre-related, 236–242
publicists, 169
    unit, 130
publicity departments, in studios, 33–
    34
Public Television, 89
Public Theatre, 95

Rabb, Ellis, 54, 74
Radner, Gilda, 95
"ragpickers," 169–170
readers, 32
receptionists, 31, 161
    profiles of, 39–41
recordists, 126, 127
regional theatre (resident theatre), 8–
    9, 14–15

regisseurs, 115
re-recording mixers, 126, 127
    chief, 126, 127
resident theatre (regional theatre), 8–
    9, 14–15
Resnais, Alain, 131
resumés, 192–193
Resurrection, 59–60, 80
Rich, Shirley, 87
Richard, Lloyd, 94, 95
Riefenstahl, Leni, 131
riggers, 111, 112
Rosenblum, Ralph, 134, 135, 136
Rosenman, Howard, 59, 80, 81

Saks, Gene, 41
salespeople, 27, 34, 166
    camera supply house, 163–164
Samnick, Norman, 187, 190, 192
Sanford, Geoffrey, 173–177
    advice given by, 177
    as agent, 173, 175–177
    background of, 173–175
Santa, 97, 101, 102–104
Saphier, Peter, 57–61
    advice given by, 61
    background of, 61
    as production executive, 57–61
    projects initiated by, 59–60
    shooting and post-production super-
        vised by, 60
Sarandon, Chris, 95
Sarandon, Susan, 95
Saturday Night Fever, 18
scenic artists, 110, 125
schools, 224–227
Schuler, Fred, 147–153
    advice given by, 152–153
    background of, 149
    as camera assistant, 149–150
    as camera operator, 147, 150–151
    as director of photography, 147,
        150
scout consultants, 70
screenwriters, 5, 71
    profiles of, 77–82
script supervisors, 125

seamstresses, 115
seasonal producers, 28
secretaries, 32, 161
  production, 32
Serban, Andrei, 95
Serpico, 150
set decorators, 125–126
set designers, 128
set dressers, 124
Seven Arts Associated Corp., 47–48
Shakespeare Theatre, 14
Sherman, Martin, 95
shop jobs, 169–170
shoppers, 114
showcase theatre, 16
Shubert Organization, 12
Simon, Mel, Productions, 5–6
Sorrow and the Pity, The, 20
sound designers, 126
sound editors, 117, 118
sound equipment designers, 165
soundmen, 126–128
  in film production, 126–127
  in film studios, 126, 127–128
  in theatre, 126
sound operators, 126
special effects persons, 128
  assistant, 128
stage designers, 128
stage managers, 128–129
  assistant (ASMs), 66, 128, 129
  production (PSMs), 128–129, 144
  profiles of, 54, 142–147
Stardust Memories, 131, 137, 139
Stark, Ray, 48
Stephens, Clifford, 94
Stewart, Ellen, 14
still photographers, 129–130
Stir Crazy, 151
story analysts, 32
story departments, in studios, 34
story editors, 32
Strasberg, Lee, 7
Streep, Meryl, 4, 87
Streisand, Barbra, 40
Strider, 146
studio executives, 3–4, 32–35

chief executive officers (CEOs), 32
division heads, 32–33
studios:
  administrative divisions of, 33–35
  films made "in-house" by, 3–4
  former power of, 3, 6
  independent production companies
    and, 3, 4–5
study centers specializing in theatre
    and film, 242–244
stunt coordinators, 170
subscription directors, 35
subsidiary rights, 38
summer stock theatre, 16–17
supervising editors, 117
supporting services people, 159–183
  function of, 159
  job descriptions of, 161–173
  profiles of, 173–183

Taper, Mark, Forum (Los Angeles),
    14, 54
teachers, 170
teamsters, 172
technical directors (TDs), 130
television, 3
  cable, 89
  commercials for, 21
  made-for-, movies, 19–20
  pay-, 6, 19–20
Tharp, Twyla, 66
theatre architects, 170
theatre consultants, 170
theatre directors, 68–69
  profiles of, 89–97
Theatre for the Forgotten, 15
theatre managers, 170–171
theatre operations managers, 171
theatre operators, 123
theatre owners, 171
theatre producers, 28–29
  commercial, 7–8, 28–29
  noncommercial, 28
  profiles of, 35–45
theatre production, 7–9
  geography and, 8–9
  investment in, 7, 36, 38

theatre production *(cont'd)*
  types of, 11–18
  unions in, 9
  see also commercial theatre; non-
    commercial theatre; *specific jobs*
theatrical attorneys, 171–172
theatrical film, 18
Theatrical Index, 39
Thief, 139
Thomas Crown Affair, The, 149
tie-in novelizations, 80, 85–86
Titus Productions, 19
training programs, 213–220
translators, 172
transportation, 172
treasurers, 25
  assistant or apprentice, 25
  head, 25, 35
trimmers, 115
Triumph of the Will, 131
Twentieth Century-Fox, 4, 19, 84

unions, 9–11, 228–229
  employees of, 172
  entry into, 10
  in film production, 9–10, 33
  job responsibilities established by, 10
  list of, 229–236
  in theatre production, 9
  see also specific jobs and unions
United Scenic Artists (U.S.A.), 113–
    114, 139, 142, 157
unit production managers, 30, 31
  assistant, 30, 31
unit publicists, 130
Universal Pictures, 7, 80–81
university theatre, 18

Urban Arts Corps Theatre, 72, 75, 76
ushers, 28, 172
  head, 172
utility men, 115

video disks, 6
Visit, The, 93
Volunteer Lawyers for the Arts, 172

Waissman, Ken, 36, 42–44
Waissman & Fox, 36
wardrobe supervisors, 130
Warner Brothers Inc., 47, 48
Warner Communications Inc., 19
Welfare, 20
West Side Story, 129
West Side Waltz, 195–196
Wexler, Haskell, 149–150
What Color Is Your Parachute?
    (Bolles), 189
*Where Do I Go from Here with My
    Life?* (Crystal), 189
Who's Hiring Who (Lathrop), 193
Willis, Gordon, 147, 151
"windows," 27
Wiseman, Frederick, 20
Wolper, David, Productions, 19
wranglers, 162
Writers Guild, 71
Wyeth, Zoya, 142–147, 195
  advice given by, 145, 147
  as stage manager, 142–147

Zarin, Judy, 92, 94
Zeigler and Ross, 175, 176
Zoetrope *Studios*, 6
Zsigmond, Vilmos, 147